Andrea AND Faber

Letters 1968 – 1980

FABER DONOUGHE

Umbrella Publishing,
New York, New York

Cover Design by Janine Agro

ISBN: 978-0-578-99804-6

10 9 8 7 6 5 4 3 2 1

Printed in the United States of America

For Lisa, with love

To alissa!
Each Became Both.

[signature]

"But Souls which are pregnant — for there certainly are men who are more creative in their souls than in their bodies — conceive that which is proper for the soul to conceive or contain."

PLATO, SYMPOSIUM (209A)

Table of Contents

OVERTURE

Dear Andrea,

At last I sit and write to you. With you in my mind perhaps I will be able to recap our years together. I tried for so long to understand what was at the core of our twenty years together. Finally, I realized that the relationship could explain itself through our letters and other written notes to each other.

After all, for the first five years of our relationship we were not living together, and it was the telephone and letters that sustained us, and through which we got to know each other. In fact, we were not physically together after our first meeting for one year. That first meeting was certainly an example of how our great moments hang by a thread. In our case, by a toothache.

It was after school had finished, March 5, 1968. I was just starting a short rehearsal with a few students in the auditorium at New Kensington High School. Sam, the janitor who also acted as a stage hand for community concerts which were held at the school, came over to me. I could see that his jaw was swollen on one side. He had to go to the dentist right then and asked me to cover on the light board for him for a rehearsal that was scheduled for 4:30. I had heard in the Teachers' Lounge earlier in the day that a former student who was now singing with the Metropolitan Opera was being honored with a welcome home concert that night. Of course, I agreed to do it and off went Sam, nervous as hell to the dentist.

My rehearsal ended about 4:15, and shortly after the main door at the back of the auditorium swung open, and in you came. Never forget that entrance you made: like a Divo — black short overcoat that had a black mink collar, white silk scarf, and a striking black fur hat. Your Russian one I learned later. You were followed by Hilla, as usual trying to take charge of everything as she came down the aisle like a fox terrier after prey. She was followed by your accompanist, Stanley.

I introduced myself as the Drama teacher at the school and explained that I was filling in for Sam and that I knew the light board rather well. You were very kind and pleased and we agreed that you would sing a few intros to the songs and I would set the lights according to the mood, and also for a degree of variety. You smiled and looked deeply — those amazing eyes of yours — at me.

When we finished setting the light cues, you walked over to thank me, again with a piercing look, and asked me if I would come to your concert that night. I hedged a bit; I was beginning to realize that you were flirting with me, which was a new sensation to me. I was flattered I guess. Had to decline the invitation due to plans with David to go to a poetry reading in Pittsburgh. I told you that I would try to go to the concert, though, and let it go at that.

The week after your concert I was in Pittsburgh at Kaufman's, in the men's department and the manager, Phil Burns came over to me. He was the person responsible for planning your homecoming concert, gay, and a high school friend of yours. He asked me if I was the "young man" who helped Andrea Velis with the rehearsal at the high school. "Yes, indeed I was." You had asked Phil to track me down and get my name and address. He said you wanted to send me a thank you note. "No need, my pleasure," I said.

You were clear, however. Phil said that you insisted he get the info for him. You made him promise. Thank you for that persistence, love, it worked. I gave him my name and address and within a week or so you sent me a very gracious thank you, which included an invitation to call you when I was next in New York. You repeated what you had said at the high school when I told you that in the spring the senior drama and choir students got the treat of a trip to New York, and I went along as one of the chaperones. You invited me to take a few students along to the Met and you would show us the backstage area and their famous stage operations.

I did not respond to your note. You probably gave up on me as a missed opportunity. What you did not know, of course, was that my life was in a sorry state at the time of our meeting. Only recently I had begun to accept feelings that I had repressed for many years, feelings that drew me to males rather than females. A college therapist told me that I just needed to have sex with a woman and then to channel my libido in that direction.

Anything was better than becoming queer in 1968. I had followed that advice and it seemed to work; I enjoyed sex with two female students, one of course, being Susan, Lisa's mom, as you know. Actually, I thought that Intercourse was like so many things in life, fine but over-rated when all was said and done. Do you believe that? Not what we were to find out with each other. But, then, at that time, I was naïve about love. Not just sex, but love itself. The body shaking, all possessing nature of desire for another person was something that I had not experienced; but I did get a peek into it through an attachment to a former student of mine. I might even say, and I have said this to you, that I loved David. It was his lips, his smile, his body that freed me from doubt and anxiety about my own nature, as a man who sought the love of other men. And that was a rebirth of my full identity, fully aware for the first time that the love I sought was a right — not a curse.

3

How you had learned that concept so early in life puzzled me. That is until later when you told me about your relationship with Jerry R. when you were only 13 years old. I am so glad that you wrote about that important experience and that I found you're written recollection of it:

> Into this little life came Jerry R… Since I was the young-est of four — separated from the third by six years — a great deal of my youth was spent in my own fantasies. Our cherry tree became in the Spring, the set for Springtime and I would sit in its branches with the petals falling all around me and sing of Jeanette and Nelson — the farms below Parnassus on the shores of the Allegheny, divided from it only by the railroad, where the Italians and Greeks had confiscated the land and set it out in flats, with lean-tos to hide from the sun — became for me with its adjoining small woodland, a jungle — a forest where my imagination was free to play out its wildest fantasy. There were prin-cesses to be rescued, and spies hid there, and only I on my bicycle was capable of finding them. Jerry showed up one day working for my father as a waiter. Here indeed was a prince — blonde and curly (still my weakness), story book handsome and from far off Oklahoma. I was entranced by this exotic youth and he saw my interest as a chance for a small diversion in this dull city his fate had brought him to.
>
> I don't know which of us seduced the other. He was 17 I think, but I had some experiences with my school mates. His stories of far off places — of his teenage wife and a small son back home — of the things he had seen and experienced completely captivated me. I took him to

visit my farms and the swimming hole in Lower Burrell where the boys swam naked — there we put down my bike on a bluff overlooking the pond and made love. He had come like a Prince into my life to carry me off from the monotony of my youth. Older parents — disturbed mother — and a vivid imagination prepared me for his arrival, and he provided me with my first complete love experience. We began to meet regularly. I would provide the places — now this farm — now the swimming hole — once in the apartment of some friends whose dog I was caring for. Everywhere we could, we would meet and make love for one glorious spring and summer — I don't know where he lived. I imagine a room somewhere. I had no phone where I could call him, we would just plan from one meeting to the next where we would meet, for he finally left my father for some other job. We were to meet at the hole at 2:00 (funny I remember the time.) I had anticipated the meeting for several days — I think I arrived early to heighten the expectation. 2:00 became 3:00, and my disappointment knew no bounds. I felt deserted abandoned there in the woods. Then 4:00 came — perhaps he had simply forgotten — then 5:00 confusion — distrust then hate filled my heart. I had been riding on a crest of discovery and satisfied love, and now I was dashed into doubt. I couldn't call — I couldn't find him. I felt lost and confused and… thirsty. I finally had to drink some of the stream that fed the swimming hole and then decide if I should cut this one last thread to him and leave. This I did at 5:30. Never has there been a more hurt, rejected, unhappy child.

All these feelings which crashed in on me were new. Who could I ask about them — no one. Who would understand? I had to bury them inside — weep alone — try to imagine what had gone wrong, convince myself that he must have felt something of what I was experiencing and would come back.

On the second day of my agony, I saw his picture in the paper. He had drowned the morning of our tryst swimming in the river. He was to be viewed for one day before being sent back to Oklahoma. I clipped his picture from the paper through tears — with all the hurt I had suffered now came loss — guilt.

I was determined he would not go alone, that I owed him my company and respect. All alone I dressed and went to the funeral home. He was there in an open coffin — handsome, blonde — alone in a room full of chairs. I sat with him, stunned. I had never lost anyone before. I was not prepared for the responsibility which had been thrust on me, his only friend. Yet, I relished the fact that I was handling the situation. No one was telling me what to do or how to feel. I had lost my first great love, he was dead here before me and at thirteen I had to control my emotions — no one at home must suspect. The funeral director, made curious by the sole presence of a child in a visiting room, asked if he was a relative. I said, "No, just a good friend." Finally, afraid I would be missed at home and certainly my return "all dressed up" would arouse suspicion, I decided to leave. I told Jerry how sorry I was, how I would miss him and left. Now, I would have added — thank you. That night at home with his clipping, which I kept for many years, I felt I should do something for him. I could not pray — for I knew my love would not be acceptable. I instinctively took some salt and threw it into the gas fire of our kitchen stove. It flamed up and as it did I wished him farewell; this flaming done three times seemed to satisfy me and I knew he too was content. This child he had taught to love, had grown enough in three days, to bid him a suitable farewell.

I think that you wrote that memory down in the late 1980s but I'm not sure.

I wish you had dated your writings, even many of your letters have no dates and I have had to guess from their content as to the timing, especially the letters which you wrote from the tour cities. They were often written late at night, after a performance, and were quickly dashed off before you crawled into bed.

Your memory of Jerry is so tender and obviously so deeply felt, even so many years later. You wrote that as a thirteen-year old, you "knew my love would not be acceptable." You knew that the love you were feeling for Jerry was a forbidden love but you did not think of it as sin, and, this I find so fascinating, you created your own ritual for sending his soul off on its journey. And you chose fire to do it, and to do it three times.

And you did have a weakness for blondes, curly headed even better. That explains your soft spot for Eric all those years. Also, you mention that Jerry "provided… my first complete love experience" and since you also mention that you had had some casual sexual experiences with other boys, so I assume, knowing you as I do, that you are saying that you had intercourse with him. And, it sounds as if

7

you had the romp all Spring and Summer. He had a wife and a son, and so we assume that he was bi-sexual.

It seems a good moment, love, to include a similar experience — not as complete an experience as you had — but my own brush with love, or at least a deep crush, without any penetration so to speak, when I was thirteen years old.

He was Italian-American and his name was Tony:

After all these years, my mental picture of Tony at 12 is sketchy at best. I was a year older than he was; I was the same age as his older brother, Eddie. We all went to the same elementary school in Garfield. Eddie was blonde, wore glasses and had a quiet, rather studious personality. Tony was the opposite. He was a small, tightly packed fire cracker. He had dark eyes, black hair, olive skin and a solid, muscled body. Sort of reminds me of what Robert Blake looked like in his childhood films. Tony was tough, at least street tough, and bit of a bully, even to me, who was older and taller. He was a bully on the playground, and a good athlete at all sports; again, I was the opposite more like Eddie than Tony. He pushed me around for a while until I realized that I was probably stronger and certainly bigger. A few shoves and pushes back, and he began to respect me, and the more we spent time together the more I was attracted to him, in all ways. He was just a lot of fun to be with, always coming up with crazy ideas for making extra money that we kept a secret so that we could spend it on movies, pinball machines, or White Tower hamburgers. Tony's mother was a lovely blonde woman, big pile of hair on her head, always wearing makeup, had been a singer at local Pittsburgh clubs. She was warm hearted with open arms and home baked sweets always at the ready. Sadly, she was pretty much confined to their small house on Rosetta Street because she had a wooden leg and I don't think it fit very well, so she must have been in pain a lot when she did walk around. His father was in prison — are you ready — for shooting Tony's mother in the leg; guess he had aimed higher and missed. He was in the rackets, as they used to call them, which I guess covered all kinds of illegal scams. When I would visit Tony's house and his Mom would carefully maneuver from the kitchen towards us in the living room, Tony abandoned his little tough guy street image. And his Mom greeted him in a baby talk lingo that startled me the first time it happened but later became part of a special relationship between them that I thought was rather sweet. He didn't mention it and I don't think I ever did either.

I liked being with Tony even though he was regarded by most people as a trouble maker. One of his money making schemes was to get us a couple shoeshine boxes so that we could go to the bars in East Liberty on Friday and Saturday nights. Tony kept both boxes at his house because that would have been a problem for me if I got caught with it. We saved the extra money so that we could play hooky now and then and go to the Triangle movie theater on Frankstown Avenue in the afternoon. It was in a Black neighborhood out East Liberty way and was indifferent about letting school kids in during school hours.

We did most of our stuff together in the summer, then school was not an issue. And, in fact, it was the summer heat at night that provided an opportunity for our first sexual relationship. We decided to sleep out on my back porch using some old blankets and pillows as a bed. It was cooler there than inside that's for sure, and at some point we were body to body for a little warmth, and then we started to play with each other. We even started kissing each other very gently. All tentative, but very pleasurable.

Thus began an intensive year-long relationship of having sex every chance we had, in movie houses in the dark, in friend's bedrooms if left alone for twenty minutes or so, and especially in warm weather on my back porch.

We were sucking each other and kissing a lot. And we were both able to come eventually. I loved being with him and felt that I loved him, whatever that meant. He got me on his baseball team (he was a catcher) and also his football team. On the baseball team I was in left field, and on the football I was just on the defensive line. Wasn't very good at any of it, but Tony helped all he could and I stayed for one season of each sport, just to be near him. Tony hung out with a gang that included his brother Eddie and several other guys, a few of them were rather wild, not Eddie though. Tony liked to hang with the bad boys, who liked to steal cars for a joy ride. This was a sort of sport among them in the '50s.

Tony and a few of those guys stole a car one night, a '54 Chevy I think, and they decided to drive over to my house and pick me up to go for a joy ride. Tony's pull on me held strong even for such a stupid thing and so I sneaked out and joined them for a ride that wound up taking us out to Penn Hills. It was mid-winter and coming down a slippery iced road we lost control and crashed the car into a snow bank. We scattered into the back yards of the surrounding houses; however, what with dogs barking and lights flashing on we were all caught by the police and taken to holding cells at the Penn Hills Police Station. We were going to be transferred the next morning to East Liberty Police Station and from there to Juvenile Detention in Oakland. Tony and I were in one cell; two other boys in a second cell.

I was scared shitless; could not believe I was in jail. After the lights were turned off, Tony crawled down slowly, quietly from the top bunk and got into my bunk. He started hugging me and touching me and wanted to have sex. "How the hell can we think about sex now!" I said. He saw no reason not to miss the opportunity and pushed for it, but I simply could not get anything going. He was pissed but reluctantly crawled back up to his bunk and jerked off. The next morning we were taken to Pittsburgh, then spent a night in Juvenile Detention. Tony stepped in to help me there a couple times. His street savvy got a few boys to back off me.

We all had a hearing a month later in Juvenile Court. Tony had had other minor offenses and therefore a record and so did one of the other boys.

I was stunned when Tony and the other boy were sentenced to eighteen months at Thorn Hill Reform School for Boys. They called it a school but one always heard that it was a terrible place, more like a prison than a school.

Because I did not steal the car but simply went for the ride (and I did take a turn driving the car) I got off with a harsh warning about what type of friends I had and should avoid in the future.

Tony wrote to me several times during the months he was away, and my feelings for him did not change. When he got out he surprised the hell out of me by showing up at my house one evening. He told me that his mother had moved to California with his brother and had come back to get him on his release from Thorn Hill and to take him back to California the next day. She had rented rooms for them on Negley Avenue which was not far from my house. Tony and I had no time alone that night; he caused quite a stir in the neighborhood, a minor celebrity and he looked even more handsome at fourteen. I was sixteen and now had a driver's license. We were not alone but we both could tell from the way that we looked at each other longingly that our desire was unchanged.

Tony told me that he was abused viciously by the older boys at Thorn Hill for many months — raped with a broom handle if he would not let them fuck him — until new fresh victims showed up. But he survived it all. I desperately wanted to be alone with him, and so I asked him to tell his mother to take a taxi herself to the airport, and I would borrow my brother's car and take him out myself. It was early summer, no school, so I got up very early — took the car from the garage without asking my brother — which later brought a messy battle down on me from him — but I didn't care: I had to be able to hold Tony and to tell him that I loved him. We sat very close in the car, a brand new '56 Chevy, and kept touching each other gently. We talked about not really understanding what was between us but that we knew that we loved each other, that was certain. He gave me a picture of himself, hot little dude in T-shirt and Levis, with that tossed curly black hair and sexy smile. At the airport, we sat in the car and kissed; then he left with a backward wave as he walked toward the terminal. I parked the car and went to the terminal roof to watch for his plane to taxi out and take off. That was the last time that I saw Tony. We wrote to each other for over a year or so but I eventually decided to tear up his picture and try to repress my feelings for him, convincing myself that they were evil and un-natural. However, I never forgot the joy that those feelings had provided me at such a young age.

You were fortunate, love, to recognize the beauty of your love for Jerry. I was afraid of mine for Tony, and repressed it for many years, hardly knowing that it still existed. That is, until it was awakened in me ten years later when I was twenty-six and married with a child.

The feelings arose in me again because of a relationship with a former student of mine, who reached out to me emotionally for reasons only he knows; however, his need, his handsome face, and his intelligence combined in such a way that I felt the forbidden love returning to my consciousness. It scared the hell out of me. I tried everything that I could to squelch the emotions; including agreeing to go to therapy to see if I could find my way out of the pain of the love. I had David, a college student then, meet with my therapist, Dr. Bistey. He tried to convince me that this was " a thing that will pass" if I simply did not act upon my feelings. Contrary to what he said, I reasoned that what I was feeling was genuine, deeply rooted in me, and, ultimately, I realized that I was entitled to seek this love, that it was an important part of my very nature. I knew that a life without it would be a lie, a betrayal of myself. I decided that I would get a divorce, endure the pain of that decision, and seek the love of another man.

And so it was at this time that I entered into the divorce-drama, that I remembered our meeting in March of 1968 and the thank you note that you sent after your concert. I also remembered sensing something welcoming in your words, warm — enticing in fact, so… it began.

The first letter:

I.
OAKMONT

November 14, 1968 (New Kensington)

Dear Mr. Velis,

Perhaps time has clouded or altogether obscured our brief meeting in New Kensington last spring. I, of course, remember but do you recall the "accidental" stage hand who helped, slightly, with the lighting of your rehearsal in New Ken?

C'est moi. I hesitated writing to you for so long because I assumed that your kindness in thanking me, and, also, inviting me to visit backstage at the Met were, although delightful to me, courtesy extensions which one should not pursue.

Nonetheless, since I will be going to New York in 3–4 weeks, may I ask if the invitation is still open? Perhaps you will be away, or too busy, or a thousand other likely conflicts, but I am so intrigued by the prospect that I had to ask.

Since my trip will be a usual low budget affair I'm not sure where I'll be staying, but if you think that it would not be an imposition of too much magnitude to show me the facilities of the Met, perhaps I could call you when I'm in New York.

If this should prove impossible or unfeasible at this time, I hope, at least, to be able to see you and hear you (if not help you) the next time you visit the provinces. Needless to say, you were magnificent in concert in New Kensington. I regretted not going to the reception held in your honor at the Holiday Inn.

Thank you for listening, I hope to hear from you soon.

Sincerely,
Chuck Donoughe

You must have got a kick out of that first letter: so formal, in one sense, so obvious in all others. I must have crafted it very carefully to sort of let you know between the lines that I was hoping you would invite me to stay with you. I was ready for the plunge. I wrote the letter a month before I moved out of my apartment with Lisa and her mother, Susan.

We had agreed to the divorce and to my departure in late December after my semester exams at Pitt, which ended on December 10 I think.

You responded to my letter right away, and you were very pleased that I had written. You asked me to call you in New York. Unfortunately, I did not save that response. In fact, I did not save any of your early letters to me. Careless of me I guess, but I threw each letter away after I answered it. The first letter of yours that I saved is dated March 28, 1969.

I did not make it to New York and to you in late 1968 as I had hoped. It was simply wishful thinking on my part. You did use my initial letter as an invitation to stay in touch and that is what happened, big time. You started to call me on a regular basis and to write often. It was a miserable period in my life for the most part; however, your letters and calls helped me to get through it. I had moved into a rather crummy one bedroom apartment over a garage on Fifth Street in Oakmont. My friend, Jane B. and her husband lived in Oakmont, and I had some family history with the town through my uncle W.J. who lived there for many years. You know me, I spent a lot of time working on the place to make it a space that I could live in. Of course, with little money, still on unpaid sabbatical until September of 1969, and finishing my course work at Pitt, and teaching Freshman English at Penn State two nights a week, I was a wreck; didn't know if I was going to keep it all together at times. Most importantly, I was miserable about what the divorce would do to Lisa, the innocent one in the whole situation. Her happy, intact life had been disrupted, and why? How do you explain to a five- year old what is going on in your heart? You try, but you really can't. All I could do was constantly reinforce my love, and her mother's love, for her, make it a reassuring reality for her in every way that I could. One thing I did was to insist that I would not give up any parental rights as Lisa's Dad, period. No restrictions on my time with her and none of that other one-sided crap that was used against Dads at that time. Susan and I would co-parent: period, case closed. Her lawyer advised against that, but Susan knew me well enough to know that I would not budge from my position, and we agreed — so to hell with the lawyer.

As for you and me, we became closer over the next several months; you definitely were a help to me through the holidays, bolstering my spirits always, even pushing me towards the idea of venturing into the gay scene more so that I could have some sex. A gay friend, fellow teacher, took me to my first gay bar in Pittsburgh, Lucky's. It was a dingy joint on the edge of the Hill District: a beat up red brick building on the Boulevard of the Allies that prob- ably had been a warehouse. Lucky, a wiry thirty-something with black hair, puffing a cigarette always, was a fixture at the door. He had to recognize you or the person who brought you for you to get into the place. Once in, there was dancing and a large bar on the street level, and a basement area for more dancing, primarily for Lesbians.

I usually managed to hook up with someone, danced a bit, and then left with him. The encounters were not very successful for me — there always seemed to be an aura of guilt or shame coming back at me from the other guy afterwards. It was get-off sex. Also, I was not into intercourse with the guys, either top or bottom. So, that was an underlying frustration for them. However, the intimacy of intercourse was for me an ultimate expression of passion; I wanted to experience it for the first time with someone who would share a complete passion with me, one that I had yearned for all my adult life, and I did not want to lessen that sensation by fucking a string of half-soused Saturday night tricks from Lucky's. That said, we did manage to have a good time always. At least it seemed that way to me, and I sleazed my way through the early part of 1969 without a break-down.

Even better: one night at Lucky's I did see this gorgeous African- American guy dancing a lot and smiling over at me a couple times. I smiled back, nothing more.

That was Oliver.

Finally, my life got a bit better, calmer. Lisa was doing well; I had managed to save a little money, and you had asked me to come to New York for a weekend in March.

March 5, 1969 (Oakmont)

Dear Andrea,

Let's hope I have better luck with this letter! Last one was returned.

I received your "care" package of incense. Thank you — I'm a bug on the delicious smells. I will try to ration it until I come to N.Y.

Yes, I can "swing" it in March. The dates are fine. If you're religious (or know anyone who is) light a candle or bonfire so that nothing short of an earthquake prevents my visit. This thing is starting to have a slight tinge of Stanley and Livingston.

Yes, Mr. Sunshine, I welcome your warmth in my life. I'm glad that you offer more than Borges. I, too, "live for life" and relish the pleasure which beautiful friendship can bring to life.

The opportunity to play host for you in the spring is an exciting thought. I'm glad that your brother lives in a "very small house." I'm a dreadful excuse for a cook — scrambled eggs and steaks — that's about it. I'm one of those unfortunate wretches who can't enjoy a frozen dinner. In fact, when I look at one, all I can think of is what it looked like in its frozen condition. Obviously, you might assume, my mother, who lives in Pittsburgh, has a frequent "extra" for dinner.

Forgive this short dribble of a letter, but I'm in the midst of "paper" time at Pitt — squeezing out profundities that have been often thought and infinitely better expressed.

Let's leave Borges — Blake says it better for you:

> "...he who kisses the joy as it flies
> Lives in eternity's sun rise."

Will confirm my arrival time later,

Love, Chuck

You wince even now, I'm sure, at the sight of "Chuck" —
the dread nickname which you would not use or accept;
you opted for Charles. You did not know for at least
another year, I think, that my first name was actually, Faber,
and Charles was my middle name.

In March I finally did get to New York and we spent
our first weekend together. By this point I knew that you
shared your rent-controlled apartment with a colleague
from the Met, Pat T. You had been lovers but now were
simply sharing the apartment as friends; though, I later
realized that Pat was more attached to you than you were
to him. But, he was away the weekend I came and so we
were alone for most of the time. I saw you Saturday afternoon at the Met for the first time: Corelli and Nilsson in
Turandot. I did not realize then how special that combination was, but the whole opera scene was just beginning for
me.

Bless you, you did save my letters, and so I wrote this to
you after my visit:

March 28, 1969 (Oakmont)

Dear Andrea,

Forgive my abuse of etiquette, and try to understand the reasons
for my hesitation in writing to you. The words just wouldn't come!
Oh, of course, all the easy ones, the casual ones which slip onto
the page, they were there; however, I wanted words which would
cradle all the joy and love of our weekend, which would re-echo
the music of Puccini, which would be flavored by champagne, and
a walk through "a John Wayne movie." All this couldn't be "dashed

off" in a "thank you so much" way. Even now I feel like a plumber trying to write a symphony. Then, your beautiful letter came.

It said, "Yes, everything really happened." And I felt all the warmth again, Britten's melodies seemed to be only ours again. Oh, Andrea, if only I could have said it all when we were together. Did you see it in my eyes? It was there gazing at you all the time.

Although I would hesitate to say either one of us "fell in love," I think I will cherish the "love" of our weekend, and let time handle our potential love.

"Hershey's Huns" have not captured me, yet. I am waiting for the draft board's reply to a letter sent by the school district which requests a deferment for me. If it fails I will claim you as a dependent. Of course, you realize that I can't keep you in the "manner to which you've been accustomed."

Love, Chuck

May 3, 1969 (Oakmont)

Dear Andrea,

If May comes can June be far behind. Let's hope not. Needless to say, the Cleveland thing was painful. In fact, I almost gave in to my desire and left for Cleveland at 12:00 Friday night, after the concert. Alas, my seldom, but of late increasing, practical side won out. The lighting for the concert by the way, was ghastly. My favorite nag, Carolyn, (the choir director), decided the day of the concert, and in my absence, to move the acoustical shell six feet downstage. Of course, she thought it would be quite simple to "adjust all the spots, etc." And, of course, I said, more or less "Shit on you — you can sing under a blood red haze for all I care." Fear not, we remain at our normal status, restrained friends, so that I can make it to NYC.

In addition to being upset about missing Cleveland, I felt terribly naïve about the S&M bit and my reaction to it. I suppose I overreact to such scenes because I always seem to be trying to walk through a coal mine in a white linen suit. One shouldn't expect to exit unsmudged; in fact, the sign or marks of the trip should be evident. I guess Hart Crane haunts me from his watery sanctuary.

Good news at last. I will be going to Vermont (July 7 – August 9). I waited to write until I heard from them so that I could include something bright and upbeat in this letter. I am very excited about the summer program. They have gathered together performers and scholars on Shakespeare & Renaissance England. All are eminent authorities on different aspects of the period. It should be a stimulating five weeks. Also, I get paid to attend; I only pay for my books and accommodations.

By the way, I mentioned to Phil B that we write to each other and have talked over the phone several times. He speaks so highly of you all the time I felt almost deceptive not to let on that I know you more than by reputation. Of course, I did not see any reason in telling him that I was with you in NYC. That belongs to us so exclusively that I hesitate to share it with anyone. It's ours and Michelangelo's.

I saw my landlord and told him I was "abandoning" his apartment. He may try to hold me to the lease. However, I also told him that my "asthma" requires that I have an air conditioner for the summer and that he would have to re-wire the apt. if he wished to hold me to the lease. The old wiring will not withstand much more than a fifteen watt bulb. I don't expect he'll cause me any trouble. I've done so many things to him already — scheming almost as well as he — that I'm confident that he will sigh from relief when I leave.

I miss you.

Neither of us, by the way, has made promises that we didn't or couldn't keep. So be it always.

I was reading one of my favorite poems today (came upon it in the process of looking up something else). I want to share the last stanza with you, possibly you know it:

Ah, love, let us be true
To one another! for the world, which seems To lie before
us like a land of dreams
So various, so beautiful, so new,
Hath really neither joy, nor love, nor light Nor certitude,
nor peace, nor help from pain, And we are here as on a
darkling plain,
Swept with confused alarms of struggle and flight When
ignorant armies clash by night.

(*Dover Beach*)

I know, it's too pessimistic for you. Thank God your brightness spills over into me.

Good night,
Chuck

P.S. I don't have asthma.

You must have had a robust laugh about the S&M encounter that I mentioned; I told you the details over the phone. All rather naïve on my part, a blind date set-up by a mutual friend who had been a student of the English prof from CMU. You remember, it was my first encounter with his type. After a night of drinking at a gay bar in Oakland, we went to his apartment on Fifth Ave. near the university campus. When we were naked in bed (along with his dog by the way) he got turned on to the idea of dripping candle wax on me, but first he wanted to wrap my body in Saran wrap, and, then, I would have to do him, which he really was hyped about. What the fuck! I thought he was ready for a straight jacket. "No thank you, fuck off and I am out of here," ended that night. He apparently had a lot of success with his male students along those lines from what he babbled at me as I got my jacket and left. You and I had a great laugh over it.

May 19, 1969 (Oakmont)

Dear Andrea,

This is the third letter I've started in the past week. The previous two were hastily written and so fragmentary that I tore them up. Realizing that your schedule is probably twice as hectic as mine, I still must complain slightly about the fourteen- hour work day I've been suffering from the past two weeks.

From famine to feast in two weeks. I've been teaching a full day and then going to the store at the Mall for six or seven hours, then all day Saturday.

I'm not used to standing that many hours, and so I've been coming home and crawling into bed. I suppose the dullness of clerking adds to my exhaustion; I don't enjoy work that doesn't demand that I use my full powers, however meagre they may be.

Hart Crane keeps watching over us doesn't he? We could not hope for a better qualified patron. I feel great empathy for Crane's "love search." I have shared the hunger that plagued him throughout his brief life. Surprising as it may seem because of my ever-present hesitation, I have not suffered a "big hurt" from a broken love affair. It is from people like Hart Crane, and lesser creatures, that I've learned to guard my heart against the heavy-hand. I suppose one must live with his personal convictions even at the price of losing some joy. The most precious possession I have is the love which I can give. If I don't defend, protect and guard it, I, too, will be swallowed in the tragedy of Hart Crane and so many others. Therefore, it is not often that I extend my talons to grasp life's joys. In fact, I'm sure this all sounds horribly romantic. It does not come from the mind of one uninitiated to the "way of the world." It comes from one who wishes to make his the best of all possible worlds.

The grand tour will soon be over and we will be together again. (We haven't been apart since March really.) I'm sure you have had some new experiences with your blue-haired opera lovers that will make amusing counterpoint over a pitcher of Sangria. So, I will be at the Taft on May 28.

You will be in Pittsburgh in June, and, then, I will be back in New York on July 2 or 3. Things are looking up for us.

I should have surprised you in Cleveland. I will always regret not seeing the surprise on your face, as well as the joy on mine.

Please remember that my infrequent letters are not indicative of your presence in my thoughts. You are with me always. (This sounds like an English teacher or some other pedant. I've been reading an 18th c. novel.)

Hurry home safe.

Chuck

P.S. I got an A on the Crane paper. (Maybe I should get a little statue made for my dashboard.)

You were winding down the spring tour with the Met. I had hoped to get over to Cleveland to spend a day or two with you, but an obligation to do a lighting job for a concert at Ken High prevented me from going. As for our sex lives, we both seemed to be getting by on tricks; yours were in the tour cities (a whole network I later found out, my love) and mine were few and far between because I had given up on Lucky's for the most part. Usually, because I worked at Cox's Men's store at the Monroeville Mall on Saturday nights I was drag ass tired afterwards, and just wanted to go home to bed.

I got hit on by a lot of guys at the store, mostly types that had no appeal what-so-ever to me. The one encounter at the store that became more than a one or two night stand was with Drew Bender who was married with two children and was a Ph.D. in theater from CMU. He was beginning an interesting program at Carnegie Institute which would include the museum, art, and drama classes aimed at students in the inner city. It was to be funded by the Andrew Mellon Foundation. We hit it off and he started coming to my apartment for an evening of sex, about every other week. Afterwards, we also would have serious discussions about his program and he kept offering me a job as his assistant. He knew that I was fed up with my job at Ken High. However, the salary he offered was well below my teaching salary, so I put off the decision every time he mentioned it. Nevertheless, I never actually said that I was not interested. Although, nothing compared to our wild times together; the arrangement did keep me out of the bars and that desperate search for sex, with its whole silly game and dance of desire that one had to go through with each score. All so boring and meaningless.

August 27, 1969 (New York)
My Dear Charles,

Thank you for your letter — the next day after receiving it, I got back a letter I had sent to Vermont — "address unknown." I thought that you might be there still. Your letter sounded sad, mind you I loved it — who doesn't want to be loved and desired, but somehow, I felt that you were lonely. Please don't be — know that I think of you always, love you, and hold your friendship as one of my most precious possessions. It's unfortunate that we found someone to love who lives so far away. That makes me love and desire you no less. You're right, our separation at the terminal was embarrassed and stupid and I felt very ashamed. Imagine, a separation like that after such a weekend. Will our feelings always be subjected to a schedule? I want very much to hear about your new apartment — I still have not been too bored — What became of your article? Please call and write. You know I long to hear from you — and love you very much —

Andrea

I was on the five-week seminar in Burlington; we had spent some time together on my way to Vermont. We were getting deeper into our sexual relationship, enough that we were fucking like horny rabbits, and it was filled with deep passion, of a degree that I had never experienced. The soul dance began.

Before I went to Vermont you managed to come to my garret apartment in Oakmont. Your visit was twofold

— sex nonstop and powerful — followed by interludes of hunting for antiques in Oakmont and Pittsburgh. I learned that after sex, visiting antique shops was your favorite pastime.

My course work at Pitt was finished and I was preparing to return to my teaching job at Ken High in September. Dreading it a bit too.

While you were visiting me in June we went to a cocktail party in Oakland and George Anderson, drama and music critic for the paper in New Kensington, was there and he knew of your career of course and said that he would like to have an article about your upcoming performance in Britten's *Curlew River* at Caramoor in July. You told George that I was going to be there and that perhaps I could write the article. He agreed; however, he wanted me to do a few reviews as tryouts first. I did that; he liked them and hired me as a stringer critic for the paper. (I did it for five years.) Thanks to you, love, for opening that door for me, one of many over the years.

So, you were asking about the Britten article.

Yes, you were right about my feeling lonely and sad when I wrote from Vermont. I was missing my times with Lisa terribly — total absence from her was hard to take because I knew that she missed me so much.

September 2, 1969 (Oakmont)

My Love,
I hope you are back in New York again. Some travel is fine but I like knowing that you are in Gotham and I can pick up a phone and

talk to you. I've missed you terribly this time — Good God! I think of you much too much. You've permeated every facet of my life. I yearn to see those electric eyes — to hold you close to me under a shower spray — to do all that is love — to stop the sun and tease the moon. You left me at such a high moment — Britten's ethereal music ringing from a cathedral of art. You were so beautiful! If only I could have held you and shown you totally how much you mean to me. Shaking hands at a terminal!! Oh, I wanted so much to write poetry to those eyes — to sing back to you in my feeble voice.

Your summer was probably spectacular. We will share our experiences, perhaps over a dinner at the Bavarian Inn on East 86th St.

I'm in a new apartment — utter chaos. I do have a shower, though, come to share it with me.

Let me know when you're home, love.

Chuck (No phone yet.)

Not sure if I ever told you how significant the *Curlew River* experiences were for me that July in New York. I went with you to a couple rehearsals in an apartment on the Upper West Side. Watching you reach into yourself and bring forth the Madwoman was a revelation to me. And then, seeing the actual performances at Caramoor transported me; you captured the essence of the beauty and pain in the role. Then and there, to my love for you as a man, now was added my love for you as a brilliant artist.

It seemed to me that you were awakening in me, and perhaps I in you, a capacity for passion that was rooted at the center of our selves. And watching you that night at Caramoor I began to understand why I was having feelings of love for you that were beyond anything I had ever felt.

Meanwhile, once apart from each other, the hormones were ever present and on the make. I must have been sending out distress signals because on the first day of classes at the U of Vermont I met Marco. What a charmer, and what a smile. After class, he offered me a ride home to my dormitory. He was a hunky Italian, thirty something, married with two sons, each a couple years older than Lisa. He was a teacher in Teaneck and his family had come up to Vermont with him; they had rented a house for the summer. Marco pitched his story to me in the car: gay, lived with a lover in Greenwich Village, gave in to pressure from family to dump the lover and get married to escape " the curse of homosexuality." A typical scenario for many gay men in 1969 as for eons before. Why then did he want to get fucked so badly? Ah, there's the rub. Ironically, on the night of the moon landing (which makes the night forever memorable), Marco told his wife he wanted to stay at the college for some extra collaborative work: that was having sex with me. Marco was very experienced with men sexually and knew all the right moves, including expecting to get fucked as a finale. Nope, not on my playbill with tricks; I would do everything but that. He was disappointed; nevertheless, I had a great time. He subsequently found another member of our group — a skinny, wiry guy who played a lot of tennis — who jumped on Marco's ass as soon as he got the chance. We remained friends for several years. You met two years later when he and his family came to the Met to see you in *Hansel and Gretel*; I took Lisa to New York to see you too.

September 20, 1969 (Oakmont)

Hello again,

It was rather thoughtless of me to call you collect; as I said it is an adjustment. One I can easily make, by the way. I love you prince or pauper, more accurately, princely pauper. I will be your agent in Pgh. if the big, bad Bing doesn't open the doors. I will, through hook or crook, arrange for concerts in the Pgh. Area (Velis sings an evening of Benjamin Britten, Velis lectures at Duquesne Music Dept., etc.). That way, I will have you with me. Seriously, I hope the damn thing is settled. You belong at the Met not in Pgh., alas.

I'm including the article and a review from the same week. I'm afraid the Caramoor piece neither reflects my style nor the exact feeling which I wanted to give it. Oh, one correction, "memorial estate" should read "manorial estate." Not a big thing, but the way they have it sounds like a cemetery. When it comes to writing about you I wilt. Only poetry will do, and that, I'm afraid, is not for public consumption.

The only good thing about being back at Ken High is the steady income. I'm afraid that my entire being has gone further beyond the atmosphere of the high school. I never was geared to it, but now I find it totally suffocating. I have been offered three jobs lately: 1. To teach in Dublin for a year (nix because of Lisa.) 2. To manage an art gallery at the mall (nix because of low starting salary.) 3. To be a co-ordinator of a drama dept. at Carnegie Institute (ditto salary.) The last one, incidentally, is very exciting. I may try to do it on a part-time basis. The program is first in the country, and could be quite a stepping stone. It's too bad that I can't afford to take a step back in salary in order to take a giant step in some other direction. One thing is certain, my days at your alma mater are numbered.

This typewriter is having some sort of attack. It won't do what my fingers tell it to. Unto thee I burn incense, the bowl crackles....

Goodnight,

Chuck

My sabbatical was over. Yes, I was back at Ken High. Not very happy about it though. I had finished my course work at Pitt but still had to prepare for the difficult exams for the M.A. at a later date.

My disappointment at being back at Ken High had to do with a conflict that I had with the administration. I wanted to continue my part-time work as a critic for the daily paper; therefore, I told the head honcho at the school that I did not want to direct plays because I needed to have my evenings free. They were pissed; my punishment was that they took most of my elective classes away, and replaced them with 9th grade English classes, level that I had never taught before.

You listened to all my complaints and suggested I take the job at Carnegie Institute.

While I debated with myself, I did have a lovely September surprise. Let me remind you of the day that I actually met Oliver. It was early in the school year and one afternoon I came out of the teacher's lounge and saw a very handsome young African American guy looking rather bemused at me. He was a student teacher he told me, and then he said, "I think that I saw you last summer in May or June at Lucky's didn't I?" Aha, I laughed, and told him indeed he had and I remembered seeing him too. We smiled that happy smile of recognition.

And so Oliver was now to enter my life. What a lovely surprise. God, he was so beautiful with that big afro, and a charm that played off his face and enticed one to take in all the rest of him.

September 30, 1969 (New York)

Dear Charles,

I'm sorry for the delay in my promised letter. The factory where I labor has kept me going day and night. This is my first day's rest in many a week. And, yet, I have a performance tonight. I fail to see why I should be the one to work so hard to put this season together, when I didn't really want the strike to begin with. The Ballet, which started the whole mess, has not lifted a foot since we started to work. Ars gratia artis...

To compensate for being so late in writing I'm sending you a fat juicy letter this time, well fat in any case. I don't know what juicy is. You cannot imagine the surprise I received to find myself offered a *Catulli Carmina* performance with the Miami Philharmonic in October. I love that piece so much that I wanted to offer it to you, shortly after someone offered it to me. It will be my first performance, and I'm very excited about the prospect of doing it the way I've always wanted it done. The period is just the week before I go to Chicago for the *Billy Budd*, so it will all work out well as far as schedule goes. I wish there was some way for you to hear it.

I've finished my book on Alexander. He had also a lover, named Hephaestion. They even dressed alike. When he took Persepolis, Alexander received Darius's widow; when she saw the two men dressed alike she chose the taller, Hephaestion, to salute. After she discovered her mistake Alexander assured her by saying, "He too is

Alexander." When Hephaestion died in the East, Alexander carried his body with him until he himself went mad and died… now there is a plot for your play or book. He was so tormented by his mother, Olympias, because of his preference, and he would sleep with all the girls she sent him just to content her, and to prove he could. She was jealous of Hephaestion's hold over him.

Tonight I sing *Rosenkavalier* with Madame Chancellor. She wants me to come stay with them in their guest room when I come next year. I admit it would be very chic to be staying there, but it is not why I'm going to Pittsburgh. I certainly couldn't ask you to come stay with me, and I certainly couldn't be in Pittsburgh without staying with you. So the Chancellery is out. Maybe we can go over for dinner or something. I want to stay with you, but I see unsurmountable problems with transportation. I think what might be a better idea is for me to take a room at the Webster Hall, and we can decide which place to stay at as the rehearsals present themselves. If I have a late rehearsal I'll stay with you, and come in late. If I have an early rehearsal, I'll have you stay over with me until after the rehearsal, and then we can go home to your house. I think that would work out best, but if you have any suggestions let me hear them. Of course, the best idea is for me to come to you, and just stay, but, unfortunately, I must work while I love.

I hope you are well my love, and happy. I think of you all the time, and want so to be with you… I may call this Sunday.

Andrea

That strike at the Met allowed you the option to book gigs away from the Met as a source of future income. Rare opportunity for you because the Met was reluctant to allow you to work outside. You were too valuable.

Bing wanted you in everything, and more or less said that in his autobiography. So, you were coming to Pittsburgh to be with me in my new apartment and I was wild with delight at the idea. You were to do Shuisky in *Boris Gudonov* and I would get to review it. Mrs. Chancellor was your old friend Marylyn Miller (Millie) who was married to the top man at the University of Pittsburgh, Wesley Posvar. We actually did go to the mansion for dinner one night; Wesley got plastered and was a riot of fuck this fuck that and Millie shut up and so on. They had no idea that I was a graduate student at Pitt; we told them that I was a friend of yours who lived in New York near you.

You mentioned Alexander and Hephaestion in this letter. We had talked about our desire to find exemplary models of male lovers who lifted their love to a noble level that defied all the obstacles pitted against them, all the condemnation placed by religion and society upon them. The culture was feeding on animosity and condemnation of gay love, and it was poison to us if we accepted it.

We refused it and eagerly looked for higher ideals to embrace, even if one had to go back to antiquity, and so we did.

You were going to Miami for the *Carmina* with the Symphony. The conductor there was a real beauty and talented. I always wondered whether you and he had had a short-lived romance. Never asked because we had made no rules for each other regarding our sexual behavior when we were not together. Free range so to speak.

Within a few weeks of our meeting, Oliver and I had become regular weekend bed buddies. He quickly became more than a diversion because he was so beautiful and sexy; it was still rather low level on my part: frottage and lots of oral sex, period. I did not mention him to you for several months I think. Wanted to wait until he became a presence in my life.

Oliver H., 1969

December 2, 1969 (Oakmont)

My Love,
It is 2:30 AM and I've just finished my TV column. Planned on writing to you this weekend — taking time to compose a letter

that would do some sort of justice to all my love for you, a love —
prose poem. Today, though, when I got your joyous letter filled with
the news of the *Carmina*, the reviews, the broadcast, your visit, and
"Alexander" I cannot hold still.

Perhaps I will burst forth with silly lines or just repeat over and
over your name — I feel childishly, deliciously captured "Here too is
Andrea." I wear not the same garments of my love, for they are mere
trappings; I wear the same soul — spiritus — alma — whatever one
calls the sanctuary of life's essence — that I have in common with
my love — and I too would be a mad desert wanderer without my
other soul — the one that dwells within my heart of hearts. Andrea,
Andrea, Andrea I love to sound those rich tones — I wish I could
sing it in a rich tenor that would bring old Caruso back by its sheer
beauty — but that, my love, I leave to you. Someday, I will sing of it
in my own way — with words.

I told you I would ramble — and I'm not stoned or anything. By
the way, if you bring some of Charles's Cure all to Cleveland, perhaps we can try again, this time with more temperance, to make love
like the Gods. Perhaps, Mephisto will let us alone this time. Doesn't
matter if you think we should leave well enough alone. With you I
feel totally safe. (He too is Charles.)

Busy studying for exams, teaching and reviewing I am enclosing the
Auden piece for you. Wish I had more time to spend writing that one.

Of course, I will listen Sat. Maybe I will cry. Not from sadness but
because there is a Met, there is a Caramoor, there are two champagne
glasses, because I stayed to turn on the lights — all those things that
exist for us. Must go before this letter becomes totally unintelligible.
Why do I grope so, when all I really have to say is "Andrea, I love
you." Sing for me on Sat.

Charles

January 2, 1970 (Oakmont)

God but I've missed you — I suppose the holidays are so filled with love that I wanted to be with you sharing ours for each other. And, then, you called and, as only you can, reminded me that our love doesn't need tinsel and holly or even "auld lang syne;" it's a constant thing and you're really always with me. I know that, love. And please forgive me If I seem foolish sometimes. Guess I would just occasionally enjoy having a real live Greek with me.

You want to know something — in Cleveland all I want to do is lounge away hour after hour in bed — broken only by a few showers together.

Cleveland — April? Oh! That's so damn long — I get a four day spring vacation first week in March. Will you be in NY or on tour? Maybe I could stay with Jane's baby, Tom, and visit you.

Wish I could get time to work on our Antinous thing. Perhaps this summer I will have time to work on something. The paper and school are crowding my time. By the way, thank you for the card. I, too, will have it framed.

Well, love, we begin another year " together." Somehow that seems so good-so right to me. I feel that I have seen into your " heart of hearts" and to my delightful surprise found a piece of me. It is a splendid feeling — Crane, Auden, Shakespeare, Britten they would all understand — Oops, there goes my romantic thing again. Most important — we understand.

Goodnight,
Love, Charles

You were so loving in the phone conversations. I was frequently depressed about missing Lisa and my whole life situation.

As you know, Oliver was a good addition to my life because he was young and looked to me for guidance; he brought stability to my sex life, and I was growing very fond of him. I was trying to understand all the issues that he confronted as an African American. The closer we got the more I learned how ignorant I was about his feelings.

January 14, 1970 (New York)

Charles,

How wonderful to receive your letter. I know how hard it must be for you to write. I know the way you feel. I am the same; you poor thing have the added problem of writing all the time. But please do write. I love so to read your letters. I keep them, and they give me many hours of joy. That is the beauty of writing as opposed to phoning. I can pull you out any time I care to and read you, and love you. And assure myself that you love me also. It's the comfort of having your letter right near me, since I am destined not to have you.

I will be in Cleveland on April 26 and stay until May 3. I'm not going to ask you if you can be there. I can only say, I want you there.

I am reading *Fire From Heaven*, Mary Renault's new book about Alexander. I found a line I want to share with you "Friendship is perfect when virtuous men love the good in one another, for virtue gives more delight than beauty and is untouched by time" — nothing new but I rather like the way she says it. She puts these words into the mouth of Aristotle who taught Alexander.

Well our *Pagliacci* is over. Our leading lady cancelled on opening night, so all our work went down the drain. We had a substitute soprano who was good... poor thing, but nothing can replace five weeks of rehearsals. I received rather nice reviews, one of which I am sending you. Perhaps New Kensington Stroller in your paper would be interested in it. I have one even better which I will send you next week. I also include the pictures I spoke to you of. As you see Franco Zeffirelli is not as you thought him. We had our usual fight. He always goes through hell to have me in his productions, and then gives me a hard time. My parting word to him was that I would not use him in my next picture. And I sang his Goddamned opening night with a cold! Bernstein and I find ourselves as close as ever. In a moment of joy at the curtain calls he said that we should never do operas but together. Good for him, but I might starve. I do love him so, and think him a great talent in opera, but he must have people around him to help him. The cast of *Cavalleria* were afraid of him and they let him conduct the opera too slow. Even Franco Corelli told me he was afraid of him. I simply can't understand them... he is like a baby. Karajan and Cleva are ogres, but not Lenny. I just can't understand fearing him.

We presented Jane's beef recipe to group of French friends. I think we must have been out of our minds; anyway they loved it and insisted we give them the recipe. We had to dig one out of Julia Child's cookbook, because we simply couldn't tell them it was made with Lipton's soup and canned mushroom soup. I have replaced the Sherry with Marsala wine. I like the stronger flavor better. You know it takes a lot of nerve to serve Frenchmen that recipe... Speaking of food ask Bill where my freeze dried food is. I've been talking all about it, but have none to demonstrate with. Tell him to send it to the above address because I have no doorman at home.

I must close now... please try and not be unhappy. You know that's not what I want for us... only sunshine and joy... remember? Be happy... you make me very happy...

Love, Andrea

My brother sent me your review of *Barber*... good for you.

Corelli, Zeffirelli, and Bernstein in one letter, you were hitting on all cylinders with me. Yes, I was astonished that my life was swinging between dwebes in the teacher's lounge every day and then coming to my apartment in Oakmont to your letters, filled with love for me and a cast of characters from a world of geniuses and glamour. How did this happen so quickly? Could this be real? Your letters and your phone calls each week were filled with Met stories and encouragement for me to reach out for something more now that teaching had become so less satisfying with my new, demoted schedule. Reviewing for the *Dispatch* was also giving me new confidence; the more I reviewed, and now with a weekly TV column added, I was having a tough time juggling my schedule. I complained and you consoled. One thing kept getting clearer, however: I was yearning for a life with you.

You met Lisa when you came to Pittsburgh; she was five years old and I remember so well your singing contest with her. The three of us were in my old Chevy riding along Washington Blvd. and I ran out of gas. I had to leave the two of you and hike to a gas station about a fifteen minute walk away. Lisa started asking you about what an opera singer did and so forth, and I guess you tried to explain about singing and holding notes and so forth. She decided that she could hold a note at least as long if not longer than you could and so the contest began. When I returned to the car with my gas can full, you two were still battling it out and she claimed to be the winner.

You were won over to her charms.

You met other friends of mine, Bill and Jane, but I hesitate to verge off in that direction of detailing places and friends; rather, I want to focus on us, on our letters, on our trying to understand how we could claim our love as something beyond the ordinary.

I want to follow our journey towards that goal. That is really the only reason for me to do this with you, love, so that I might understand our beginning and the path that our love took for so many years.

February 18, 1970 (Oakmont)

Love,

Did you see me in the house at the broadcast? God, if there is anything at all to sorcery or witchcraft, I was there. I felt your eyes on me during that glorious little song. How marvelous you were — that distinctive, absolute clarity and lovely tone. Was it to me, really? I believed it so strongly (and always will) that I closed my eyes and found us together, you singing, warmly pressed against me while I turned the pages. Our little Columbian friend smiled in his niche as if wisely approving our love. If I have ever been happy, love, it has been in those stolen moments when we cheat the petty whims of fate and capture what is ultimately the only glory of being a man — the kind of love of which he is capable. Beyond passion lies the sea of your soul / it is there we drowned in copulation / Permit me voyage... (with apologies to Hart). Poor Hart, do you think he ever managed to have what we do? It could have made all the difference. Unfortunately, his poetry probably would have suffered if he had. For his work grew so and depended greatly upon his pain and hunger.

I think the Beppe picture is marvelous. It now faces my bed, framed of course, and at this moment I am being seduced by your eyes. It keeps me from sadness in many forms.

Turandot, Saturday. That is a special one for us. A beginning. I will meet you again Saturday. Same time same place.

Put some incense in our friend for good luck.

Persephone will be coming back to us again. We will share her in Cleveland.

Yours, Charles

April 11, 1970 (Oakmont)

My Love,

Once again I am away from you, except for the mails. I would have written sooner; however, I've been looking for those gas things for you, and wanted to write when I sent them. Can't find them — I will though. I thought I'd get three or four and you could give one to Pat and to Robert.

I was a little nervous for the last couple days of my visit. Pat is a dream and is always beautiful with me, but I do get a little up-tight when he's around. He is a reminder to me that you share your love with him — and I must learn to do that. It's strange but when I am back home, it is clear to me that I share a unique portion of that love only me, no one else. In your apartment, perhaps after we have had our tea and scones, when we embrace — it is at that moment that I want to possess you solely that I deny to others voyage to your soul. Its futility makes me cry — as I did.

Will you ever really know the full degree of my love? No affidavit, oath, vow or x- ray could truly convince you of how totally you have become part of me.

45

You asked me whether I thought our love was "immortal" — maybe you have asked that before — and, also, maybe you have seen " immortal" love come and go in others. God, I know how easy words fly back and forth on the breath of desire — but, love, believe me that if a man can know truth as well as love then accept the measure of my heart. Alexander had nothing on us — except renown.

Delightful surprise yesterday to be teaching Crane, and up pops Page 11 and "Nov. 11-15, 1969....and you beside me...." It brought back those glorious few days, only the two of us — cut off from the outside world. Will Cleveland be like that? I hope a little anyway.

Another surprise. I think I saw a bronze statue of Antinous at one of our Pgh. antique stores. It has all the signs you told me to look for — turned down head, curly hair, wide separation of breasts. It's beautiful. Would you like to see it? Maybe I can take a picture of it. What do you think would be a good price? They were asking 325.00. We stopped at 225.00.

I would try to get if for 150.00. What do you think? The figure has a goat skin over his shoulder, and some sort of berries or grapes woven in his hair. Is it David? Dionysus? Dealer says that it is definitely Italian late 19th C. I shouldn't get worked up about it, but you know what a thing now I have about Antinous & Hadrian (we both have!)

I've thought about what you said about my "taking a lover," so to speak.

You're right, I'm best alone ("I was born to be alone, I am best so..." Roethke) — if I can't be with someone whom I love totally. You're damned hard to top; I was never one to settle for second best. Perhaps someday I will be driven to a compromise. We often are. But until then, and even after, I know I will have had a love relationship that pales 99 44/100% of all those around me.

Write soon,
Charles

Well, you know that the bronze bust was not there when I got back to the shop. I had gone first with a friend, some-one much more into the antique thing at that time than I was. He was sneaky Jerry, my companion that day, and he went back before me and bought the bronze. Never saw him again. Silly man; waste of time. He was a window dresser at Hornes and among his predecessors was Andy Warhol which thrilled him no end indeed.

It seemed the time had come for me to tell you about Oliver so that you could realize that I was having sex on a regular basis and with only one person. No more Lucky's for me. Oliver went on his own regularly to Lucky's for the dancing and "girl" talk with his friends; but he came back to me in Oakmont afterwards.

You and I had spent a week in New York; Pat was there part of the time, so we kept a weird low profile. I'm sure he thought I was just another one of your "out of town" boyfriends. I felt uncomfortable.

You had cautioned me often about the wild west char-acter of the Upper West Side with muggings, and shootings and you asked me to get some cans of mace for you and your friends. I referred to it as "gas."

Robert Leonard liked to hang out at your apartment since his lover, another Robert was an actor who was always out of town. We called the actor Robert "Big Robert" and, of course, our visitor, was "Little Robert." You loved Little Robert (Leonard) dearly as I did the more I knew him.

Robert Leonard, 1979

April 14, 1970 (New York)

My Love,

I knew today would be a great day after I finally found you at home. What a joy having you for those few moments. Then I found your letter in the mail; there it was like the cherry on my already sweet day. How ironic it all seems. I spent so much time convincing you to love me, to open up your arms and accept all the love I had for you, without reservations, only with trust and joy. I've convinced you, but now you seem uneasy, unsure. Please don't be. Pat can't change the way I feel for you, any more than you can change the way I feel for him. We have so much for each other, you and I, and it is too beautiful to question. Beauty is immortal, and we must do nothing to mar that beauty, we must try to leave some trace of it. You must die as I must, but for an eternity our love will exist; we will circle each other, you and I, like two spheres in space and reach out and touch and embrace forever. People will look at us as they have so often in the past, and say, "with such a love how can we doubt..." I think only two things exist in the universe: beauty and love. And they are the same thing.

They are you, and they are me, and they are all the loves such as ours that have ever been or will be, whatever their names may be. Smile and enjoy me my dear Hephaestion. Love and hold me my dear Antinous for we have found each other again.

Come to me in Cleveland on Thursday... it will be a joy.

> Animula, vagula, blandula et amorosa.

And you reminded me again, love, of Hadrian's final poem to his soul with the addition of beloved. Your sending these extraordinary images to me, calling up profound comparisons to our love made me feel increasingly blessed at your presence in my life. And, then, when we were together the images became kindling for the pyres of our love making. Each time we were together we etched deeper our bonds and passions. I had no idea what was fueling it all; yes, the grass helped, but I believed it was us reaching into a place that was profound and sacred.

April 18, 1970 (New York)

Charles....what a beautiful love letter that was...I feel so terribly inadequate in trying to answer... What I should do is fly to you, and give you your answer in a murmur in your arms. I shall treasure it always, what a shame it is that I can't show it to someone, or publish it; how proud I would be to have everyone know that I received such a love letter, and that you love me.

I also like the reviews very much. What can one say of Auden? Why should anyone have to ? Did you like the music of *Carmina Burana*? I like it rather less than *Catulli*, but still like it. City Center is showing Lucie Rosen's production from Caramoor with quite a bit of success.

At Caramoor it was paired with the *Songs of Bilitis*, which made for quite a wicked evening. The type of thing Lucie loved so, just a bit of shock. Mildred Dunock narrated the *Bilitis*.

I'm rather glad I received your letter after I called you. I would have been rather speechless after reading it, such beauty.

I think you should come to Cleveland on May 1st just after school as early as you can. Perhaps you could take Friday the 1st off and come Thursday evening. We will leave Cleveland on Sunday morning so try and come as early as you can. I would like to have Friday,

Saturday together there. You could see my *Pagliacci* on Saturday night. I'll bring the stuff and all the trimmings, candles, incense and all, if you will really come. Our sex has always been of the Gods... if it works out this time we will transcend the Gods. Now that you will not fight it, I will come along with you, and together we will wonder, who knows what fields. I will sing for you this Saturday, every note for you. I may say Colombine but I mean Charles. I sit in a cart under a tree with a guitar, strumming my love song "Open your window, show me your face and your eyes which torment me, come to me it's your Harlequin." I sing it early in the second act... I hope you like it... for it's for you my love.

Even this early in our relationship, Andrea, we were always adding the spiritual link to our sex, which we both believed added to our sensational sexual experiences. We were smoking grass but that was all, at least all that I was aware of, unless you spiked the grass. All I know was that when we were in bed in Cleveland, and New York we wrapped our naked bodies in a sexual writhing embrace that took us both beyond ourselves into climaxes that echoed through every pore of our bodies. Those experiences scared the shit out of me in New York, you remember, and I found it hard to reach into my innermost soul and open it to the passionate love that was offered by you. We talked about my thoughts, and by the time we were in Cleveland I had accepted you as my Beloved, the one who was meant for me — with whom I would share the great love of my life. All the poetry I had ever read, all the novels, all the movies, all the myths that I now called forth in my own life seemed to coalesce in our passion. And you lay there, my love, with arms wide open. And in Cleveland of all places.

I remember, in fact, that the sex in Cleveland was so sensational for me that I asked you if you had put some drug or something into my wine or food. Crazy, but it was that good. Cleveland included seeing the *Norma* with Sutherland and Horne. Even in that vast civic auditorium with its ghastly acoustics that experience was one that has stayed with me all these years; opera was getting into my blood.

May 5, 1970 (Oakmont)

If I had known what Cleveland would be like, I'd have hitch-hiked up last year. It was as beautiful as one could hope for. My only regret is that you didn't share the museum with Pat and me — or that we lost that afternoon together.

I wish you were here now. I always need you so much after we're together for a short time. Today is particularly bad because the weekend was so glorious.

Also, the Kent State business is so depressing and tragic. The whole scene is another nail in the coffin of a hoped for, but growing ever weaker, dream. The love children will go mad or be shot before the country reforms one iota.

Thank you for leaving the oil. It may not do anything but my skin loves it.

Wish you had kept the money — simply that I don't want you to feel that if I ask you to do me a favor that it will cost you something. But I love you too much to fight. Thanks for Cleveland.

Love, Charles

July 21, 1970 (New York)

I didn't want to call you — I felt so close to our departure my call would sound like a farewell; Pat and I are going to Costa Rica — where did that come from — who knows. I think from what I have read, I will like it — in any case — from there to Mexico and home on August 23. I'm writing this on the copy of the *Rubaiyat* which you took to bed to read to me from — now it has moved into my bedroom, and has become one of the many things which lie around and remind me of your visit. Little pangs of memory. This morning as I lay in bed, I thought how strange memories are. I got up and wrote in my memory book: "Time has become flat through glossy pages I remember the past." Even "nothing" reminds me of your trip — the nothing I see in front of my house — Mon. Wed Sat — makes my heart jump, and I turn to send you on your eternal journey. I must confess to you that the most tiresome thing we did together was that endless search — still I would like to do just that — now, just to have you with me.

I hope you were not too upset by the Robert situation; in the future, I shall not let anything like that develop.

I hope your August will be fun and trouble free — remember, people bother you only as far as you allow them to. Say no!

I will think of you always, and will call when I return.

Much love,
Andrea

You told me that though you and Pat were now only apartment mates rather than lovers (you had been together about fifteen years when we met) you still liked to travel together as a couple. The main link — as with so many New Yorkers — was the rent-controlled apartment that you shared.

The money you each saved on rent provided most of the funds for travel off season. Also, of course, you both worked at the Met. Pat was on the Directing staff of the Met.

The eternal journey you mention is of course the alternate street parking on the Upper West Side. Mon., Wed., Fri. or Tues., Thurs., Sat.; which side this time? And now where to? It was a pain in the ass, as I guess it still is, but we did it together and then went for breakfast at the Greek's on 84th St. It was an annoying ritual.

Robert had come to the apartment every night for dinner and sometimes stayed way into the night; loved him, but we wanted to be alone more.

August 9, 1970 (Mexico)

My Dear Charles,

I'm sitting in a small rose garden by a swimming pool, on the outskirts of Puebla. It's quiet except for birds and a few distant sounds of the city. Very sweet and fresh air. In the far distance over the tiled domes of the city I can see the snow covered peaks of Pococateapetle and Ixtaccihwatle. Costa Rica was a strange experience, we found ourselves driving to the Volcano Iraqu through some of the weirdest scenery I have ever seen. Forests of tropical vegetation, but cold and foggy and covered, rather strung, with moss. Some of the plants have leaves that are three feet across, and ageless trees lost in eternal fog banks. Then you drive out into the sun, find yourself in a crater where you can see both oceans. One of the things we have noticed is that even the smallest centers have an air pollution problem. Rubla is a nightmare of belching busses and smoke — yet it's so small. Fortunately, we stay out of the cities, where the air is a dream, and there is no noise. But this experience has brought home to me what I have always believed, the only pollution problem is people pollution.

If half of the population were to disappear so would all the pollution. I think that is what nature is doing. Our leaders sit around blaming one another, and hoping it will go away before their term in office is up, the industrial complex will see us all dead before they will stop, and they will ignore the fact that birth control is no longer of any use — we must stop births. Here in these poor countries the church has mounted a merciless campaign against birth control. Families which are starving must have 7 or 8 children to please the Pope, put their 20 pessos in the box, and prove their father "un machio." Man really deserves whatever nature has in store for him, and I fear this summer has proved that it is not far off. So breathe all the fresh air you can. I for one from now on, will no longer vacation for rest, but for air. I didn't mean this to become your problem, but if you stopped smoking you could help!! Today we went to a dry, dusty village called Cullula. It was a great Aztec center, and the inhabitants planned to kill Cortez as he passed on his way to Mexico City. He heard of this and killed everyone at night, and levelled what was once the greatest Aztec city. Now all that remains is a church built in 1565 on top of what seems to be a hill, but what is in reality the largest pyramid in the western world. We climbed it today; you can also drive up. It's covered with trees, but you can tell it is man-made. Its base is larger than that of Cheops's Pyramid in Egypt. Now, centuries later, the Indians still climb all the way to the top to seek help from a small doll dressed in crepe, and leave their pathetic 20 pesos as a bribe. Their ancestors left their beating hearts, and had their bodies hurled from the top in order to bloody the steps and prove their devotion — how very far man has gone.

I've thought often of our "two weeks." I've had a lot of time to think. I wish you were here to read to me, these poor brooding lands need words. Then I could tell you to drive me to the end of the street, and turn right, and we could ride off together — what contentment.

I'll be home on Sunday the 23rd — very late —

Much love,
Andrea

August 25, 1970 (Oakmont)

Love,

Thank you for such a welcome surprise — your voice always lights my world. I remember Jane commented to me once that I seemed so "changed" around you — "happier somehow." Of course, I passed over it casually as a result of my interest in you — your exciting personality and life.

She was absolutely right though, you know. I do react physically as well as emotionally to you. Your smile and touch are enough to bring instant warmth to me. Although we did have much that was beautiful during our weeks together this summer you know that I was pretty low as a result of the <u>test</u> and an accumulation of several things. Not the least of the "things" was the creeping realization that your world — the public one which includes your friends — is so interwoven (and naturally so) with Pat's that I seem to be some sort of "appendage" — something that must be explained away. Everyone you introduce me to is polite and genuinely gracious but still I am aware that "our world" is at its best as a private sphere — one which rests in seclusion and romantic dreams. Perhaps, Cleveland was such a "high" because there were no Roberts, no Hillas, no Moes, but only two lovers who laughed at "Tarzan and the Aztecs," had ice cream in bed, and ravaged each other completely.

Love, I'm sure you understand that I enjoy and cherish meeting your friends and sharing them with you; however, I think it is important for me to understand us as well as I can. Oh, I know that you are right when you caution me about <u>thinking too much</u>. That isn't what I'm doing this time. It's only that I want to understand and protect something that lies at the center of my world. You and Lisa are my loves and ironically I am in some way separated from you both. Do you have any idea how I long to walk into my apartment and have her run into my arms again — or to sit and look into your eyes across a dinner table night after night. As life would have it, I also know that those moments become mundane when one has them every day. Is it better then to keep the flames of love bright by rationing its pleasures? Perhaps, so. Well, for better, for worse, for richer for poorer, with stones or without, your love is what I want. With all your friends, with Pat, with opera, etc. I share a major part of that love, but there is a certain part of Andrea Velis a part that I have seen through the haze of a "trip," or through the eyes of a poet, that I alone enjoy. It is mine forever. Funny, you know the only time I feel that I am sharing that part of you is when you sing " the Madwoman" or even play the tape. I told you when I heard you sing that role I realized that you were firstly a great "acting" tenor and secondly one of the most beautiful men I had ever met. Please don't think I'm being foolishly (and unnecessarily) gushy. Seriously, when I heard you at the rehearsal and then at the performance (also on the tape) I realized that there is a point at which you transcend the role and reveal, what I feel, is a very private spirit of Andrea Velis — my beautiful secluded part.

Well, at least you're back in NY again and soon we'll be sharing Sat. afternoons — just you and me, Milton Cross and several hundred thousand people. That can still be surprisingly intimate — "Columbina" was mine alone last winter!

It will be hard for me to walk into that school come Sept. 8. I will look on the bright side though — my salary was increased $600.

Write often my love,
Charles

You had your kidney stones operation and I had failed my French Reading exam in prep for my MA exams, and we had had some fantastic solo time in New York that summer.

The summer time together had brought me more and more into your circle of friends and especially into Pat's company. I liked him, as I indicated, but was struggling with where I fit into the whole picture.

I had a few sexual encounters with Drew B., the man who offered me a job in the Drama Dept. at Carnegie Institute. It was purely for the sex on both our parts. The job offer was a separate issue, and I was considering it. I was naïve about Drew's sexual needs as time would show.

And so I decided to ditch "Chuck" and sign off as Charles as you preferred.

September 3, 1970 (New York)

My Dear Charles,

Thank you for your wonderful letter; as usual it was a joy to receive and re-read. I believe had I never met you but somehow we had begun to correspond, I would love you only for your letters. There are so many parts to you, like my Olympia doll in *Hoffmann*. I have seen many of them and I love them all. You remember, our love began by letter and our letters sustain and nourish it.

I think during your visit we discussed at length how things were going between us, in regard to my many friends — I still maintain that a lot of the coming and going was envy — it can't be that a love like ours was unnoticed. In any case, I enjoyed the luxury of taking you and our love for granted. There you were, my most desired object, and I knew you would be there, and I could savor you anytime I pleased. I know you were under a terrible strain. I tried to understand and help you. I hope that in some way I did. I wanted from the bottom of my soul to make more demands on you — but I couldn't bring myself to add to your distress. I wanted only to comfort you. I was very proud that you confided in me, although I felt inadequate. I wanted so much to take you in my arms, and to wipe away all memory — take you away into a land of love and forgetfulness. I think the most blessed gift is to be able to forget.

I can't tell you how moved I was that you include me in your love for Lisa. I know how you feel for her.

Must I wait until January to see you? Perhaps. But be with me in your letters. Perhaps you can come to Chicago. I leave on October 16 and stay for six weeks. Can you come? Please — much love.

Andrea

In this letter you talk about "envy" that your friends had and that that was why they were so intrusive the whole time that we were together in New York. You even write "There you were, my most desired object…" and you did not pick up that what I was feeling, the stress that I was experiencing when we were with them was caused by that exact description — I was feeling like an "object" in their eyes — a treasure from Pittsburgh, of all places, that you had charmed from the steel valley to come and play in a world of opera, antiques, champagne and grass. That was what I was sensing in their company — not that they were obvious — on the contrary they were all charming, fun, and likeable — but what I was sensing simply oozed out of their pores and became part of the air and smoke in the living room on W 89th St. I doubt if they or you, for that matter, had any idea of what I was sensing and did not quite understand; nevertheless, I knew that what I was feeling made me uncomfortable, and that the discomfort was only relieved when you and I were alone, because then I could look into your eyes and see in them that the love was as true there as it was in my own heart. Yes, I would go on this journey with you. Fuck your friends and those "object" feelings — I decided I was in for the long ride of our love.

September 23, 1970 (Oakmont)

Heat exhaustion grueling time schedule and a taste of despair have kept me somewhat occupied lately. I'm very unhappy right now. School, of course, is at the root of the problem but there is very little I can do about it right now.

I agree that I too would love you through your letters alone. But the very thought of never having looked into those fiery Greek eyes — of never having experienced your arms around me and our bodies intertwined — is enough to dispel any ideas of fulfilling love through letters. Our letters are merely sustenance compared to the feasts of Cleveland, 89th St, and Oakmont.

Chicago sounds great. Are you sure you want me to come, though? I know that you'll be very busy. You know I would love it. Let's talk it over after you know more about your plans.

January will be all ours. It's the thought of that week that will make the coming winter bearable.

The paper continues to serve as my only creative outlet — reviewing the local scene. Nothing terribly exciting so far. Covering the Pgh. Playhouse production of "Your Own Thing" this Sat. Real heavy stuff!

Write and tell me everything that is happening with you.

I wish you were here, my love; as always, I need you.

Charles

Obviously, my Love, our relationship had changed my life. It had opened up new avenues of experience and reignited my interest in the arts on a level that I could never have imagined before I met you. Returning to my teaching job — after a year sabbatical to complete my course work for the MA — was a bump back into reality. Teaching now was difficult because my greatest teaching tool, which was being myself, honest and open with the students was no longer possible. Accepting myself as a gay man impacted all my roles in life — teacher, father, son, ex-husband — the whole bag. To identify as gay was to be labeled many nasty things but the most egregious was the one of mental illness. Here I was, happier emotionally because of love in my life for another man, and the culture was pissing all over me at every turn. Only you, and the environment you had in New York seemed able to operate independent of the general condemnation of us, and that was mostly due to having a mostly gay clique of friends on the Upper West Side.

So, back I went to the regimen of the 8:00 AM punching the clock — did you know that Ken High required the teachers to clock in and out? It was the only school I ever knew that required that. I used to have to get Carolyn Bruno or another friend to clock me in sometimes because I often had to deliver my copy to the paper before going to the school. I was miserable. Susan was teaching French at the Junior High, and probably would transfer soon to the High School. I felt that I was cheating the kids — something I had never done — and that made me feel so dishonest each time I got in front of them. I prided myself on being a good teacher and that seemed beyond me now because I was unhappy with the persona that I had to present to them each morning, and that made me feel like a phony.

September 28, 1970 (New York)

Yes, you're right, having been together, letters are sorry substitutes, but then you don't receive your letters. Nothing can replace your presence right here in my arms; however, your letters are incredible works — I almost wish I could share them with someone. Hold them up and say — you see he loves me — here is the proof — and I love him. I'm reading a new book on Hadrian written by an Englishman who questions the physical relationship between Antinous and Hadrian. He doubts it, in spite of Hadrian's "Like of males" but then he also used all forms of show as shew — shewed — I'll bring it to you.

My performances in Chicago are November 6–9–12–18–21–23 — I arrive there October 16, so you can come from then on — I won't be working so hard that you can't come in Oct. I may come to you between the 12–18 performances, if I can. I'm returning your check — I don't remember <u>lending</u> you anything. In any case put it all in a kitty to fly to me in Chicago — that we can both work for — what a joy that will be and what fun we will have. Please don't be sad — soon you will be out of it all — Smile and laugh for me.

Andrea

> I told you that I was on the brink of resigning and accept-
> ing the job with Drew at Carnegie Institute. Within a week
> or so I did resign and started the job in the Drama Section,
> which was funded by a large grant from the Mellon Foun-
> dation, and was geared to providing interactive programs
> in the arts, particularly drama related, to inner-city schools
> and youth groups. With us in mind, before I started the job
> I told Drew that I had a commitment to be in Chicago the
> last week of October.
>
> I think that our relationship was becoming more impor-
> tant to me than my career. Only Lisa superseded you at this
> point.

September 30, 1970 (New York)

I can't tell you how happy I am for you. Not because you "quit your job" but because you seemed so happy on the phone. I'm sure your new job will be much more in the direction you want to go. Certainly teaching has very little future, yet you always have it there if you should need it. You will now meet the kind of people who can be of value for you, and of interest to you. I do hope that you intend to go ahead with the M.A. Everyone may have one, but you're still better off with it than without it. Drew B. I'm sure will be a shit to work for, but I'm also sure you will know how to treat him. As I see it, there is nothing but sunshine and joy in your decision. It's a step you had to make, if not now, very soon, so congratulations. I'm so excited as I'm sure you are about your prospects. I will help you in any way I can; I only wish I loved you less, so that I could love you more… unfortunately you now have all my love. So all that is left to me is to reaffirm what you already have. I'm proud of you, and love you. I wish I could be with you so that I could share your joy in a more physical way. Don't be too happy now. Save some joy for when we meet. Then we shall celebrate, and the heavens will resound with our joy for each other.

Andrea

You were right, it was a good move in the right direction, even though Drew B. was a problem from the get-go. He hired me for the right reasons; I was good with our events with students in the city and I was good with the Saturday morning drama classes and so forth. However our relationship had a short honeymoon for the first six months; then, nasty, jealous Drew started to emerge.

October 1, 1970 (New York)

It's now 7:30 A.M. I don't know why I got up so early. Perhaps some commotion on Broadway — I no longer sleep in the back bedroom as in happier times — perhaps excitement at the imminent arrival of my new refrigerator. I am not jaded after all you see I can still be excited by a refrigerator — perhaps nerves over my *Hoffmann* performance tonight — I think a cold is on the way — perhaps it's irritation over Hilla's insisting on my coming to Connecticut for her last weekend — she plans a large dinner tomorrow night. Ravioli cooked by her Italian maid just for me — Perhaps it's knowing that week after next, I must leave my quiet little womb, and go live in a hotel for six weeks. I don't really like Chicago. I suppose now with your new job it will be difficult for you to come to me there. Or will it be easier? Can you tell them that you had already planned two trips to Chicago? One in October and one in November? That way you can visit me during rehearsals, and then again to see the performance. Will you try?

It would give me reason to be happy about leaving home. I have not been back here long enough to want to leave yet, and I am a dreadful lazy pig about leaving my safety and comfort. Do tell me you can come twice. That would hardly be enough to last me until January. Also in Chicago I will have endless time, but in Pittsburgh I will be on the go constantly, what with two trips back and the two demanding roles I must perform.

There, I think I've said enough to melt even the most obdurate heart. Therefore, yours which is kind, and sensitive and all mine, must by now be completely convinced.

I talk of "quiet womb" — Hilla's for the weekend — dress rehearsal of *Chenier* 11:00 A.M. Tuesday — *Hoffman* performance 8 P.M. Tuesday — dinner Monday night — friend from Rome — right hand man to Dino de Laurentis, and a very good friend — actor type with A.C.T. in San Francisco — Thursday dinner for faggot type dancer with Met, and his wife — must find another guest who "understands" preferably female type — perhaps Chicago will be rest. Meanwhile, Pat wants to paint and paper the kitchen before I leave.

I have been reading *Billy Budd* — I must say Herman could really turn a phrase!

By now you must have thought many times about your new job. Any doubts? Don't have. If my intuition is to be trusted at all, and it has served me well enough, you have done the right thing. It's as though you have thrown open the door of your cage of false security, and allowed your creative soul to fly free — now it will soar unbounded and give the only true security — fulfillment — my only fear is, that it may outshine the brilliance of our love. Will success (i.e. happiness) make Charles love Andrea less?

Andrea

This was you at your most seductive to me. I loved getting these long rambling letters about your life in New York. I had seen enough of it to fill in the blanks, including Hilla — the camp follower of opera, as Zubin Mehta called her once to you — and had seen her big house in Cos Cob. You were hedging a bit as I would later learn. Yes, you wanted me to come to Chicago for all the right reasons of love, including our passion; however, you had a fear of being alone, not a paralyzing fear, but enough that you avoided it whenever possible. Of course, on my part, I was so swept up into my love for you that whatever opportunity presented itself for me to be with you I would agree to it regardless of the heat I got at a job, any job, even a new one at Carnegie. You were going to Chicago to do a role in the American premiere of Britten's *Billy Budd* and

Theodore Uppman was reprising his role as the first Billy. And I would get to go to rehearsals and be there for the opening night. Wow — yes, indeed.

October 7, 1970 (New York)

Charles — I'm rather surprised not to have heard from you. I was sure that by now you would have written full news of your new job. I have an indulgence to ask of you — since these reviews are rather stunning I would like them to be mentioned in the New Ken and Pgh. papers. Perhaps you could do the New Ken one, and send George Anderson the one for the Pgh. papers. I hope this doesn't put you out too much, or embarrass you.

Marco and Ruth are coming to dinner tomorrow night. They are being used as a foil for one of our ballet dancers and his wife. I thought they would "get along" since their "history" and "lives" are somewhat similar. My long-awaited refrigerator arrived last Friday, and was pushed out the back of the delivery truck onto Broadway so now we try anew this Friday. There are so many chores I must do before leaving for Chicago next Thursday — I'm sure they will never be done — and to tell the truth I will not miss having to do them for six weeks. I'm becoming rather bored with responsibility — will I see you in Chicago? Don't write me here. I'll let you know the address there — many thanks and love.

Andrea

You and I had gone to visit Marco and his wife in Teaneck; I told you that I had a summer tryst with him in Vermont and had promised to visit him in Teaneck. You and I drove out in August I think. They both were teachers in the Teaneck school system. Marco and I excused ourselves and went upstairs on some probably obvious ruse so that we could kiss and touch a bit, and you two were left downstairs. You probably looked at each other with knowing eyes as to what in fact was going on upstairs. I think that you too were a bit attracted to Marco — an Italian beauty with all the assets that one expects, and a charmer of rare talent.

Neither you nor I could resist physical beauty, and even though, yes, our love transcended it and we knew it, we liked to clasp it when fate stopped us momentarily to enjoy it. So, Marco was that for me, and, I am sure without your confirming it, that when you kissed him in greeting at his arrival and at his departure, your tongue found its way between that lovely smile and slid quite easily as far as he let it.

George Anderson was the entertainment critic for the New Ken paper who hired me, and he left for a job with the Pittsburgh *Post Gazette* a year after he hired me. Good critic and great admirer of yours. I did get the "stunning" reviews to him as you requested, and loved doing it. I was even going to get to review your performances next year in Pittsburgh.

December 8, 1970 (Oakmont)

Again, I have let time sneak between our moments. How selfish of me to look in the mail box every day for that familiar "Velis" when I have not written you since you left Chicago. Perhaps because I think of you so much I expect my thoughts alone to be answered.

Thank you for *Hadrian* — I prefer the " romantic" view, however. But I guess it is nice to know the more objective facts.

You seemed pleased with the *Budd* in spite of the confusing reviews. By the way, you must have a friend in Dallas. I've seldom read such a paean for a performance which you didn't even give. Tell Robert — the usual 35 copies!

I didn't mean to give the impression that the Chicago people "messed up" our visit together. Everyone you've ever introduced to me has been worth meeting — and usually enjoyable. I guess we needed more of each other in Chicago — more than just making up for time lost — we needed each other in time present — so much so that when I was on the plane I felt as if I had never got around to "now."

When you come to Pgh. I promise only myself. I suppose since this is an official visit there will be commitments but I will snatch you back to Oakmont at every opportunity. I want to hold you, make love with you, and talk of all those things that are ours alone.

I am not foolish enough to think that no two lovers have shared what we cling to. You have known more love than I and you know the ravages of time and familiarity on love. Antinous knew them and that is why he shackled Hadrian's heart to his memory. I dread every lapse of time because it means our love moves farther from the moment of its white heat.

Shakespeare spoke of this loss in a sonnet to his young friend, and he captured the sense of eternal love as only he could when he expressed the idea of love merging souls in its ultimate form. There are times when I feel we are lovers on that scale. You will never lose your "sexuality" in my eyes because I shall always make love to your soul as well as your body.

Perhaps, that sounds like something I concocted from a book on

Zen, but, regardless, I truly believe that only love on a "mystic" level (complete with icons, incense, and champagne) weathers the "whips and scorns of time."

All I want to say is that I will love you always — even if the Met closes and you come and teach music in Arnold.

Drew is more than anyone could ever believe. He is the Black Spiro Agnew.

My love always,
Charles

You remember the Chicago visit went very well and *Billy Budd* was a success. I spent a week with you and we did a lot of socializing with the gay A-list in Chicago, mostly museum types. I felt on display, rather uncomfortable as I had felt early on in New York. Many of them knew that you had a lover in New York, and so I was picking up the vibes from their "latest member of your collection" attitude. I shot down a few queens with my own "don't pull that silly shit with me" attitude. But I did resent that our time together was wasted with those social evenings, when time alone with you was so precious to me, and I needed you to reassure me of our love as it existed in our letters to each other.

December, 1970 (New York)

I can't thank you enough for your letter. What a marvel it is. I hate to part with any of them, and keep them safe, but these last two I carry with me — they are with me always — ready to inspire me when I need it.

Do you remember when I had to drag you out of your loneliness? How wary you were and afraid. Not wanting to be hurt as you had been hurt before. Now you know that what I was offering was not love alone — sometimes I think that what we have should not be called love. Man has used that word to mean so many things, most of which are not at all what we have. Where will we find a word to mean what you said in your last letter? Where will we find a word that stretches into the past and on into the future? Our meeting was not a meeting, it was a reunion. I'm sure when Hadrian found Antinous, it too was a reunion. I wonder if they knew when they were last together. I only hope that I shall not have to endure another lonely existence without you. There is no question of promises between us — no arrangements nor chains. You are Andrea and I Charles.

"Pepsi Cola" kid indeed! Tommy — Oliver? These are fauns we find in the forest on a sunny afternoon. They nuzzle us; we stare into their sad eyes; we play with them. But they are free and wild — we must not, can not have them. They are creatures of nature, and we are gods — we would destroy them.

I hope you like the print. It is by a friend of ours in Rome — I think it is universal.

Andrea

The Pepsi Cola Kid was a trick of yours from one of the tour cities, a cute blonde; Tommy, who was in the wings, on the other hand was really a beautiful young man; he danced with the Joffrey in New York and had one of those amazing Nureyev butts. I did agree that we should be free to play with as many fauns that came along and wanted to romp a bit. We were separated too much for any other approach, and I certainly realized very early on that you were not a man to deny his urges or his needs; fortunately, however, your romps were not indiscriminate and casual; they were always done with genuine affection and passion, and discretion. And I too, played a bit early on, but at that time I enjoyed Oliver so much that I had no desire to seek out any other fauns in that gay forest.

This letter was the first time that you mentioned your good friend, Larry Cabaness's art; he did the Christmas print that you sent to me.

January 2, 1971 (New York)

My Love,

Thank you for the *Carnegie Magazine* — the more I read about that damned lecture the more I don't want to do it. Your article reads like a love letter — did you know that? I spent a hectic New Year. We did our *Perichole*. Hilla decided to have a party and of course it was in my dressing room — three cases of champagne — packed in ice — all my rugs are now wet — jellied donuts (German tradition) — everything covered with powdered sugar — melted lead put into cold water for fortune (German tradition) shit — a real mess — only gay note was the arrival and departure of Spiro Skouras and his effect on Cyril Richard — quite a laugh. Last week we visited Mary Curtis Verna for dinner — I thought of you often and laughed — Germane was there —"My husband the famous Viennese doctor who invented (Con-ed?)" and poor Bill Taylor — who will now always remind me of W.C. Fields.

The fifteenth is not so far off; I dread it, for it seems the Saturday return on the 23rd will be a close call, 5:10 the curtain, 5:40

plane from LaGuardia — what do you think? I am thinking at this point of a charter. Perhaps the Met can pull a V.I.P. and make them hold the thing — perhaps not — we shall see — in the midst of all this with auditions and Drew B.'s damned lecture, I must spend as much time as I can with you — and that is my reason for coming — and the only thing I want to do!! So besides being tired, rushed, et al; I shall also be frustrated by not being able to do anything I want to with you. So my small plan to come and spend a week with you has turned into a nightmare because of other people. Enough bitterness!

Here are a few phrases I would like to share with you. "One or another is lost since we fall apart endlessly in one motion, to part from each other." D.H. Lawrence. Isn't that beautiful? This I like also — "there shall be such oneness between us that when one weeps the other shall taste salt."

So my love I hope your holidays were very nice for you — I thought of you so often and wished so to have you with me — to hold you close and toast a new year of our lives together. Who knows what it will bring us — so much joy I hope — I want that for you — joy — joy — love — laughter and then I want to share it with you. To take your hand in mine and lead you through clouds of joy — all illuminated with your laughter — buttery yellows and orange —

      Until I see you, remember my love for you —

                Andrea

Oh, my, Hilla, yes, she was a permanent fixture in your life, no question about that. She went to the Met every night that you performed, and spent every intermission in your dressing room, and after the opera provided champagne for the guests who always came back to see you. The result was that there was always a party atmosphere after the opera in your dressing room.

Drew had persuaded me to ask you to do a lecture on your career as a Comprimario, and you had agreed. However, it became a sort of event for the Pittsburgh Opera, and all of your old friends from the company. Our plans got sidelined again. And a good bonus was that I got to see you do the character of Shuisky from *Boris G.*

January 10, 1971 (Oakmont)

My Love,

From the sound of your schedule, it seems our moments together this time will be as preciously stolen as they usually are in New York. A far cry from the plans for our week together. At any rate, we will be together between flights. I'll settle for that! (Thank goodness winter nights are so long.)

Pittsburgh is experiencing a "strike plague" comparable in effect if not in scope to what is chronic in New York: no newspapers, no school, no garbage collection, no city services. Perhaps, things will be back in order by Friday and everybody's greed will have been alleviated.

Needless to say, I have made no plans for us — have discouraged Jane from being "hospitable." As far as I know, I have one event to review other than the opera, of course. Emlyn Williams is doing "An Evening of Dickens" on the 18th. It sounds like a nice evening.

The poetry was beautiful in your last letter. D.H. Lawrence was a master with words of love, but your thoughts for us in the New Year were lovelier to read. I, too, hope that love and joy wait for us throughout the year. Until I die, I shall love you — without melodrama — without fanfare — it is as simple as that — I shall always love Andrea.

Until Fri at 1:52 PM

Take care, love
Charles

Don't forget to burn some incense for your safety and our joy!

January 11, 1971 (New York)

It's so early — I awoke at 6:30 — Perhaps the noise on Broadway, perhaps worries over my impending trip — many problems will be solved or not today. I wanted to say so many things to you over the phone — but Robert was lurking in the background. I had tried to reach you so often — that I had stopped being selective about situations — when I finally made it Robert (bless him) was there — (remind me to tell you of his *Hansel & Gretel*.)

I'm so happy about the afternoon lecture being cancelled — can you arrange to do the same for the evening — then we would have all day alone.

On my desk as I write you are a million tickets representing next week's coming and going — quite a stack — it tires me to look at them. My only consolation in all this is you — you — you —

In this month's issue of *After Dark* there is an article about a ballet done to the poetry of Leonard Cohen — some of it is so beautiful — although I wonder how you dance to "when you wrap your tongue about the amber jewel and urge my blessing" or "kneel love a thousand feet below me, so far I barely see your mouth and hands perform the ceremony" — I like this, and had never heard it before "and the real and violent proportion of your body made obsolete old treaties of excellence, measures, and poems" or "you have lovers, they are nameless, their histories only for each other."

It pleases me to think that someone is saying such beautiful things. It's comforting to think that we are not alone in the beautiful things we say and do to each other. It never occurred to me that the beauty we have and which we consider eternal could be on such a vast level that others feel it.

Is it possible? Why have I not felt it before? Why was it Faber who awakened it in me — was it Faber? Or was it something that stretched down over the centuries to touch us — to make us take each other by the hand and gaze into the constellation of our eyes?

Andrea

Ah, you learned that my actual first name is Faber. You began to push me to reclaim it and to use it again. I was reluctant.

February 1, 1971 (Orlando, Florida)

I can't tell you what a surprise this place was — I expected warm — but had not envisioned what I found — palm tree flowers blooming everywhere — 70 degrees every day. It's as though someone knew what I needed and sent it to me. Today I played a Donoughe and slept until noon. My room faces a large lake — no traffic — only the play of a large fountain in the distance. The city is a horror, but the flowers, the sun, and the endless orange grapefruit, and lemon groves are a joy. Yesterday we looked to the east and saw Saturn 14 blast off. I can't tell you how happy I feel. If only I had you to share it with — then my joy would be complete.

As I sit here in the sun, by my pool, I wonder why anyone would live in the north. Why should I go back? Why should I leave this to go back into the snows, and wait three months to find it again? I am definitely a creature of the sun — I need it, and love to survive.

Our opera is going well — parties everyday — everyone is a real study — but quite nice. They live for this week of opera, and treat us like gods who have come down from Olympus to bring them gifts. If you happen also to be nice to them, they make you a super-god. My room has been filled with oranges — tangerines — grapefruit — and flowers and I love it all.

To think this is all so close, and we sit up in our horrid snows and ignore it.

Not me — I'm going to be like Baudelaire and return to the sun and let it consume me...

Much love,
Andrea

Andrea, 1971

You could no more have left New York for a sunny spot somewhere in Florida or any other place, than Fiorello LaGuardia could have. But you were being celebrated and I don't blame you for loving it. And, of course, your charm was on full display, no doubt.

February 11, 1971 (Oakmont)

Love,

Glad Florida is so restful — I hope that you rested enough for both of us because I need it too! I'm tired in every possible sense of the word.

I won't go into all that your visit meant — all I'll say is that If it took me the rest of my life to recover I'd still want it to happen again... and again... and again. It's after you leave that is the most difficult time — the emptiness is (dare I say it?) Hadrianic. God, I slip into the past easily. Sometimes, I get the feeling that I'm on an island and visited occasionally by a god with a crazy fox hat. Melodramatic? It's either the French exam or my love or both. I'll write — coherently I hope — next week — will also send the spray.

I got them at a cheaper price — so you have a refund coming in the next letter. I met Emerson — Miss Gosetti brought him over — nice but no thanks. He wants to get together and keeps calling "What is someone like you doing out there in Oakmont all by yourself?" At least, as Capote said, "you don't have to look your best for masturbation."

Thought you might get a few chuckles from the review. Considering everything — I was kind.

Yours (alone)

Charles

I think this letter included my review of a rather awful production of *Boys in the Band* in Butler. You remember that Emerson was a friend of yours from Ken High; Miss Gosetti had taught you both English, and had followed your career very closely.

February 16, 1971 (New York)

My Love —

Thank you for your strange letter — you sounded very tired. I don't know what to think about the exam. I feel that if you had passed you would have called — yet I feel you did pass — Christ, I all but incinerated poor Zippy — in any case, you know that to me it makes no difference — so let me either share your joy or console you.

I have not been doing much since my return from Florida. Attended a few rehearsals and will sing on the 26th for the first time — I feel very guilty, but here I am waiting. I have had a chance to read, study, and think for a change.

Today I saw Franco Corelli trying to portray Goethe's "Werther." I wonder if he has ever read a poem.

Last week I saw the Beaumont do Synge's *Playboy of the Western World*. I didn't like it one bit. Do you know it? Should I have liked it?

Poison my dear, absolutely poison — where do you find in that sweet, gentle loving person whom I love so much — poison!! Can it be that deep inside you is something I haven't seen — Poor *Boys* and their band — and they thought they were being so avant garde — along comes my love and smites them.

I love your drawing — I would rather be on that lovely island with you — than any old Allegheny cloud.

Then I could protect you from all the Emerson Milligrams of the world. "Alone in Oakmont" indeed — tell him you are never alone — not for one second. Tell him I hold you close always and that we are united through time -space — and love — tell him my love for you knows no bounds —

Andrea

I had taken my French exam (for the third time, I think) but was still waiting for the results. If I passed, then I could take my MA exams.

February 19, 1971 (Oakmont)

My Love,
You were kind to say that I sounded "tired" in that last distraught note. I was that, but I was also quite low about a number of things — not the least of which was missing you.

It was so beautiful sharing that wild week with you — all those lovely memories made it difficult to exist again without your actual presence. Although, I will not pass on the message to Emerson — the knowledge that you feel that way assures me again that there are not enough Emerson Milligrams in the world to replace one moment that we have shared. Incidentally, my last conversation with him sort of did the poor thing in. I was quite pointed — or poisonous if you prefer — and don't expect him to call again. I don't give a damn for people like him who approach every male as a phallic plant. I even realize how dreary and naïve seem my feelings at times to "chic folks." Again, I don't care. We each find a way of coping with the absurdity of much of our existence and I have mine. The

80

only choice we have is to write the dialogue for our own tragedy, I suppose. My how Beckett-like this sounds. — " I can't go
on.....I must go on...." and all that.

It hardly sounds like the love song I intend it to be. You have
touched my very soul as no one has ever done and I shall treasure
that touch and desire it as long as I live.

Thanks to Zippy and all gods known and unknown I passed the
test. I should have called — always hesitate because I want to talk to
you when you are alone.

I will be off work for a few days to prepare for my next exams.
Everyone who is aware of the difficulty of the exams says that I
am foolish to attempt the tests with so little concentrated effort —
normal procedure is to study intently for six months. Since I never
do things the easy way, I will attack them head on next month and
probably fail –then have to take them again in June. Sounds like a
defeatist attitude but I'm only trying to prepare myself for what
everyone thinks is the likely result. I will do my best to prove them
wrong.

Work... Work... Work.

By the way, I think I have out-flanked Drew. Through a series of
moves which he unknowingly precipitated, he has lost the authority
over me. So, he is much less a threat in all areas. In fact, I think he
is worried that I want his job — which I don't. I prefer to let him
self-distrust.

From what I read about the Beaumont's *Playboy*, you were
right not to like it. The play itself, however, when properly done
is excellent theater — a taste of Chekhov with blarney instead
of borscht.

Hope we talk soon,

Love, Charles

81

P.S.

Missed your Beppe on the *Pag* broadcast. — No more Schmoor! He may copy everything you do — but he will never have the clarity of tone and the poetry of phrasing — every syllable an emotional expression — which is all yours.

March 15, 1971 (New York)

You were very strange on the phone yesterday. I wonder if it was because I had awakened you, or if you were tied up with the Bill thing. I would have liked to be with you, to talk of death. He was lucky, Bill was. He was cut down with no lingering pain — no tormented years of blindness, and slow loss. He had a successful life, was comfortable and left the world an heir.

Of course anyone's life can be happier — one can love — art — so many lovely things. I always feel that when I go, it will be a loss only for me — for there are so many wonderful things to see and do, and so much love to share. I'm not sure that that continues afterwards. One thing that will always last will be our love. I know I will still feel that, and I hope I will be able to share it with others later on. That has made my life complete — that is my heir.

Your letter was marvelous — such a howl of protest — such outrage. You are right, and you must continue believing in Zippy and beauty — that is all we have — that is our god — beauty and love, joy and laughter. I have been thinking about your statement of the Phallic Plant. You are again right, and perfectly put. I have quoted you several times — it's a perfect put down. Reminds me of my favorite graffito, "The pope is imphallable."

From what I can glean, Rudi will not dance here — but come — come when you can, come as often as you can — come, for my soul and body long for you. My heart yearns to be led by you again peacefully — hand in hand, through that land where our souls reside together.

Andrea

Yes, I was upset about Bill's death. He was a good friend — Jane's husband and only 52 years old. He died on an Oakmont golf course.

Rudi Nureyev did dance with Fonteyn in the spring at the Met and I shared their magic with you.

"Zippy" was our little Mayan terracotta figure which you had brought back from Mexico in the 60s. He had a special cup-like area in front to be used for burning incense to him. We did it for good luck all the time. (And I still do.)

March 16, 1971 (Oakmont)

Dear Andrea,

It's very late and I'm tired. I shouldn't be writing this now, but I need to reach out to you — this is the only way that we have.

How beautiful it would be if I could just turn to you beside me and talk and look into those eyes. I often wonder if you realize how deeply I miss that part of our relationship — the sad realization that there is always a plane ticket or a schedule lying on the desk waiting to take one of us away from the other. You have many people to replace me but I have no one when you go. Oh, I see people; I go out, but half of me is lost. I've been going out quite a bit with the student teacher at Ken High, Oliver, as you know. He doesn't know you but he is jealous of you because he knows that you have a part of me that I will not share with anyone else. Oliver can have a part of me that requires companionship and daily activity, but the totality of my spirit is released in your arms. I've told you before that you and Lisa are the two treasures of my life.

Death is a wretched intruder and it spins us into a total awareness of time, futility, and love. Bill was a lovely man — Jane asked me to choose several poems to be read by the minister at the funeral. All the ones that I suggested have a central theme of living life to its fullest by being sensitive to the world around you. *Fern Hill* by Dylan Thomas is one I particularly hope they use.

Jane has already started to lean heavily on me. I've thought a lot about the possible situation that could develop there and it worries me. I'm not sure whether we have ever talked about my relationship, but with her son, Tom, in New York, things may be very difficult. I'll need to talk it all over with you.

Tomorrow is the funeral — it will be the most painful part for me. Finality is never so real as when they place a casket beside a hole. Despite the flowers and phony grass, you know that when you get in your car that casket will thud into that freshly- turned earth.

Perhaps it is in the light of such ultimate finality that I long to cling so frantically to you — my consolation is in your words to Emerson — "I am never alone because I am loved."

Hold me close to you in your dreams tonight my love.

Charles

March 20, 1971 (New York)

These last weeks before the tour will be a nightmare — every free moment has been filled with some function or the other. My friend from Athens is in Washington so I'm cajoled every day with invitations to come down to their day and night parties — they will all arrive *en masse* on Friday the 26th and the only thing I can do for them is a midnight supper that evening, after we have all left the theater. The Noh company is here and I have an entire box for their *Curlew River* that night — then on Sunday they will drag me off to Greenwich Village to a lunch — this is five parties later — mercifully — they will leave on Tuesday. Do you see why I long for the quiet of your arms? Oh, that land where we lie on soft grass together — and I can rest so deep in your eyes — my love — know that this beauty we share will never end. I feel so sorry for your student teacher — but I can't understand anyone being jealous of what we have. We don't possess each other. I keep no part of you from other people. I would be very unhappy if that love and beauty which I find in you was hidden and reserved exclusively for my use — of what use is such love? We didn't come together to hide our love — but that it show like a beacon over all time. Would a Hadrian be jealous of us — I think not — he would be proud — just as we are of his love.

Please don't envy my crowds — I so long to be in the quiet of your arms. My body is here in this maelstrom of horrid activity — but my soul lies there beside you — listening to your deep breath as you sleep waiting to wake up —

I have never left you, you know that.

Andrea

May 17, 1971 (Dallas)

Hi my love —
How often I've tried to call you — every time the urge moves me I call — no avail. You must be very busy these days. Atlanta was a ball — I met a lot of very nice new people and the weather

was divine. I've become Chestnut brown and glowy. I skipped Memphis and stayed one day over in Atlanta — then flew here ahead of the company — now they have gone on to Minneapolis and I have stayed one day longer — a quiet day in the sun — my two friends here continue to be more outrageous every time I see them. This year it's a new $20,000 pool, complete with whirlpool bath and vast plastic garden. One of them I have named Luther Burbank of the plastic set. He goes out every morning and plants a new garden. He also spends time ripping up any grass or weeds that might be so audacious as to try and <u>live</u> in his plastic garden. This is all complete with a sprinkler system — which I claim waters his garden with silicon. In the morning, we have coffee with Sweetah — milked with fake powder — and heated in a microwave oven. I suspect that they themselves are not real — I sincerely hope they are not, our civilization cannot all be going plastic, can it?

I have missed you, and so am looking to New York in June — with you — I'll continue calling.

Much love,
Andrea

August 23, 1971 (Corfu)

Charles my dear —
I'm sorry to have been quiet for such a long time, but with Robert along there was little time to spend alone. Now he has returned on a 6 AM flight to Rome. We have a pink villa on the island of Corfu; it sits in an olive grove, and we can see through the grey green trees all the various bays of Palaikastritsa. We have a little car, and drive to all the lovely beaches and sites on the island. This

morning in order to get Robert to the airport, we got up in the dark silent middle of the night. Dawn came up as we drove into Corfu city, and silhouetted all the cypresses and weird olive shapes against the skyline; one needed Beethoven to complete the fantasy. This is quite a place; the hillsides look like what we ideally dream of as Elysian Fields. Pat and I have two weeks more to rest up from our Robert trip.

Yesterday was the end, when he asked if we ever felt locked up on this planet — He really does go-go-go despite it all. I will be calling when I return — I hope you have had a peaceful summer. I now have Cavafy in Greek — we may be able to share it soon — much love,

Andrea

You asked me originally to go on this trip to Corfu with you and Pat. However in late spring Robert was diagnosed with what he said was rectal cancer. We were all stunned, but you were devastated. You loved him very much; at the time, I did not know that you and Robert had had an intimate relationship; Robert had a lover — an actor who was always on tour it seemed. You and Pat were shaken up by Robert's illness and so you both got complete physicals just to make sure that you were both all right. Robert had never been to Italy or Greece, and so you wanted to take him in my place, which of course I understood. Eventually, after some treatments back in New York Robert quit his job at the Theater Guild and went off to Hawaii (he said that they had the best health plan and the best pot); after an operation in Hawaii and six months of follow up care, he survived that crisis and went on to many other adventures, including becoming the most cherished lover of Peter Shaffer.

August 30, 1971 (Oakmont)

Dear Andrea,

Today was my first day back at work after vacation and my spirits were quite low at the prospect of facing what has more or less become an intolerable situation with Drew. And when I came home, depressed, needing kind words and love, your letter was waiting. It is uncanny how timely you are. At my most forlorn hours you come to me — either by letter or phone — you reach out over hundreds or even thousands of miles to touch me with embracing love and my troubles are made lesser, my life brighter.

How I burden you with my minor tragedies! I won't bother you with a listing of Drewsiana. Suffice to say that I am getting out if things don't improve. In fact, I went to Phila and Hartford to be interviewed for jobs set up by a local placement service. Neither job was worth making the change for. However, with luck I will find something by January (because I have set that as a deadline at the Institute.) Either things improve or I quit. Never again am I going to endure years of a job that I am unhappy in.

Lisa was with me (or rather she stayed with my mother) for most of July and August while her mother was in Europe. The two of us spent several days at a motel near several Disneyland type parks in Ohio. Lisa was thrilled to be staying at a motel. She kept insisting on making the beds up so that I'd save money on the room. Directed by her own logic, she figured that we should get a deduction on the room if she handled the maid service. The trip was fun but exhausting. Can you imagine riding roller coasters, logs on wheels, antique cars, etc. for eight hours at a clip. No, I'm sure you can't. It took me a week to get my stomach under control.

Corfu sounds like a poet's haven. I envy Pat for sharing so much of the beauty in the world with you. Robert was on my mind so much during the summer. Often, I thought about the crazy mishaps and treasured moments which you were sharing. He is beautiful in many ways, and one is because he does wonder if you "ever felt locked up on this planet." Tell me soon how he is doing.

Peaceful is a euphemism for my summer. Dull is more to the point. Lonely is another good one. If only you could understand how deeply I miss you. At times I feel that only when I am with you do I exist fully, completely.

In Oakmont, I am half of a dream — the other half waits in a darkened room — broken only by the light of a small candle beside a bronze bust. It is your love that makes Oakmont bearable.

Heinz Hall is ready for unveiling and looks magnificent. It is all they expected and more. Hope you can sneak away for weekend visit in the fall.

Write soon, my love. My need is great.

Charles

August 31, 1971 (Oakmont)

Zippy did it again for us! I now am a Master of Arts! Don't ask me how but I passed the exams. Tried to call you with the news all day (Fri.). Wanted to share the comments by the examiners with you, so I'm enclosing them — most are quite accurate — last page is funny — what does he mean by "cavalier attitude?" When you finish — return them so I can "press" them in my Bible or something.

It's over! I keep walking around telling myself that I really did pass. I had thoroughly prepared myself for failure — thoroughly — and now I have to convince myself that someone didn't make a mistake. They said it couldn't be done — but we did it. All hail love, Crane, Blake, and Zippy.

We will celebrate soon I hope!

All my love,
Charles

As you know, the MA was a major step in escaping the harassment from Drew. It helped me focus on a next move, but I was still confused as far as the direction I should go.

September 1, 1971 (Corfu)

This island has been an enchantment. I hope I can share a few of its experiences with you. This is our fourth week in the little pink villa overlooking the bay, and our last. Two days remain. Often I pass through a long wide valley called the Ropa. I stop halfway and look across the dry fields dotted with olives and cypresses. The silence there is absolute; you can see people moving far away but no sound reaches you. The slow movement of the animals makes only a dry, hot sound. The only intrusion is the passage of an insect. Being there has made me realize that I have never heard silences.

My next favorite spot is a beach called Myrtiostissa which means in Greek "Lady of the Myrtle" for a small white chapel which stands among the myrtle trees halfway up the cliffs. The beach is practically inaccessible; it's remote and the cliffs very high, so it has become a haunt of young people — hippy types who camp out and bathe nude. We went there because it was Lawrence Durrell's favorite spot. Fresh water comes out of the cliffs in various spots causing lush vegetation, and falling in large pools on the sand below. This makes the hippie's life possible there for they can bathe and drink without leaving their beach. They parade around in naked splendor proud and free. Our first day there, one young giant, bronze from head to foot, with long thick black hair and full black beard went to the cliff face to shower in the falling water. He mounted a small rock and stood there glistening in the sunlight. Man, proud and beautiful using nature as she offered herself. A sight I shall never forget.

Now I must tear myself away from my bay, my olive grove. I must close the doors and shutters on my little pink house, and return to another life. Newspapers, television, telephones and problems —

Much love — my return to telephones does mean I can talk to you again, one of the only pleasures that accursed instrument gives me —

Andrea

> You were at your most romantic in that letter, love. So Idyllic: naked young men among all the unspoiled splendor of nature — very you, my love. And me too, of course.

September 7, 1971 (New York)

Charles —
How lovely it was to find a letter from you waiting for me. You sound so unhappy, yet until something turns up for you — you are stuck with that monster. Still if he succeeds in bugging you, he has achieved his goal — you must try to ignore him, and make him realize that anything he does-cannot touch you — then you will be victorious over him. He can only harm you through yourself. Do all you can to get away from him and when you have — then give

him a parting blast and walk out. He can only bug you if you take him seriously — try to pretend he doesn't exist — you know you'll be out of there soon — and he will only be a bitter memory to be laughed at. If I could only be there to shelter you; I want so much to not have you hurt — I want so much for you to be happy. I know I can do that and I want to.

Nothing has changed here — I'm beginning to doubt the value of vacations — they hold up a false life to us and we love it — would I really be happy under an olive grove in Greece? Everyone there wants to be here — where I am (excuse my breakfast all over this) I close you in my arms — be happy —

> Drew was the "monster" in question, and he was really giving me a hard time at Carnegie Institute. I guess I told you that he was jealous over my relationship with Oliver, and angry that our previous sexual adventures were ended by me so abruptly. Remember, also, that he was doing some really sleazy stuff with the Mellon Foundation grant through which we were funded. I discovered it and he decided to undermine me. So, since I had been writing for *Carnegie Magazine*, I asked to be transferred to the PR department.

September 21, 1971 (New York)

Charles Love,

I hope you feel much better now. I feel so helpless when you are ill and I'm so far away. If I were nearby I could be a Jewish mother for you. You know — make chicken soup and force you to eat. That's a warning to you should you come to live nearby. I hope you have written to Marco. You know I would love to have you near. If only near enough to spend weekends together; the nearer the better. Don't you think though to move to another small city, isn't very much of a move? Wouldn't it be better for you in all ways to move to a large city… say New York. All the world is here… theatre, art and me. Not to mention Robert Lowell.

Tell Jane the 27th of November I do sing… I can get her tickets if she wants.

The 30th of December is fine for you. I do sing *Hansel* that night. I want you and Lisa to stay here, if you can sleep in my bed. I think it would be wonderful to have you both here. We will have our usual big tree and all. By then I will have my new Baroque bed… you can feel like an opera star when you sleep in it. Phil Mathews gave it to me. He asked if I would like to see it, and I did. He needn't have thought that I wouldn't like it, it is all me. Cascades of gilt angels and follies all over my head… much. If I ever decided to give it all up as you are doing, I would have to have an auction to get rid of it all… be happy my love, you know all will go well. You know that Lisa will always need you, as I also will… one always needs the person they love.

Andrea

September 29, 1971 (Oakmont)

My Love,

Again I hesitated for awhile before writing because I dread coming to you again with unhappiness oozing from my fingertips. Of course, your advice is so right. I should endure Drew until something better shows up. But, somehow it isn't that simple. Need my life be a series of such endurances — quiet desperation — relieved only by bits and pieces of happiness centered around you and Lisa?

Now, at 30, the desire for some things has mellowed but I'm still faced with enduring yet another unpleasant phase of my life. I know all too well that most people have little more than that in life — that I am blessed in many ways — that towers of steel courage like Hilla scoff at fools like me who writhe in circumstance. I have not been ruthless enough in life to grab at what I wanted at other's expense. Even now I could not leave unless I felt that Lisa would not suffer from my absence.

But please understand that I cannot endure this one. I have never regretted leaving Ken High, perhaps that was a first step towards the feeling I have now. Andrea, I see myself being boxed more and more into a corner at the Museum that I don't want. In order to escape Drew I've been working PR and writing press releases, etc. I don't want to go in that direction — it's unreal to me.

Perhaps only I know what is happening in my head right now and it isn't good. It scares me to be this unhappy — to lie awake with my bedroom walls seeming to enclose me.

In the midst of all this stands the oasis of our love. That remains a positive part of my life.

Meanwhile, I think that I am going to Fla. in January and teach for six months or something. I have friends in Tampa.

Think I will give up my apartment at the end of October — take two months to get things settled and leave for Florida after Xmas.

I will bring Lisa to NY to see you triumph as the witch in *Hansel and Gretel*. I wish I were with you now, love.

Heinz Hall is magnificent — wildly mixed reactions as one might expect — some people miss Syria Mosque if you can imagine that. Your article was delightful against the cover story on the Kennedy Center. Mrs. Hillman must be pleased at the fruits of her tour arrangements.

I was at the opening and it was quite an event for the city — so great to see so much happening in town unlike most cities (other than New York.) Possibly this fall within the limits of space of the downtown area there could be a world series game, opera, touring stage play, event at the arena, etc. all on the same night, bringing hundreds of thousands of people into the area night life.

Sorry to burden you with such a weird letter — it was written at the nerve ends of my head. Your love helps tomorrow as you know. May it always be so.

Love,

Charles

> "Weird" letter indeed. So over the top but I guess I was that unhappy. Mentioned Heinz Hall because you and I toured it prior to its completion with one of the Symphony Board member who was a friend of yours. I covered the opening for the New Ken paper. I was looking for teaching jobs again; this time hoping for an up-grade because of my shiny new Master of Arts degree.

October 20, 1971 (Oakmont)

Love,

Quick note to let you know that I'm all right — whatever that means.

Still trying to get a job — although I haven't contacted Marco I have registered with a teacher placement agency for the East Coast area.

As I thought, Susie informed me that she plans to marry within the year. That I can take. However, there is the possibility that hubby-to-be will be transferred to Denver, CO. God, I can't see Lisa going out of my life that way — being swallowed into the blankness of the far west. Can't cope with that right now. Wish you and I were at the Villa Rosa now!

I've been hearing my PR stuff for the museum on the radio. That is kind of fun. Also, my articles have been getting into the papers. It's much too plastic a thing for me, though.

Other news —

Drew doesn't fool as many people as I thought — the Mellons plan to end his program at the end of '72. I was talking to a member of the PA Council of the Arts who "gave me the word" as he said. Also, talked to head of Art for Pittsburgh Public School who told me that they will have nothing to do with that "con artist". Needless to say, I'm delighted.

I'm trying to tie in with reviewing for an artsy weekly paper — remember "two dimes." It would be a good move — more immediate area prestige and coverage for my writing.

Made reservations for Lisa and me for Dec. 29 — arrive NY at 5:20 PM. We will leave afternoon on Dec. 31 — OK? Wish I could simply stay on forever and forget my problems with Drew and Susie in your arms.

Got caught in the turmoil after the World Series victory — only for a few minutes though. I don't understand why they made such a big deal about the "riot and looting." Seemed like nothing more than a large version of a South Side Polish wedding minus the potato salad.

I didn't like the opening opera — bad lighting, awkward staging and tacky production. Music was good, singing too, but I can get that on a stereo record — and even better.

Have been busy with reviews — lot happening here because of the new hall and availability of the Mosque. Saw Fonteyn last week with the National Ballet. She still has exquisite form but attempts less and less. Hope she has the wisdom to hang up slippers before she slips into a mere parody of her own greatness.

Had to break down and buy a used tuxedo for all these important events. Thanks to my Bank of America card and changing styles I now have a thin lapelled, shiny black suit, with built-in dignity — it probably has shared many a prom night and absorbed its share of coke and peach-fuzz semen.

Guess I sound rather cynical — only bitter with life's jokes on me.

But then, there is you! A gift of love to soften all the harsh jokes. That makes tomorrow possible.

"When in disgrace with fortune and men's eyes, I all alone contemplate my outcast state... think on thee — and then I would not change my place with kings"

Love, Charles

A little more upbeat, Love. Guess I was looking forward to leaving the museum after two years and going on to the next stage of my life, where that would be remained a mystery.

October 20, 1971 (New York)

I have been thinking that the time is approaching when you will leave your apartment — The thought makes me sad I like thinking of you there, safe — where we have loved. I love knowing that I knew what your surroundings were. I loved to know the bed you slept on — where you rested, ate — worked. I felt that way when you left your garret — then I became used to your new home. I'll always remember the morning we woke to find snow out the living room window. Now I won't know where your are. When I call I'll not be able to see you come to the phone. Mind you, I would not have you stay — I'm sure your reasons for wanting a change are good.

I'm sure you are right in wanting a move. How pleasant it would be to have you closer.

I'm sending a photo of a new statue of our Antinous. New to me that is. It was moved to the Vatican museum where I found it. It is perhaps 12 ft. tall — How beautiful he was — even with his lap full of flowers — he seems to be very unhappy and tired.

Think of this year — all the things you have done — just passing the test is more than most people accomplish in a year — I'm very happy for you — now be happy for yourself — know that I want you and I need you –

Andrea

November 3, 1971 (New York)

Charles my dear —
I have talked to Marco, and he promised to write you with information as to who to contact about work up here — he seems to think a man would have little trouble.

Enclosed are the tickets for Jane — I seem not to have her address which is strange — I shall write you a more coherent letter later — Pat is waiting to take this out into the rain and mail it saving me a trip.

Much love,
Andrea

November 9, 1971 (Oakmont)

Andrea Love,

Thank you for calling. I hope you have some idea of how much those calls mean to me. The love in your voice and words minimizes all the "overwhelming" problems that plague me right now. But, I'm not going to write about all that this time; it's too heavy. Will say only that Drew and I have reached the breaking point and I will either be moved or fired within three weeks. That's all.

Jane will send a check for the tickets. Thank you for getting them. She is flying to NY, so a ride up is out for Thanksgiving. Too bad, I'm so anxious to see you.

Couldn't resist enclosing the article on Pgh. from *Life*. Thought you might enjoy reading about all the excitement that you're missing here in Steel City.

Did you read about the Caravaggio exhibit in Cleveland? *Time* couldn't resist slipping in a tidbit of homosexuality so that inane comment about the homosexual version of the Ecstasy of St. Francis resulted.

I would love to drive up to Cleveland simply to see the show — it is unlikely that Carnegie will get it.

You would love the exhibit at Carnegie with 2,000 pcs. of 16th and 17th century furniture, porcelain, and silver. Nearly 3,000 pcs. were given to the museum by the Mellons — making the collection one of the finest in the country. It's all in preparation for the new art museum which is being built currently next to the original building.

By the way, there has been a lot of talk about cleaning the bldg. It is not pink stone (as someone told you); the consensus, however, was that cleaning would speed up the deterioration of the limestone. Also, the American Architectural Society protested that cleaning would "destroy the soiled splendor" of the five-acre structure. The money was ready and everything, but the protests caused such an uproar that I doubt whether they will do anything.

Marco has not written yet. I doubt very much whether he can be of much help.

My landlord is trying to rent my apt. I plan to be out by the 30th (Nov.) Then I will stay with a friend until I make a definite decision. At any rate, even if I should stay in the city I don't want to live in Oakmont anymore.

Too much trouble driving back and forth — especially when I have a review to do. I, too, feel a sense of loss about leaving the apt. because we shared love here that was solely ours — a secret love time with snow and champagne.

Before I leave I will drink a bottle of champagne to celebrate a new beginning as well as a toast to us — may we love in many more places so beautifully.

Jane is quite upset — almost refusing to accept that I'm moving more than a few blocks away. She has been so good to me that I feel guilty — as if I'm abandoning her. She does have many other friends, and, of course, I will keep in close touch.

Wish I did know what was happening — I'm optimistic though. I got love!

Charles

Haven't called because the "code" is too outrageous. When it's rough I think about you.

November 13, 1971 (New York)

Charles —

I'm so sorry my last letter was so curt. I had to run and wanted Jane to have her tickets. She has already sent me a check. Actually I wanted her to bring me some of those "tear gas" things. Could you get four and have her bring them? Have her pay you, and I'll pay her. Or better still bring them yourself. Has Marco written? He promised he would. If he hasn't let me know, and I will call him again. Perhaps now that Lisa is staying, you don't want to leave Pittsburgh. How nice it would be to have you here. But I shouldn't be selfish — I know that Lisa is very important to you, besides — should you really pack up and leave until Susie is actually married? So much could happen.

Here is a picture of my new bed where you and Lisa will sleep, and eventually we will. The base, which is not in the picture, is just as Baroque as what you see. I hope to be photographed in it for *After Dark*, which is doing an article on me — Do you like it? I hope so — much love.

Andrea

November 17, 1971 (Oakmont)

Love,

It's the middle of the night — I'm crazy to be sitting here writing at this time — 7:30 AM comes too thunderously. But I had a good day today and I thought I just had to write for once when I was up a little. So often, I write to seek comfort from my beloved.

Today was an exception; in fact, the past two days have been rather good. I've been planning press receptions for the opening of an Abstract (early American) show at the museum — also, I've been introducing a visiting Danish lecturer at special engagements. The reaction has been quite good — Christ, they have so little idea of what I can do.

Anyway, I've been doing a lot of writing — press releases, public service announcements etc. There is a chance I will present info. lecturers to Women's Clubs, Jaycees, etc. explaining the history and various activities at the Institute. Public Relations is still not my bag — (even though some old lady called our office to ask who was that beautiful young man who introduced the speaker?) "Beautiful," "young" — god! — no wonder I had a good day. The poor dear must have had cataracts. I consider myself beautiful and young only in your eyes — you look at my soul.

Drew is still trying to push me out — although I'm not working with him at all — it is a complicated matter because my salary still comes from his budget which is a grant from the A.W. Mellon Foundation — no part of it can be used for purposes other than those Drew approves. That's the snag! My plan, of course, has been to make myself indispensable to the PR Office — unofficially my new title is Asst. Public Relations Director. But that is a matter that won't be settled for several weeks. If Drew wins — and I certainly don't underestimate his Machiavellian tactics — it will be a sticky matter. Being an Irish fighter from way back, with lots of crazy IRA blood in me, I have compiled a complete file on his scams bordering on outright criminal offenses. I am not beyond using it as a weight to balance my power against his outrageous actions. The Mellons as well as the Institute would shudder at the thoughts of a scandal.

Drew's art opening, which poor George Shirley participated in, was a disaster. It is a long story — cost the Mellons close to $10,000 — you wouldn't believe the things that occurred.

I've ordered the "gas" — probably won't be here before Jane goes to NY; however, I will bring them with me. Had to get Jane one too.

That bed is wild — I can't wait to share it with you. In fact, I can't wait to share anything with you — even a cot would do! Lisa will love the whole adventure. She told me she told her friends that she was going to NY to see this famous opera singer and she was going backstage to see him and he is her friend and her daddy's — the kids didn't believe her — so I better get a camera so she can "show off" with documentation when she comes back. I miss you so, love, please call me this weekend.

Charles

When will the *After Dark* article appear?

November 18, 1971 (New York)

How strange to contemplate your affair with Drew. It began with him chasing you around the table, and has ended with him chasing you out the door. Anyway, you have had what you wanted from him, and he has not had what he wanted from you. That is the fate of all who are attracted to great beauty. Yes, my love, you are a great beauty. And you know it. And you don't like it. Any hang ups you may have about sex and your reaction to people who come to you for it, is because of your beauty. I think what you are — what you have made of yourself, is all a reaction against being only beautiful. What I see in you once past your physical beauty is what you have done to make people love you for other reasons. That's why you are offended by quick affairs, because they are based on appearance.

But you should be proud of your beauty, you know you are not only beautiful, you are the many other things which make you the person you are — still to be beautiful is a marvelous thing. Just think of all the beautiful things in your life that give you joy. You are one of those things to people — when someone sees you, they stop, admire you and you have done that wonderful thing — so rare — you have made them happy. After all, it's the stunning beauty of the rose — that stops us in our tracks, makes us go over, take it our hands, and only then are we aware of the aroma which we cannot see from afar. That's what happened to me — on a long, dry desolate road I saw a flower, whose beauty stunned me — I took it in my hand, pressed it to my lips and have been intoxicated by its perfume ever since. Don't deny me that beauty; it is mine.

> That letter showed me that you had really been studying
> who I was in so many ways. You called me out on my reac-
> tion to being hit on by men all the time. You were right.
> I was both aware of and reluctant about such encounters,
> and confused I think.

December 7, 1971 (Pittsburgh)

Love,

Sorry to be so long in writing — particularly after your "love letter."

You, my love, are one of the few if not the only one who sees the "rose" in me. If I ever feel beautiful, it is when I am with you and bathing in the warmth of your eyes. You give me beauty as you give me love. Oh, I readily admit "a hang up" about being valued as an object (if I may borrow a phrase from Women's Lib.) and it goes back to dark recesses of my childhood — I was "too lovely to be a boy" I remember hearing that a lot — my mother kept my hair long and curly as a result — the whole bit. But all of that — including the beauty — is long gone. Only the essence of the "rose" remains — the potential of being loved and loving. You have always and will continue to be beautiful to me. For too many reasons to even try and cover — for *Curlew*, for "Zippy", for a walk along our "monument park", for all those moments when you held me and I wanted to cry because I was leaving you again, for just being the <u>consummate</u> Andrea, my Greek with the Blakean eyes.

I can take anything — knowing that we are once again going to triumphantly make love and share our world of private beauty.

Even Dreadful Drew can't get to that. He is managing to mess up everything else, though. Would you believe he has insisted that I return to his department — accused the PR Division of "stealing me from him" — even went to the President of Carnegie Institute with his story. Naturally, they knew he was lying but they are so ridiculously intimidated by his black magic that I was taken from PR and put back in his realm. It's really absurd. Obviously, he saw that I was escaping him — moving to a better position within the Institute and it scared and angered him. He knows that I know too much about his theft, etc. to be safe to have around, so he wants to force me out. Well, the Mellon Foundation is afraid of a scandal before his grant runs out in July so they are treating him with kid gloves. I was told by one of the important Mellon people that they plan on booting his "ass out of there" when the grant is up. Until then, they can't do anything. Of course, he has tried every rotten trick in the book on me — even tried to get my keys to lock me out. I just want out — nothing there seems worth fighting for. The PR was a relief from Drew but I'm not the type. (Jane brought me the article from the *NYT* by the way.) So, I will leave at the end of December — have told the ulcer-racked Director that I will solve part of his "Drew problem" by leaving — but only as professionally as I came — with a proper resignation giving two-weeks notice, etc. The whole business is a ridiculous joke — an insult to all concerned — black and white alike.

Oh, I didn't even tell you about giving up the apartment. The apartment was rented on the 30th so I had to do a crazy rush job of trying to get everything together and out in 2 days. I unpacked the last box today — sold the stove and fridge — stored many things with Jane and my mother. If nothing turns up here I will go to Florida for six months.

Talk to you soon, I hope.

Love, Charles

January 4, 1972 (Pittsburgh)

Love,

What can I say? The short visit was all more than I ever hoped it could be. What was missing — our cherished intimacy — waits for another time. A time when I come not as a "Daddy" but as "a flower, seductive, tender and searching for the warmth of the beloved's arms." Antinous, cast forever in stone, is pinned over my desk, a constant reminder of love that transcends the frailty of bodies and time.

Lisa made me promise that some time we will do the New York thing again. She will never forget her first trip though. Raves about "the gold bed" et al.

She beams at the mention of your name. Also, made her friend Bonnie a pal for life by remembering to bring her the picture and witch-cookie.

You and Pat were spectacularly considerate, kind, loving, and plain nice about the whole thing. I hope you enjoyed Lisa; I've always wanted to share her with you.

The picture arrived from Mitchell; I'll send the article to you. It will be far less impressive than you're used to at the *NYT*, but remember I'm writing for a slightly different readership.

Miss you again! I wait and wait and then swoosh! It's over, and I'm driving; back from the airport in Pgh. Andrea is not a touchable reality now; only a feeling inside, a photograph of a clown over my desk, a warm memory, a sense that hovers through my body of love — these are what I accept as tangible until I hear your voice on a groggy Sunday morning or until I feel your touch on my hair and once more know your body with mine.

Oh, mustn't forget to mention the clothes that we left — in your drawer — sorry, love, I should have double-checked. Also, I forgot my scones. Seems the only thing I remembered was Lisa.

Love,
Charles

Lisa and Andrea
(as The Witch in *Hänsel und Gretel*, Met Opera, 1971)

January 12, 1972 (New York)

My love,

Thank you for your letter, and Lisa's note — we all loved it, and it has taken its place in my fan mail folder — along with others from children — one signed herself — "yours forever" all sweet. Lisa is a doll, we all loved her — Robert still comments on her intelligence and charm. She is all I would have expected a child of yours to be like, many of the things I love in you, I found in her then even if she were not what she is — I would love her because she is yours. She was not one bit of trouble — actually she helped get over the trauma of the performance. I'm glad you saw the last performance; I think it was the best. It was strange to have you here, and not have you alone. It was as though an image of you was here, and not you — still one moment with you alone in the kitchen — or perhaps a touch in the kitchen — these things thrilled me. I would have wanted to be alone with you, to rest in your arms at night — how comforting that would be — how happy that would have made me, but you were here — I touched you — I loved you.

I have spoken to Deek of the poet whose poems you read. Turns out the American Poet's Association paid for that publication — he said they considered him a promising young poet.

Wasn't Jack Mitchell nice to send you that witch picture — Keep it after you have used it — I'll send Lisa a smaller one — signed. Make sure the paper gives Jack credit and send me two copies — I'll give him one — I think that would please him, this will be the first time it will have been used, and he is very proud of it. He had me to dinner last week, and invited the editor of *After Dark* — a very nice person — I have settled down a bit now — only *Fille du Regiment* and *Countess Maritza* to learn. Much love to you, I'll write again soon.

Andrea

You made Lisa's first trip to New York a dream come true. When we got into the taxi to go to La Guardia, I asked her if she had a good time. She said, "Yes." Then, she paused and said, "I'm coming back you know!"

I think you had so much fun with the children who came backstage after the performances. Even giving them delicious witch shaped ginger cookies.

My favorite story was the one about the little girl who took the cookie, smiled at you a bit and then said, "Thank you, Ma'am."

January 19, 1972 (Pittsburgh)

Love,

Delayed writing because I've been waiting for the article — I'm rather disappointed in it because they left out a few paragraphs and messed up the sense a little; also, after I specifically got assurance that they would credit the photo, it is uncredited! I planned on sending the piece to the photographer, but I am embarrassed at the oversight.

Anyway, the picture took well and was well placed — it should please your legion of local fans, including all the bushy haired boys, future music majors, who will someday pursue you. Please tell Jack Mitchell that everyone raved about the picture — too bad they are so damned second-rate in their attention to details. I attached a note reminding about the credit — and there was a note on back of the picture.

Money is the answer to so many damned things, isn't it. No matter what our ideals, it lurks under the surface, a constant threat.

I remember the time, while you were "unemployed," when we were riding through the park, you talked about realizing how the only thing you missed about the Met was the money. We all "miss the money." Working at the Institute, constantly confronting the power of big money and the protective layer it puts on its owners, I fully realized for the first time the scope of that different life style. Not that they have more fun — not that they dress better, look better, or that matter live that much better; it's that detachment they have. Being a Mellon, a Hunt, a Hillman, etc. gives you a base of security that creates detachment from the mundane concerns of the masses — except as the occasional patron or "savior" of a cause.

Referring to the Hillmans by the way, the Met auditions are Saturday and Theodore Uppman is judging here. When you were the judge that was a fun day that we shared. I'll never forget that pathetic girl who failed so miserably and stood around afterwards on the verge of tears. Such a forlorn, crumbled figure. You tried to be kind, but it was a hopeless thing.

Well, let's get off the hopeless stuff.

Nothing much is new in way of a job. I think I'm going to take off and go to Florida to see about a job at a community college there — maybe the market isn't as saturated. If I go — possibly next week — I'll give you a call before I leave.

Maybe I can get a job with *After Dark* — in spite of what you say about critics — they do need writers. Can't wait to see the spread on you.

Lisa is a lovely little girl — thank you for seeing some of me in her. I often worry that my influence is being squeezed out by all the others. Her clothes arrived — underwear and all.

I'm afraid if I move to Florida for a while that we will lose even the brief days out of a year that we now share. The years are long enough already. You and Lisa are the joys of my life and I would be depriving myself of both. I don't know — wish I could get my life together — I'm confused by the whole thing. Sounds like Holden Caulfield talking. One thing I'm not confused by is that I love you, completely and without reservation. If I am always touched by loneliness, it is because I need you to look at me or to touch me. But perhaps that need is part of the poetry of our love — it is unresolved, continually seeking — and dreamlike.

Write soon, love, (Are you more attuned to Faber?)

> How did you manage to be so patient with all this? You were so tolerant of my confusion and moods. You were amazing — so tolerant.
>
> Florida popped up because I had friends who lived in Clearwater and they told me that I could easily get a job at one of the local community colleges.
>
> I think I just needed to get away from Pittsburgh and my surroundings for a bit to clear my head. The past six months had been very stressful.

February 1, 1972 (New York)

My love,
I'm sorry I have waited so long to return all this to you.

What an abyss of work I have been plunged into. I actually have conductors and stage directors fighting for my time. I should perhaps be flattered, but I am only tired. In the midst of it all, I must do a roundtable during the broadcast this weekend, and a lecture later in the month in New Jersey. Also, Boulez wants to hear me next week for a Haydn opera with the Philharmonic in '73. Pat has gone and come. I kept the apt. closed tight, never left my bed and saw nobody

— I really relished those days alone. I worked and rested — and being alone and quiet really helped. Then my friend Olive dropped in out of the sky to upset everything, I couldn't turn her off, for when I am in Vienna she does all for me. So the lights went on, the noise began. She will be here until Tuesday. You would love her; she is one of my dearest friends, and most sincere. She was in Pittsburgh last Sunday. She went down for lunch with her family.

I should confess to you, that at moments like this, when I'm so harassed I begin to feel very sorry for myself. It's then I would like to run away from everyone, to a quiet island, where the sun shines, but the sea is cool, and you are by my side to console me, to hold my head against your chest and talk to me for hours. That is the only music I need now, the sweet sound of your voice — the only consolation I need is your hands. You are all my love.

Andrea

February 2, 1972 (New York)

Charles,

Thank you for your letter — as always sweet comforting — just what I need right now. If you look at your Met schedule week March 27 you will see that I have 6 out of 7 shows. I'll say no more about how busy or tired I am.

You are so sweet to make plans for us if I direct in Newport, you know it can't be — there will always — be a Hilla, a Robert or a Pat — Newport is run by two friends — Glen and John — who are worse than everyone else put together. What you want or what I want for us is of no importance — there will always be someone else pulling strings on my life. I suppose if they stopped, there would be no life left for me. I haven't decided yet about the directing, it would kill any vacation plans I may have had. Still what are those plans worth anyway if you can't be with the people you care for? Perhaps I'll throw it all over, and work! Perhaps by some strange chance your plans might just work out — perhaps for just one short period — the strings will go slack — and I can move myself for a change.

Love, Andrea

This was a playful dashed off note more than a letter from you. You were at the height of your career at the Met; you loved that and you loved that they used you all the time. No chance you would ever give that up, my love. But you were playing with a romantic fantasy, which you loved to do.

II.
FLORIDA,
PITTSBURGH
AND ZANESVILLE

January 30, 1972 (Lumberton, North Carolina)

A quick note after a tiring, rather nervous day. I'm halfway to Florida at this point, and what point it is. There's a huge sign which greets visitors with: "You are in the heart of Klan Country" "Fight integration and Communism."

This admonition shouts at you from a painting of some guy who looks as though he was doing a white knight commercial for Ajax cleanser and ran through a back yard clothesline, entrapping himself in one of the sheets and still brandishing his jousting piece. By the way, this lovely town's motto is "Lumberton, the all American city." Too bad they fail to appreciate the pathetic irony there. No wonder the arts as well as artists and other sensitive types find they can exist only on the slightest edge on both sides of this vast continent.

Anyway, here I am in Lumberton going to god only knows what tomorrow.

Just as I was leaving today, I got a letter from Greece (Thessaloniki). The President of the college wants to interview me in Philadelphia on February 9. How's that for fate. I hope he is scheduling some interviews further down the coast, because I absolutely cannot afford to fly up to Philadelphia from here.

I'm reluctant about this Florida thing, but it is an adventure of sorts, so I'm going to play it that way.

Send the witch photo to Lisa (she's expecting it).

Until I see what develops I'll be at my friends' place. The address is on the envelope.

Miss you, my love,
Charles

117

February 1, 1972 (Clearwater, Florida)

Well, love, here I am in "God's green waiting room." The weather — aside from dampness — is so far the only bright side of the trip. I'm afraid that Ron and Gerry were too enthusiastic about the job market and that I was too desperate for a change. The colleges are losing enrollments here and dropping teachers — one I went to, though "excited" about my credentials, is letting three English teachers go in June. And the paper hired someone a week before I got here. That, of course, is no one's fault, perhaps mine for bad timing. I have been offered a teaching job (high school) for September, but I can probably get one of those around Pittsburgh. Aside from the money situation, which is pretty gloomy right now, I don't regret the trip. It was good psychologically because it proved to me that I could "extract" myself from the Pittsburgh scene of family and Lisa and not fall apart. Certainly, if I had a job here I would stay for a while, but it seems silly to stay when there is not a distinct advantage and many drawbacks. For the rest of this week, I will look for a job, but I plan to leave to return to Pittsburgh.

If I make another move, I think it will have to be closer to New York and you. Please continue to be tolerant of my misguided groping a little longer. I'm trying damned hard to get my life together so that neither one of us has to worry about me.

Don't bother writing to this address, unless I should write and tell you of some phenomenal break I got. Chances are I will be in Pittsburgh by February 7. With all the address confusion, I have been missing the *After Dark* editions. If you're in the February one I hope I can pick it up when I get back.

Hope the new roles are going well. I am so hungry for you again — so lonely.

I dread the long ride back by myself — I shall think of ways to pay for the gas I'm charging as I drive back.

Also, I shall think of you — my love,
Charles

February 14, 1972 (New York)

The only bright spot in this dark damp day was our phone call. I wish you had come up last week — we couldn't have had much time together alone, but I would have liked to have you by me for a while — I know you had to get back, and set things in order. I hope the Tampa paper works out — I know it is farther than old Pittsburgh, but I would like more visiting you there. New York, of course, would be the best. In a way — other than the financial drag, it must be fun to just cut loose and set out — to try and find a new life — that's a joy that will never be mine — no matter where I go there is always a new opera just over the horizon — now *Salome* and *Otello* — then just out of sight *Countess Maritza* in Cleveland in June — *Prodigal Son* in July — a Haydn opera next year with Boulez — all waiting there to be learned. All waiting there like Cavafy's candles — waiting to be lighted, waiting for me to look back on them — how much glory is there in an extinguished candle? Then there is you — always bright — ahead of me — there somewhere to go — somewhere to lift my hands, and warm my soul.

Andrea

You refer to the newspaper job; I had applied for the entertainment critic's job at the *Tampa Tribune*, but I left before they got back to me.

119

February 20, 1972 (Pittsburgh)

Love,

I'm already excited about the possibility of the short time together in Maine. What a hiatus it would be. You would be away from the phone, the chaos, the schedules, the Hilla, etc. and I would be just away — I know where there are so many spectacularly untouched places in Maine along the coast. That is if they haven't been turned into amusement parks or something. Let's play it by ear — you already have a dazzling summer ahead of you.

You sounded tired — but in a fulfilled kind of way. Unlike my tired spells which frequently represent a total collapse under the weight of mental frustration at the general mess. There are so many exciting things coming up for you — I hope I will manage to share a few of them with you.

The more I think about it, *Tampa Tribune* is my best bet — full-time writing.

Lisa keeps asking me about the picture — I shouldn't have mentioned it. Know that you're hassled but if you can send it to her soon — or that is when you get the prints — I will be a grateful daddy.

I was stuck with a dead car the other night — Saturday after I talked with you actually — so I had to buy a new battery ($30) — thank god for credit cards and minimum monthly payments. I'm sure that I will be paying $10 a month to someone for the rest of my life.

I've thought about "Major/Minor" and I can't see referring to you, whether softened by a cute coupling or not, with the word "Minor". Perhaps, that is my main complaint. At any rate, I hope that you're the center fold in April so that I can post you on my bulletin board. Can't wait for the article.

You know I love you so much — I miss your touch so much — holding you close to me. Oh, I hope Maine works out — that we are totally cut off from the outside and left with our poets and our love.

Take care my love and write soon.

Charles

P.S.

Do you take min. monthly payments on loans? Again, thanks for being there when I need you.

You sent me a lay-out and possible title, etc. for the *After Dark* piece.

March 1, 1972 (Pittsburgh)

Love,

"Master of Miniature" — now that's a title for *After Dark* — How about the "Mighty Major/Minor Master of Miniature?"

Lisa loves the picture and I'm relieved that she has it. She thinks you should have used one of her cats, though. I'm so happy that you seem to enjoy Lisa — perhaps she can be a treat for both of us in our old age. (That is if we ever decide to let age intrude on our sanctum — I won't be the first.)

Like Pound editing Eliot I'd like to say, "Perhaps be damned!" but I realize too well that New England is at best a perhaps thing — that your summer will never be mine, just as your falls, winters, and springs are not. Somehow though we have had them. We have squeezed the fall into a single walk along the lake in Chicago with a stop at a crazy museum on medicine, the spring into a walk around "our park" on the Hudson, the winter into a touch in the back while riding through a snow covered Central Park, and the summer into an afternoon of car-washing in Connecticut. There have been other moments — more precious, more intimate; many spent in a limbo — a seasonless place with a candle that serves as both sun and moon. It is there that we defy all the Hillas the world thrusts at you. I shall always be waiting for you there. For without extravagance, Cavafy, Crane, or Shakespeare to help, I love you. It's that simple, that factual. Like writing that I have brown eyes, and am 5'10" tall. It's a statistic of my life — an extension of what I am. As I cannot imagine my eyes changing color, I cannot imagine not loving you — not delighting in your presence, your touch, your entire being.

So, my love, I am glad that you're busy because you are too talented not to be. Remember, if God didn't want you to do all these things he would break your leg or something. Seriously, I am delighted by all the great things coming up for you. I know that you're beyond caring much about breaking new records at the Met or whatever, but you have to live up to all those things the *NYTimes* said.

If possible lock yourself in your room and unplug the phone as a last resort for rest.

Nothing heard yet from *Tampa Tribune*; I have been substitute teaching at Penn Hills. But I do wish something would happen — an offer from somebody would, if nothing else, keep me from going unglued. I should be able to relax, read, etc. while I have time but I'm too uptight about a job.

Of course I'm still reviewing — Roberta Peters opens in *Romeo and Juliet* on Thursday — her debut in the role — your "buddy" Capone blasted her selection for the role. Karp is enlarging the schedule next year — maybe you can — forget it — you have more than you can handle now.

I'll write soon again, love; meanwhile, during this "gush" of your talents — try to relax and enjoy it.

Miss you… Let's dream of Maine just for the hell of it.

Love, Charles

March 6, 1972 (New York)

I loved your last letter, it had so many of your moods in it — all you. All loved by me. I'm glad you don't like teaching, it will give you more push in the direction I would like to see you go — writing. I think the Tampa reaction has shown you how talented you are in that direction. Never sell yourself short — that's the direction open to you — follow it.

You'll never guess where I am — Allegheny flight 901 from Newport, NY. Do you believe that? In the midst of my mad schedule, I have to fly to Newport and settle the directing job — for July. It seems all set for now. I will do everything, train the chorus, singers — help the designer and pick the singers — I think it should be a ball — my main problem will be Pat. It's a good theatre, 650 seats — good stage (new) and a pleasant setting. I think you can now start making plans.

I'm amused by your saying I should lock myself in my room turn off the phone and rest. When I'm not on the stage — that's exactly what I have been doing — such a din of people trying to break in. Then what do I do about Franco Zeffirelli? For him I must give all to repay the faith he has always had in me, and because I love him. Speaking of love, it has filtered down to me that Bernstein is insisting I sing opening night *Carmen* with him next year. Mr. D. Gentile would prefer new people (whatever that means). I think Lenny will win out. But Mr. Gentile puzzles me a bit. He has not fired a single person — even the older artists, yet he feels <u>that</u> way about <u>me</u> and *Carmen*. I look forward to working with him, and having the chance to prove to him that I am the best person for the role, even if Lenny shoves me down his throat.

I will be glad when *Otello* is finished, but alas — we have not yet begun — Franco is very demanding — and I grow weaker by the day — even the tour will not be a rest — I must learn *Prodigal* again — *Countess Marritza* and *The Wreckers*. Speaking of Countesses — I met one last week who is a dream. Contessa Nadia de Navarro — 50ish — jet black hair — red moist lips — endless millions from oil in Brazil — three apartments in New York — a Stanford White home on Long Island — a castle in Switzerland where she keeps her art. Her third husband — and a 28- year-old handsome Italian lover, who lives with them both — she has covered him with fine lace and gold. She loves Pat (calls him Siegfried) but a mad woman — with the worst taste I have ever seen. I cannot believe she's for real — we will discuss her more later — we must land at Newark now — I must rush to bed — up for Otello at 10 — then *Salome* opening night —

Much love,

Andrea

Oliver was now teaching in Pittsburgh; he wanted to do something else though. I was staying with him; I did not tell you because I thought that it might upset you. It was for a few months. I had a phone installed so that I had privacy for all my calls. Oliver was happy to have help with the rent, and the arrangement allowed me to delay looking for a new place until my job situation was settled. My furniture was in storage.

March 14, 1972 (New York)

I wonder what I'm doing up at seven AM. Still, the way I've been going anything that might happen would not surprise me. And true to form everything that can happen is happening right now. Friends from Georgia — friends from California — friends from Greece — Robert has been no end of worry for me. He thinks he has fallen in love, should he leave Robert, who doesn't help him with the rent or bills? Should he give Mime away?

Meanwhile, he has a woman living with him downstairs, and has not told his new love anything of his illness, which gets worse every day. Sound familiar, or don't you watch daytime TV?

I have been working on my *Wreckers*. I'm beginning to like it. I will have a friend, Bud Poisal, a student of Miss Taylor's, sing the lead for me, the voice is right, and he is physically correct — husky sailor type. Perhaps I can make a beautiful love- story out of it. I think Newport will be my vacation. After the performances are over, not much will be left of the summer for me. Pat is pushing Mexico and Guatemala, but I almost don't have the heart for it. I probably will need a complete rest, and short of Corfu the only place to do that is right at home in my gilt bed. Do you know where I would like to vacation?

I would like you to cup your hands together, and place them on your chest just over your heart. There I would like to curl up and rest, secure in the warmth of your love — secure in the sound of your heart. I could hold my breath until our hearts beat exactly together, then I say, "he too is Andrea and I am Faber." Lisa likes me to call you "Chuck", but I don't want to. Not because I don't like "Chuck", but because you are not a Chuck. The person I have loved since the Time that there was love, is a Faber. No one knows him;

they don't even know how to call him. I call him love — Antinous — Hephaestion — Hadrian — Faber — love —

How long since we have loved, how long since I have found my voyage in your hands, peace on your breast — soon you will come to me, promise. I have done much, I am arid, my soul uncultivated — come and give me life — bring harvest to my heart —

Andrea

March 16, 1972 (Pittsburgh)

Love,

Well, here I am facing a hostile group of acne-covered rebels without causes.

They are answering questions on some story which I'm sure is totally irrelevant to their lives. As is most English that they study, and for that matter all of education. My God it's terrifying! One probably always looks back and thinks "I was different" but in reality there was little difference. Although, honestly I believe it was much more agreeable when I went to school. I went to a private boys' school so that made a difference, but somehow I remember distinctly finding some excitement in learning — there was a fascination about life — about ideas — about poetry. And I was not a terribly "bookish" type, nor was it uncommon. Maybe the despair was there too, but I was too concerned about the prospects of life to be troubled by it.

Today the kids seem totally turned off to any hope to eke out the slightest beauty in life. I've looked out at so many blank faces in the last few years. The spark is so rare — when I've seen it; it has only been a flicker. On those rare occasions the student frequently shuts off the school environment to such an extinct that he goes a bit mad. Perhaps, being a "bit mad" is the only way to protect the spark of life.

I didn't mean to get off on a tangent like that. It simply troubles me to see so many lives exhausted of joy at 16 or 17. Lisa must be protected from that kind of bludgeoning.

So, love, you are probably running yourself ragged by now. I wish I could help by doing something for you — like rubbing your back — making tea and scones or any one of the daily trivia that shatters the greatest of adventures. All I can do is send my love — my thoughts. I am so delighted when you take on the challenge of a new role, even an old one. I could see your ruffled feathers at Gentile's inane idea. Luckily, Bernstein is heavy enough to change his mind. As you said, you will show him <u>why</u> you are right for it.

New England seems very far away — but I hope that it can work out for us.

It would be fantastic to watch you create the entire thing — every aspect with your stamp on it. Oh, I hope Zippy comes through for us. Burn, baby, Burn!

Just back from feeding the troops. I'm sure that Napoleon's troops, crazed with hunger, entered St. Petersburg with much less noise and savagery than these dears enter a cafeteria. Even the little things are made difficult because they hate the system so passionately. They lose all sense of respect for everything around them. Enough!

No luck so far with the writing — what little prospect there is in the area is sewn up tightly. I'm discouraged — no news from Tampa — and the money situation is bad again. I didn't make enough to handle things. Once I get my income tax done I should get some money back but that won't be for a while. There must be a way to see this through to some positive point. Let's hope something will happen within a couple weeks. Meanwhile, I have only you to turn to again for help. I will need to borrow $150.00 to make it. However, I should get that much at least back from my income tax so I'll be able to return it soon. I hate being in this position. Maybe I should settle into some quiet desperation — maybe this is my *Last Picture Show*.

Saw Roberta Peters in *Roméo et Juliette* last week. Found the opera pleasant but uninspired. Perhaps it is the libretto; it seems absolutely void of dramatic impact. Putting the Ball scene first is inane — the feud is crucial to the entire story and it is not apparent on stage until Act 2. Oh, well, maybe I'm too concerned about the dramatic integrity of a work. It seems to me that opera is the ultimate fusion of music and action. Just as the music and sense of a poem ideally miter one to the other, so should opera work towards a similar unity.

Maybe I am all wrong but, for instance, one reason (other than you) that I am spellbound by *Curlew* is that Britten wastes nothing. Everything, each gesture, each note works toward a culmination of operatic artistry. *Peter Grimes* has that to a high degree — Oh! That does it. I am taking this whole thing — including me — too seriously. Guess it's from being in school today.

The world is too much with me today. Take care — all will go well!

Yours, Charles

P.S.

I wrote the yellow sheets (above) in school, and, when I came home, found your letter waiting. Again, on a very low day — one in which even the rainy weather conspired — your love was waiting to embrace me again. Thank you for loving and knowing me as only you do. You saw into my deepest soul perhaps many times but particularly on our night with whistling Mephisto.

And what do I send you — a whining bit of chaos — another segment of a soap opera. Oh, love, I wish I could write to you only of my soul and my love — I wish for you only to be happy in my love — my "Faber" side. But I am forced to impose the "Chuck" so frequently — though, even in my eyes, to you I shall never be "Chuck."

Did Antinous have to borrow Dinarii (or whatever) from Hadrian do you think? You are so put upon by others that I feel like yet another disturbance in your life. Good that you're getting enthusiastic about *The Wreckers*.

I truly wish that I could bring such joy to your spirit. If love is the answer then there is no question, for it is all I have and I give it willingly — my hands are open, cupped to embrace you on my heart — to melt into our single world.

You made today beautiful in spite of man and god.

Faber

Poor you, another long letter filled with such an array of thoughts popping in and out of my head as I wrote. Let's blame it on substitute teaching.

March 20, 1972 (New York)

I discovered after my two shows this Saturday that I wasn't physically tired, but that my mind was going. I don't mean insane, but just a little loose. I must now cop an attitude as Robert says, and retreat into it. I can think no more of *The Wreckers*. I wish it would go away, and take Robert, Hilla, and Pat plus Miss Taylor along. She called me between shows to tell me how tired I must be. Robert has now laid suicide on my head. That's what he will do if things don't work out. Hilla insists on being around even if I plan to fart. Pat, bless his soul, has decided right now, at this moment, to paint the hallway. Portnoy had only one. Perhaps I've become paranoid, I have good reason.

Don't miss this week's broadcast; you will love the *Fille*. I have several broadcasts in a row now — Don't stop writing. I need your letters more than ever now. You know how much faith I have in you. This will work out, just as our problems did — meanwhile just to be safe, Zippy is smoking up a storm — much love.

Andrea

March 22, 1972 (Pittsburgh)

Love,

In school again, love, and baby-sitting in what is ridiculously called a study hall — a euphemism for dumping several hundred kids into an auditorium or cafeteria to clear out the halls and ease traffic a bit.

You are being put upon from too many directions not to wind up a little "loose." Robert is too much, but Pat painting the hall too! Your mistake, love, is coping too well under all conditions — Andrea seems indestructible — ergo Andrea is indestructible. Thus, everyone feels safe in chipping away. But this is one of the beautiful — if mixed — blessings in you because you have such an incredibly consuming — absorbing — character. It is inexhaustibly inquisitive about life — including all facets of people — their problems and triumphs.

That'll be .50 please — didn't mean to give you a reading — I'm sure you know Andrea Velis as well as anyone — what I meant to do was offer some solid advice — like stand in the kitchen at 12:00 midnight pouring hot coffee over the table while screaming for the mad hatter to stay in his seat or start the day off by throwing copies of old Time magazine out the window — subtle moves like that may ease your tension as well as hint to others that you are being abused. I'm glad that I am not there for I too would be a distraction at a time when you need rest and solitude. You are loved too well — remember what it did to Desdemona.

Oh, I hope that I get to see the new *Otello* — I heard *Salome* Saturday. I'm sure that seeing it beats Down's description of the dance.

Have to teach the monsters now —

Clive Barnes gave an informal lecture in Pittsburgh yesterday and I covered it for the paper. I was surprised that he is such an unassuming man — he doesn't seem impressed by his importance or the whole business of criticism. In fact, he said, "it's not terribly important." I seriously doubt that he believes any of that; it's a good pose though — much better than coming across like the Oracle at Delphi — especially in Pittsburgh.

(At home now.) Well the day is over.

Looking forward to the broadcasts — think of our next time together — whenever or wherever — and if possible rest in the knowledge of my love.

I can only hope it offers you a token of the comfort that you give me. Again, I am in your debt, love — in so many ways.

I'll keep writing — don't worry about answering until things calm down to a roar.

Charles

March 24, 1972 (Pittsburgh)

Again I'm in school — right now on what they call "Corridor Duty" — i.e. I'm supposed to check students for hall passes and chase them out of the rest rooms — boys that is. It is one of those demeaning chores (necessary evil they say) which rob teachers of their dignity.

Well, it does give me a chance to write you, perhaps to comfort you. At least to reassure me that as I scowl over these sterile halls — sweaty and reeking from over- flowing puberty — I have touched the heart of what throbbing life is all about — so much more than

all of these Tonys and Marias. There was only one Romeo and Juliet
— there is only one Andrea and Charles — a unique, profound
enjoyment of living, loving.

Tomorrow I will listen to you — again I will thrill at your voice
— name and presence — for I take pride and joy in merely vicari-
ously sharing your life. What a precious treasure our love is — I don't
even mind the abuses of time — I shall grow old gracefully –living
and loving.

Perfect timing — Buzzzzzzz — so with that and the tax return I
should be all right next month. Then I shall have to get some kind of job
to survive the summer — teachers stop getting sick midway through
April. Perhaps the Tampa thing will come through. If I take a job I hope
it doesn't mess-up anything that might develop for us this summer.

Also, I will probably have to move somewhere in May unless I
can work something out with another short-term roommate. The
fellow I'm sharing the apartment with is taking a job with Pan Am
and leaves May 8 for training in Miami — then he will be stationed
on the coast. Well, maybe everything will be settled soon. My spirits
are up a little because I'm teaching and getting some money to keep
above the water line. And I simply can't bring myself to borrow from
my family — they helped me through the last seize with the divorce
and all — at that time I was left with $1,200 in debts. Fortunately, I
have kept my bills under strict control — my car is paid for my share
of the rent is only $50.00 — and of course I have the child support
and a few misc. debts (like the Xmas plane fare). Well for a while
anyway, the wolf is not at the door.

Now I must concentrate on making the most of this period. Must
go — take care my Harlequin,

Love, Charles

This was the low point financially for me, as you well remember. The substitute teaching was what got me through it.

April 5, 1972 (Pittsburgh)

Love,

Sorry for the silence — again waiting for good news before writing but, again, the wait was futile.

The PR job is still in limbo — getting dimmer than ever. The woman I spoke to you about got sick and was off work all last week so we didn't get together — although I called her office every day and gradually asked some info. out of the secretary. I'm afraid the job would not pay enough for me to consider it. Finally, today she is back at work and I have an interview scheduled for tomorrow. After talking further with her today, I don't think the job will be something for me. In fact, I think what they really want is someone who is rich enough that he doesn't need a job — but likes to do "something for the 'arts' — a Mr. Hillman" who could help out with PR — anyway, I'll go.

Also, tomorrow, I have two teaching interviews — both for private schools. I wrote to Tampa — have heard nothing yet.

On to other things — enjoyed the broadcast — wish I had seen you mugging your way around Big John. Again, this Saturday! No wonder you're anxious about not getting a vacation this summer. You always work hard but these past few months have been ridiculous.

Finally got my *After Dark* — I hope you don't attract art thieves after that audit of your collection. I'm afraid I didn't feel that they captured you the way a feature in such a magazine should. In fact, your own article for *Opera News* was better. I can hardly be objective but I think the story should have tapped your charm, wit, and knowledge in a more personal and perhaps straight interview-style. As it was, it was more like a newspaper feature — bordering on straight PR. Still, I enjoyed seeing you seductively lounging over that bed.

I hope something happens soon in way of a job because I am sort of hanging in mid- air about plans for the whole summer. I'll call if anything new develops.

Charles

After Dark, 1972

April 24, 1972 (Boston)

My love,

Now it has all begun — my only consolation is that every day brings me closer to you — I will call before you get this, but I wanted to send you my schedule with phone numbers. You remember to write me at the Met now?

I will try to convince you to come to Cleveland — I feel very desolate about not having seen you in such a long time. My head has been such a mess — We had to have a big brunch yesterday which meant closing the apartment at night for we also had a dinner to go to — I can't believe it's all done — will I ever get to sit down? Will he still be alive to fly to Cleveland, and to the arms of his beloved? Wait six days and see...... love

Andrea

The Met spring tour had begun: Boston was the first city. You used to joke about the bad reviews that the main critic liked to dump on the company.

May 14, 1972 (Memphis)

The sun as it set over the Mississippi tonight was an orange ball of flame. It turned many of the distant streams red, but the main body of water stayed blue from the reflected sky. The contrasts were unreal — and then it was gone — like spent love. Only the cool gray evening remained, and a memory — restful after the flame.

I was thrown out of the "Heart of Atlanta" along with sixteen others who had neglected to send one day's deposit — something we had never done before. I ended up at the "Cabana" and enjoyed it nonetheless. Many parties, many friends — now I'm away in the country — no city to go to, and maybe now I'll rest. I wonder if you will come to Detroit? When will we know? Anyway I'll expect you. It will be a surprise for me. If you can't come then you must come to New York.

Robert is home, all finished with his operation, up, out and around — claims he hasn't felt better — only he must eat only baby food — because they removed intestine and he won't be able to digest food for a few weeks. Big Robert is home.

You see my love, I have come to half of the tour — I miss you as always — how lovely these shores would be, if you could share them with me. When will that be?

Much love,
Andrea

May 25, 1972 (Minneapolis)

My love,

Thank you. I don't know how but your letter did get to me in New Orleans. With the luck I've been having with hotels — I'm surprised it was even there. I loved New Orleans — what a city! — what characters — they close Bourbon Street to traffic at 6 PM and all hell breaks loose — nude females are seen dancing through open bar doors — male sex changes are seen doing the same — males are also — joy roars day and night — beautiful hippies in various states of dress wander about loving each other — male & female — the quarter is much like a Caribbean setting — palm trees, banana trees — flamboyants. The food is extraordinary. I loved it and will return. Now I am on the plains of Minnesota watching a storm march across the fields — we are very exposed here. I can't believe next week is the last — Boston seems so very long ago. I'm sorry about Detroit; it will be better elsewhere, however. I should be spending quite a bit of time around New York this summer.

I loved Lisa's invitation, and I would have sent her a card but it was too late. I also like your PR release — that sort of thing is very valuable for you, and should build quite a valuable portfolio.

I did a bit of antiquing in New Orleans — many of the things you will see later and are quite good — one I'm very fond of. It's a seated Buddha — about five inches high — very restored. It was brought to the shop by a man who claimed to have found it in a bombed temple. I would think Thailand.

He sold it to me as base metal and as I suspected it's massive silver and very valuable. I'm very proud of it and have burned several cones of musk to him — both to welcome him to our pantheon, and to remind myself of you — perhaps he will help us end this long separation.

Finally the tour of 1972 was over; I guess I had to cancel plans to go to Detroit because of Lisa's 8th birthday, to which apparently she invited you.

The PR release you mention, refers I think to a job I was doing for the Pittsburgh Wind Symphony. I did all their press releases for summer concerts as an assistant at the PR firm that handled them and other Arts organizations in Pittsburgh, including the Pittsburgh Ballet.

June 2, 1972 (Pittsburgh)

Love,

And now summer — still no Andrea. This is the longest time I can think of since we first met that I have not been alone with you.

Tomorrow I will call you, but I wanted this letter to be waiting for you in New York. I am excited about the idea of being with you again but I'm not sure that this is the best time for me to face the strain of holding in my feelings. My need is too great now. Of course, my problems are incredibly small when compared to Robert's or thousands of others or the starving millions or whatever, but I can only approach my own turmoil, projecting it to "Well, what if I…" or "Look at so and so…" doesn't help much. It's as ineffective as trying to console Lisa when she falls and cuts her knee by suggesting that she is lucky because she didn't break her leg. Her only concern is the cut and its pain. So, it is my "cut" right now. I'm not trying to justify self-pity — and I certainly hope I'm not wallowing in my tears. Rather, I am quite objective about my life. I know what I value and what I don't. Though the past 2 years have not been easy, I don't regret any decisions or experiences. They were all based on my attempt to achieve, not money or fame, but involvement in my own destiny. Boredom, repetition, and apathy are daily diets for many — perhaps most — people. I refuse to accept them — ever. If they are the inescapable results of "facing the adult world" as I've been told by a few well-heeled psychologists (who, by the way… avoid them), then I choose to remain a child who dreams for the life that could be. Artists rarely face them because they live in a special make-believe milieu. I don't mean the glitter, money, etc., but the very act of "playing" has child-like overtones. If it is too much to ask of life that it offer one the stimulation of maintaining an interest in his own life then who needs the aggravation — Unlike Hamlet, I do not fear the thought of something after death — I fear death in life… the slipping away of my unique identity because I've stopped attending to it.

The greatest enforcement of that identity is love — you love me because it is a celebration of my unique being — a paean of my very existence. That is the "total need" I often speak of. I can go to bed with other people — I can even enjoy being valued by others — but only Andrea can touch my heart of hearts — only you make me feel loved because of our intense awareness of each other's beautiful singularity. In all other cases, I think that merely circumstances create a transparent moment — an affection called often love for want of a better word — but for us the "moment" — Crane's "Wink of eternity" — is unique and stolen from the depths of time.

Does this all make sense, love? Perhaps, it sounds like romantic drivel from a teenager's diary. If so, it is only due to my failure to communicate as well as some Greek philosopher.

The point is that love is a crucial part of this whole "cut" I'm talking about. It is the most important thing in my "chain of being." That is why New England was so important to me — I am being starved for your free, open touch — I know that our love doesn't require that we be together always or daily or monthly; I remember the beautiful line you told me to tell Emerson about your always being with me because your love was here. I cherish that love and I try to subsist with its memory when I am away from you.

Run your fingers through my hair and let me talk of dreams…

Love, Charles

You and I had taken a two week vacation together and we went to New England. Pat was in LA directing, so we had a couple days in New York on our own and then we left for Maine and New Hampshire. We visited Caleb Gray, a writer friend of yours who lived in New York, and had a cottage on Moose Lake outside of Bridgeton, Maine.

Caleb was a small dynamo — guess he was around your age then, 40ish — had written one successful work, a one-act play for TV — and he was working on a novel — and re-working it — his main stay was secretarial work, and writing for *Current Biography*.

I wanted to show you camp Takajo in Naples, Maine not far from Caleb's place on the lake. That was where I had worked while in college as a Drama Director for two years. Still had a great attachment to the place and the experience. Also, we drove into the White Mountains and to Franconia Notch.

June 24, 1972 (Los Angeles)

Well how long has it been from pine to palm? So far from Franconia "Gulch" — so far from those northern climes — here all is flower and sun — palm trees waiving in the breezes and vulgar, vulgar Southern California — San Francisco was fun — my friend had several parties for me in two days — saw *Godspell* again because all of Ken's friends were in it — fun kids and the show was very good. Ken and I came down today — we are about to have chicken delight and champagne here in Pat's apartment — then the *Barber* — then a friend of Ken's (a dancer) is making Paella for us after the opera — tomorrow we fly off to Mexico — I am actually anxious to be home, for this Gentele thing has me a bit up tight. I found San Francisco after 15 years very much like N.Y. but very provincial — very! — but my friends old and new were sweet, and I felt very much at home, but it is not <u>home</u>. Actually, home to me now is where my heart is, and that is with you — perhaps in Franconia Gulch — perhaps astride the Ohio Turnpike — perhaps at the open page, but there — Now I must up and off — see you soon I hope — I will look forward to finding a letter from you — with your phone number. I will call you there as soon as I can —

I will miss you
Love,
Andrea

Off to Mexico you went with Pat for a couple weeks. Meanwhile I prepared to move to Zanesville, Ohio and a new job.

July 28, 1972 (Mexico)

Now I have come south to Cornavacca. I'm in a strange room all very Spanish with tile floors, and a stairway that goes up to the bath, and another small bedroom. The door opens out into a large walled garden, where red flowers cover trees and bananas and palms lead down to a pool. All terribly far from Kennebunkport. What a funny name, and now I must keep that silly strange name locked up in my heart forever. Like the mystic turning of the cosmos — billions of stars spin round each other — attracted and repelled. So we turned and spun, and joined finally at, where? Not Antinoupolis — not Arcadia — but Kennebunkport — that moment in our lives — our love, when we made our bodies one — that moment when we completely surrendered every bit of our being to each other, destiny placed at Kennebunkport. Should we change its name? I think not. Shakespeare went through all that, and didn't make out at all. So It's Kennebunkport (notice how it always comes at the end of the page so I can't even write it right) forever. Its beauty is here in my heart. Its beauty is in my body still warm with love. It's as beautiful as Faber and Andrea — Antinous and Hadrian

— Alexander and Hephaestion. Poor thing, how I pity it, for that's quite a company to join. The immortality of our love and theirs is placed squarely on its back. It can no longer say, "it's always been that way;" it never will be "that way" again. A hand has reached out of Arcadia, out of Egypt, out of the sands of the East, hot and dry, and placed a moment of our love on those strange shores. For a moment Antinous stood straight — tall and naked among the lobster pots — looked down on us in our love, and said, "where have you brought me?" then strode back to tell an age of loves — "Kennebunkport." How dear — how sweet it sounds — now it is ours, and we have made it theirs —

Let my love surround you and carry you through these difficult times —

Andrea

We were weaving the fabric together, trying to see ourselves in male relationships of mythic or historical figures to bring forth deeper and deeper passions that belied the vile stereo types and bile that the larger culture was spewing out against same-sex love.

We sought a new context; we found it; and it seemed to respond and nurture our love. By freeing ourselves from societies' contempt — spiritually separating ourselves from it — we transcended the guilt and self-hatred that that attitude pounded upon gay lovers; we sought models of our love among those whose love was so exalted that it soared through time, through myth, through legend into our hearts and into our bodies.

August 4, 1972 (Guatemala)

I'm sure I'll find it hard to describe what I see all around me, but I'll try. I'm sitting on the porch of a thatched hut where we have been staying for some days. We are at the Mayan ruins of "Tical." If you find a map of Guatemala, find the city, then go north east about 2 hundred miles. You will find the city of Flores on Lake Flores, a bit north of that is Tical. We left Guatemala City in the plane which shot King Kong down from the Empire State Building. The inside was like one of those old refrigerators one finds discarded on the streets of New York, all repaired with rusty nails, and its floors were wooden. You were forced to pull yourself up by the seat backs for the slope of the body when it was parked. Anyway, we flew over the jungle for several hours and landed on a dirt strip cut out of the thick jungle.

Here the wife of one of the excavators (from the University of Pennsylvania) had a few thatched huts to rent, and she cooks for us. The ruins are about a mile from here through Tarzan like jungle where paths have been cleared, with vines hanging down which can support the weight of a man (we swung on them). Overhead, parrots and monkeys chatter constantly — joined on the ground by peccaries (wild pigs) and jaguars. The noisiest of all are the toucans. When going along the jungle path you can hardly see the sky — then suddenly through the towering trees — you see the back of Pyramid #1 — 250 feet high. It stands at the end of the main square facing Pyramid #2, not quite as high but as impressive. This square is bound on both sides by massive complexes of buildings — decorated by grotesque mammoth masks and designs. Pyramid #1 has a huge seated figure on its comb, and if one has the courage (we did) you climb the front and view the entire complex from the

top — everywhere you turn Pyramids soar up out of the strangle
hold of the jungle — some cleared — some covered with trees and
lived in by animals. Today from the top of Temple #2 we saw a storm
approaching. We let ourselves down the 150 steps and started down
the path. Suddenly we heard a roar, like a herd of cattle stampeding
— we realized that it was the rain hitting the trees above us and it
soon was upon us in cascades — everything turned to mud and tor-
rents swept by us — we made it back but if you think my Levis were
wet the morning we parked your car, you should see them now — I
have them in a banana tree — Tomorrow morning we will board
our rickety plane, and head back to civilization. Right now I would
give anything for some of Caleb's cold water —

Much love,

Andrea

August 11, 1972 (Oakmont)

Hart Crane could not have written more beautifully about love —
you are the bard of Kennebunkport — and we truly have shared a
new and strange land with Antinous. Your last letter is pure poetry. It
came to me as you always seem to do, when my need was great, and
I cried — the tears came for many reasons — because I miss you
more and more as time continues to rob us — because my plans to
come closer to NY and share more of your daily life were aborted
temporarily by Zanesville — and simply because I love you.

Your words and love have helped me through many rough periods and this one is no exception. Right not I'm suffering from some
lousy bug — fever, sore throat, aches, the works. Fortunately, I am
staying with Jane and she is taking care of me with the fastidiousness
of a Jewish mother. Thanks to her I have a place to stay until I move

to Zanesville. I rented an apartment — it's new, clean, and comfortable — has no character — but I can't move in until the end of the month. The school is not too far away. As soon as I get settled I'll send you the address and phone number.

Love, I'm sorry but I'm going to stop here — I'm in pain — call me at Jane's.

Faber

August 30, 1972 (Zanesville)

So here I am, love, in the glorious mid-west. Tomorrow, Thursday, I return to Pittsburgh to ready the big move on Labor Day. I can't get in the apartment until then because they are painting it. Then, on Tuesday, this phase officially begins. My title, incidentally, is Curriculum Coordinator for English for the city of Zanesville, Ohio. Even now as I write this I can't believe I am actually going to live in Zanesville — even for a year. Not that I can't survive, sure I can — but that another year of my life will be spent away from you — away from the vitality and delightful paranoia of New York.

Fortunately, I do believe in old Mary Williams's prediction that I will write.

But enough of that for now, there will be time to bore you with my Zanesville hiatus all through the winter.

Thank you for welcoming Sal and particularly for the birthday business. Needless to say, he appreciated everything, and will probably take you up on your invitation to return.

Perhaps I am being harsh on Sal, but he surprised me on this our first trip anywhere together. I never realized before how much of an "old maid school teacher" he is: petty, negative, and soft on life. Sal should, and undoubtedly will, settle in to a continual boredom of living with Mom and Dad on Ridge Avenue in New Kensington. Too bad.

We were not together this time at all, love — but at least I was in your arms, if only momentarily, and I looked into your eyes. As always, they enveloped me with a warm love. Even in Zanesville, alone and frustrated, if I can hold your love close to me — rubbing against my body and soothing my spirit — then I am never away from you and my true life. It seems so pompous to try and write coherently of our love — I, too, want to call upon Antinous — to bring him to Zanesville, no less — to include Alexander — say "he too is Faber" — to shout to all great lovers that Andrea and Faber know their secrets, but the words tumble over each other in cascades of metaphors which blur the vision and assault the senses. Beautiful, yes, but as eventually fruitless as Hadrian's poetry after Antinous's death. The beauty, the essence of that great love existed only in Hadrian's eyes when he gazed over Antinous's face, perhaps after they had made love while Antinous slept soundly in his arms. Their love — like ours — is not to be found in poetry — though it may celebrate its joys — but in our stolen moments and in our hearts. The delirious love in Cleveland after we had chocolate fudge sundaes — the total love that swept over me when I watched you do the Madwoman — the oneness of Kennebunkport — all the joyful riches which you have brought to my life — these are the matter of our love. Our poetry, our incense, our Britten, are celebrations of what only we experience. Everything is a pale reflection of the experience itself. We, alone, know that joy — that totality. Its reality is always with me, love, and with that I can hold on to the golden dream of our tomorrows.

September 6, 1972 (New York)

Welcome to your new home. Your letter and card came yesterday. I hope you can like Zanesville even a little bit. Of course I can't place you there in my mind since I've never had the pleasure. In my mind you are always here with me, happy, content. I've never thought of either of us having to be in beautiful places. Our beauty has always been from situations we created ourselves. A word, a poem, a caress — the immortality of our love — these are the places we live in. After all, Zanesville can be made a more beautiful place for having you there for a few months. How can any place be ugly to me if it is the custodian of my love. Can any place where Faber is be ugly? No more than a desert can be ugly if one rose blooms there.

Your witch was right, you will write. You know that. We knew that when you started with George Anderson. I want you to write more than magazine articles and reviews. Good, you should do the articles which Caleb told you about, but just to get here, to keep alive until that beauty which is there and which I love so, can be seen and loved by everyone. I will be so proud, so happy for you. You know you have that, it's right there at your fingertips. It's only a question of time and work. What can stop you — what has stopped us? We will have what we want.

What do you think of this crazy business in New Hampshire? I can muster up enthusiasm if I see us up there together. What a quiet place to work and love — and be alone. We will set up a temple to our gods, our eternal lovers. They will all come there to us. I can hear Antinous now, "Where in the hell is Tamworth?" They will learn — we will send that name soaring down the ages to them. Tamworth is love — Tamworth is Faber and Andrea!

I wish I could be close to you now. I wish I could hold you to my arms and comfort you. You know I am with you — my every thought is yours. This greater distance brings us closer together. My love, rest, for I hold you…

Andrea

Zanesville, Ohio put me further away from Lisa and from you, love. The irony is that after I signed the contract for a year because the money was good and I had not had much success in other areas I got a letter from Tampa offering me the job on the *Tampa Tribune* as a critic. Too late.

I was hired to create a new curriculum in English for kids from middle school through high school in Zanesville — a challenge to change lives for the better. Off I went.

And you mentioned the idea of a cottage in Tamworth, NH for the first time.

September 16, 1972 (Zanesville)

You are beautiful, love. On top of rehearsals, "house building," and Robert tending, you remember that I wanted a canvas bag. As they say, it is exactly what I wanted —thank you, love — moreover, thank you for brightening my life in Zanesville with a message of light — love — joy. Again, you have confirmed that I am with you — in your heart of hearts — that when the night comes — when darkness makes our worlds one again — then in that silence I am gathered in your arms and the day is justified.

Often, I think back to that night when I tripped out on Robert's stuff, and I remember that even though you were holding me — (in the symbolic state of my mind) — I actually could not reach you and so I cried and was lonely — though in your arms.

I was experiencing, then, the reenactment of so many empty

nights away from you — so many sleep troubled nights when I searched for you in my dreams. Now, I still search, still long for your touch during the night — but I have learned the way to you through the black loneliness. All that we have shared — our love — our witness gods — has made the search an easy journey to your arms.

The days, though, are not easy and, at best, my dreams are poor substitutes for the reality of your arms. God, the years of stolen moments are decades when love is the prize.

Sometimes, love, I think that like your young call-boy friend, Rocco, I am selling myself here in Zanesville. Unlike him, however, who sells only a fleeting touch, smile, sensation — a mere wink of marketable beauty, I sell a deeper part of me than flesh: for $50 a day I peddle my spirit, my unique human identity. But I will hold on to my dreams and my love — even in Zanesville — because… well, because of you and because tomorrow we will need them.

Wish I could share your joy everyday — Best for the opening of *Carmen*.

Charles

Next year in New York — Shalom!

> As I indicate, Zanesville seemed like I had left the planet; it was so far down the belly of the mid-west that it was hard to breathe.

September 30, 1972 (New York)

I can't tell you how relieved I was to finally reach you. I was beginning to worry. Now I have gotten through. I'm sure it will be all right in the future.

Perhaps that particular line had never been used before. I have a new goalpost in my future — October 20 — I don't want to fantasize too much about that weekend, but as always with us, it's hard not to. I promise you this, however, those three days will be ours. I think it might be a good idea not to let Robert know of your arrival. When he finds you, we will invent something to tell him. If we don't, he will spend all his time up here with you. However, Big Robert will be home, and his time will be taken up a bit — he does like you, and wants to be with you — I plan to be very possessive of you and jealous. These are our three days. I do want to go up to the Cloisters.

They shall be like a retreat — we will retreat into each other. We can do quiet personal things — there will be no day or night — just three days — together.

I have your ticket for the 20th — that will be Bernstein's last performance — I want so much for you to see it. The recording will mean more to you.

All my love — it's three weeks away — I've started offerings to Zippy and all our friends —

Andrea

October 8, 1972 (Zanesville)

Love,

Do you really think it's possible for us to be alone for the weekend? I am willing to stay locked in for three days — with you my world and your apartment our universe. It has been so long again since we shared only each other with no interferences from the reality of our two separate worlds.

Do you think Antinous has lost us somewhere between Kennebunkport and Zanesville? No, I'm sure he hasn't; he is captured in our hearts and like some captive wanderer must follow us until we are together again and he finds rest in our celebration of love.

I miss you so deeply, love. Every day is such a chore. The loneliness, the boredom of Zanesville, the futility of this job are endurable, but the crushing despair comes when I realize how each day represents the loss of more precious time for us — days, weeks, months which cannot be recaptured.

Time is such an insidious, devastating enemy. Slowly it devours us while we delude ourselves with dreams. Only through love — full, wild, consuming love — do we humble time. Only you have been and are that love to me and time defeats us only by keeping us apart — we shall never conquer it, but I shall laugh at it when I am in your arms again.

Time is playing its most dreadful game with Robert. With all my heart I hope that he can fight his way through this second attack. I know how much he means to you, love. When I get depressed over his illness, I remember his own incredible courage and his nature — and I put Robert's destiny back in his own hands. More than most of us — certainly more than I have — Robert lives in his own universe filled with a kinetic energy that few know in a lifetime that spans four score and ten.

Two weeks until I see you. I will arrive as early as I can — I'm not sure but there is a possibility that I could come on Thursday night. I thought that only the students had Friday off and that the teachers had a meeting, but someone told me that none of the teachers go to the meeting since it is held in Columbus and they don't check on attendance. I'll let you know.

This weekend I'm driving to Washington, D.C. I promised Lisa a weekend away so we are driving down on Friday and returning Sunday night. I can't afford to go — charge cards again — but if I wait 'til I can afford it, the weather will be too bad.

The piece about "Street naming in CT" was unreal. Are there really people still around in CT like that? I thought they all moved to Ohio and Indiana. Poor O'Neill — his life wasn't bad enough while he lived it; it still haunts his memory. This country is so ridiculous, so foolishly uncivilized. O'Neill is the only great playwright we've ever had and he is almost totally ignored — but, then, what American artist isn't? — whether dead or alive. Our idea of "artistic recognition" is putting Johnny Carson's star in cement or something on Hollywood Blvd.

I will talk to you before the 20th.

Charles

October 9, 1972 (New York)

I have not heard from you about our weekend. I have chosen to assume that it will take place. In fact, I would now be very unhappy if anything went wrong. Please don't let anything go wrong. Everything I do is now predicated on "our" weekend. I am working mightily to defend it. It's being assailed from all sides. Gerson and Miguel who live in Washington and with whom I stay when I am there, will arrive on the 20th. Caleb wants to stay here on his way to Florida — when? That weekend. I have fended all these attacks, and the people who always insert themselves between us have not even been heard from as yet — Hilla — Robert — Oliver, etc. I should line the wall of this paradise with lead to protect us — How will I explain to Robert? — Big Robert is home, and he (Little Robert) runs up here to escape. If he learns you are here, he loves you so, he will be offended if he doesn't see you. Gerson and Miguel will beyond a doubt have a big party somewhere.

But I will hold fast, no matter what — those days are ours: Faber and Andrea. I will summon up our gods to defend us. I will offer up to them. If they will show us this mercy, our eternal love. I will show them Faber and Andrea perched on the edge of the ages, and they will laugh to know our love.

I want you, my heart — be strong — come to me — the next ten days will seem like years — these three together — a life.

My love,
Andrea

October 25, 1972 (Zanesville)

My wonderful love –

Still, when I close my eyes your name –
Thundering through my body like the cry of a racing charioteer –
Sweeps my spirit high – higher

Cleft to you I fly into, around, over, beyond my body.
Crane-like our sun winks as I am born in your arms.

Burned into new existence – we ride, my love, we ride
Into Blessed chaos.

Laughing we clinch our slipping mortality
As wind rips past muscle, hair, taut flesh
We peak at the edge of each new-fledged identity.

Knowing now that not tomorrow nor the next second
will ever be the same
We fall
Blessed in the Sun's Baptism.

That doesn't do us justice, love. Another time I will celebrate our love.

Did it all really happen? Was that weekend so totally ours — unimpeded by friends and foes? Did I really almost destroy our new rapprochement with the Chinese? How wonderful every second was — I am glowing:

"For I on honey dew hath fed and drunk the milk of paradise."
Thank you, love.

I will write again soon — I hope I never come down...

Charles

I have to laugh at the reference to China. You remember that I am referring to us going out to a nearby Chinese restaurant, one of the few times we actually left the apartment that weekend. I was still under the influence — not sure exactly how it worked — but I was still stoned. We ordered a lot of food I guess; I chowed down too fast and within a few minutes projectile vomited all over the table, splashing across the booth too. You were stunned into silence as was everyone around us, but the waiters flew from back rooms with towels and big pans and within minutes we fled back to our secret weekend on 89th St and the Baroque bed.

October 27, 1972 (New York)

My love,
I thought it would be like a dream to have had you here — but the rush, the torrent of our love is still sweeping me along. Yesterday, I saw our movie of the trip to the Cloisters — and I felt weak again from our flight of love — I want much to have you here with me

to climb those heights again together. To try this time to savor our ecstasy. Not the wild impetuous plunge of our virgin flight — but the gliding, soaring, scorching love duet which will unify us for the ages — have any lovers, loved as we do. You asked if everyone feels as we did — no my love — in order to soar to those heights lovers must love as we do. Let us go to that country again, there our gods await us — there we will see and love them — there we shall dwell in each other's souls forever. I send you my heart, cupped in my hand — it is an offering — for you alone.

Andrea

November 13, 1972 (New York)

This *Sunday Times Magazine* was dedicated to a new Greek Krater bought by the Met Museum. It's quite a beautiful thing, but my interest was drawn to its creator, a painter named Euphronios, considered the greatest painter of 520 BC. Only one of his vases is shown at the Louvre. Now the Met has the second. In that period it was the custom to inscribe the vases with "love inscriptions" to the favorite youth of the artists. This is inscribed to "Leagros the beautiful," so far there are sixty inscriptions to him which make him one of the handsomest youths in Attica. He died while leading an Athenian army in Thrace in the spring of 464 BC, so the vase has been placed at his prime which would have to be about 515 BC. The vase shows the Gods carrying away the body of Sarpedon from the field of Troy. Since he is a youth, one would assume Euphronios used Leagros as the model. Here again we have another example of what we discussed of Shakespeare and Michelangelo — perpetuating the names of their lovers in their art. Here, however, we say "Leagros"

after 2500 years. I wonder what he was like — was he worthy of
the love of Euphronios, or was he only beautiful? Interesting that he
became a general and lead troops. Still, if sixty inscriptions remain,
many thousands must have been written. Perhaps he was the beloved
of all Attica, and Euphronios never had him, but only longed for
him. Perhaps he used the inscriptions as a lure for him, or perhaps
the vase belonged to someone else who loved Leagros and ordered
the inscription — we will probably never know. We do know he was
beautiful and much loved. I envy Euphronios — my art is like the
wind or sand, I can't write for the ages "Faber Kalos." No one will
know 2500 years from now the beauty that I love — I can't write
or draw or sculpt our love. It's a very selfish thing which I keep
within me to give me joy. I feel though that <u>they</u> know, our secret
gods. Who needs graffito to record love — ours is already recorded
through the ages — ours is theirs. Our love is impressed on time.

I'm so glad for your writing, it's what I wanted for you, and sets
you up with a moveable income — plus it keeps you writing —
don't give up hope for us — hope and love.

Andrea

November 20, 1972 (Zanesville)

You said — and so beautifully — that your art, unlike the poet's or
sculptor's, is fleeting, not capable of holding in time its precious love
moment. But, for most artists, love as we know it has been a secret
passion or remembrance of past passion. Shakespeare, Michelangelo,
and Hadrian turned to their art as consolation for unrequited or, in
Hadrian's instance, lost love. Defeated by reality, they sought perfection in art. Only there could the celebration occur — sanctified by
an inspiring and compassionate muse. In your art, however, our love

celebrates its reality. When you sing — whether the Madwoman, Franz, or whatever — I share in the moment — in itself your art becomes an act of love. Once I told you that the afternoon that I heard you sing the Madwoman at Caramoor was the beginning for me of what I knew even then was a total love. As you sang, I saw not only the art but also the depth of the beauty in you. It was to become my home. At first I thought it was love like I had known briefly before — fleeting, but this time more glamorous. How totally wrong I was. Our love became for me a consuming eternal flame that needs no "artificial artifact" to preserve it — it is its own art. Perhaps, in years to come we shall both " sing of our glory."

Then came our flight — our release into the world of Antinous. It was always ours; we had lost it in time. Now it is ours again — part of our experience. In *Psycho- Cybernetics*, the author writes that an imagined experience or journey complete with sensations is exactly the same physically as the experience. That is why I was so exhausted — so utterly drained. I had literally soared with you to another level of consciousness. I don't love you more now — that is impossible — but I do understand our love vastly more than I did before. Now I know that we actually do share a unique, ultimate love. That the Word has become reality — that the dream of ecstasy a state of existence.

Would the rapture stay with us on a daily basis? Would the showers become a bore and then silly? Perhaps we will never know. I only know that I shall never know love like ours again — that fate has brought me my poetic dream of the impossible love. If infamous-time should invade and disrupt our love as it lashes out at our bodies then I shall seek refuge in my first love home — that home I found at Caramoor — the beauty inside you that not even time can destroy. I shall be gathered into your soul and there the celebration will continue even beyond the day when all Greek vases shall fall to dust.

Share me with Oliver? Impossible. No one can share what we have.

Oliver and I do have an affection for each other — a shadow of what you and I have. I never wish to hurt him. Perhaps I do use him as a buffer against total loneliness — it keeps me off the streets and out of bars. Because it is unlikely that we shall ever live together, love, I will probably have to have this type of relationship with someone. Oliver is committed to living in New York now and perhaps I will live with him when I come. Maybe that would only confuse the situation further. I don't know. Let's talk about it.

I hope to make it up for the weekend. I wish I didn't know that you will be alone over the Thanksgiving weekend — that makes it more difficult.

Until then, my love,

Charles

Your friend, Caleb was a freelance writer, helped me to get my first assignment for *Current Biography*.

December 7, 1972 (Zanesville)

And so today when I needed you — to hear your voice — to hear you say, "love," you called me. Nothing can convince me that it is coincidence that you come to me at moments of such low tide. Surely, if our love can fly us into the heavens as it has done, then it can span 500 miles to bring comfort.

You are right, of course, about our weekend. There will be others as glorious as our first. In fact, we don't <u>require</u> a stimulus to reach the heights of our love. We both realize that. No moment I share with you is less important than another. Each is a cherished instant which forms the continuing beauty of our love. As we walked through the rooms of Greek vases, I thought how much like these rare treasures is our love — we too celebrate the physical & spiritual union in our love — we too have risen to the ultimate of the Greek love ideal — and we are joined to the spirit that inspired the creators of the vases — the commitment to life as an art form in itself. Our love is even a treasure beyond the gathering powers of the Metropolitan — no glass cage shall hold our beauty in hermetic purity — our treasure shall be shared only with our peers — with Achilles, Antinous, Alexander — we shall burn it into the heavens "Andreas Kalos — Fabros Kalos."

I shall listen for you on Saturday — be well my love — I wish I could be there now to take care of you.

I plan to write about several jobs in the *Times* just to see what the prospects are for making the change later. Another year here is out of the question.

You were so thoughtful and far too generous last weekend — how excited I am with my first new razor! Thank you for all the beauty you constantly shower on my life — whether the unicorn print — the jacket — the *Lucia* performance — or the touch of your body on mine. Someday I hope you and I will give to each other in a more equal way. I often wonder what I can bring to you beyond my love to make your life easier, happier, or whatever. Until that time, I give you my most precious possession, my love, my identity.

Charles
Goodnight love

December 22, 1972 (Zanesville)

"...but because he's more myself that I am. Whatever our souls are made of, his and mine are the same... he's always in my mind... not as a pleasure, any more than I am always a pleasure to myself — but, as my own being."

These lines are from *Wuthering Heights*. Stripped of its Gothic qualities, their love is as transcending an emotion as Hadrian's for Antinous, Alexander for Hephaestion, or mine for you.

My wonderful Andrea, I shall grow old loving you, and in that grayness, still when you hold me in your arms, my youth shall rise up like the Phoenix to once more be consumed in our passion.

Then what is this dried weed that I send to you? When Jane and Bill were in England two years ago, they visited the Yorkshire moors where Emily Bronte lived and set *Wuthering Heights*. The "weed" is heather, taken from the moors surrounding the house used as the model in the novel. You have half the piece now — as you should. A symbol — though we need none — of a love like ours that prompts "because he's more myself than I am."

I delayed writing because I wanted to send you the Pavarotti piece but I will wait. Oliver called this morning. He did not get the job.

You more than anyone know how painful separation from you is for me. I am incomplete without you. Someday, not only my spirit must be with you when you need comfort, but for now I send that and this meager symbol of my love.

Charles

Oliver was in New York applying for jobs.

January 15, 1973 (Zanesville)

A few lines, love; it's late (1:30 AM) but I've been thinking of you all day — missing you, that is, because I think of you every day. Today was strange though — can't explain the urgency that I felt. Now as I tried to go to sleep it was more intense.

Many reasons, I suppose. One is that I framed a picture of Antinous (which you gave me) and also put in the tobacco ad and behind both a cherished green piece of construction paper with three beautiful red and gold leaves on it. Naturally, I can't sleep. I want you here to hold me.

Also, wanted to tell you that the check came from *Current Biography* — with what I think is an indication that the sketch will be in the February edition (it states: Feb 73+ after the article's title.) Hope they send me another one right away.

Thank you for your last letter. You have no idea what it means to me to know that on rare occasions I can in some way offer you a small piece of the support which you constantly show me. I want you to be happy, love; I shall always want that and I hope that I shall always be a part of that happiness.

Heard *Fille* — wish I could have seen what camping was going on — no pun intended. The music was like a light, rich soufflé — fun to hear even with all the static in Zanesville.

I'll try to sleep now. I will bring you to my bed in my dreams and we shall make outrageous love — outrageous to all but gods.

Charles

January 21, 1973 (Zanesville)

Love,

You sounded much more relaxed on the phone. It was a heavy strain to bear and I'm glad you have begun airing it. Strange, yet so typical, that Pat too wanted to discuss things, but didn't know where to begin. How do we estrange ourselves from others that way — reduced to children by the fragility of our egos. That shall never happen to us.

Loneliness is a strange, many-shaded thing. I have experienced it all through my life. Before meeting you, it was an acute loneliness in my soul. What I thought was a permanent condition which one simply adjusted to as he got older. Life seemed rather normal for me; I had friends, had loved and been loved in return; and so I thought the untapped, lonely area of my being was merely a condition one endued, or a notion lingering from my romantic view of life. Then you came and I eventually knew that I had been wrong. Your love reached into the depths of that loneliness and wiped it away forever. Then, loneliness became not being with you. Counting weeks before we would walk together through the park on the Hudson, or before you would penetrate my soul with your eyes and say, "My Charles, my love." Though intense, this loneliness has never had emptiness as part of it because you are always with me. Your arms are always one step beyond my dreams at night.

Now in Zanesville another side to loneliness — still endurable because of you. Here I have made no friends — a few professional acquaintances, but no friends. Perhaps the price is too great. I have sold too much already to go farther and pretend that I'm taken with all this provincial shit. I prefer to, like Shakespeare, "think on you" and let my mind wonder away from the land of Babbits and corn, and seek the land of unicorns and enormous heads that get caught in bus doors. You are my life-line to that reality and our love sustains me even here. Cut off from so much though, I find myself requiring a new type of discipline. It takes will-power for me to not just say, "Fuck it" and give in to things. Dumb things like cooking dinner for myself each night instead of going across the road to a hamburger joint — cleaning the apartment — becoming addicted to TV and on and on. Little stupid things become battles. Forgive the outrageous comparison (you know I always dramatize) but in a minute way it's like the loneliness of a mystic like John of the Cross. I feel that I must forcefully overcome this "night of darkness" before I can take the next step.

That next step will bring me closer to you.

Sorry, I got carried away with that whole business — probably doesn't make much sense.

I can understand Pat being jealous of Tommy, but I don't see what being a dancer has to do with it. As for me, my one seizure over the "Pepsi Cola" Kid was enough. You once said to me that not promises, not arrangements, not chains, but only love can bind two people. I agree.

Somehow — maybe my ESP — I feel that our greatest time is coming soon. That a period lies ahead which will be a constant high — bringing us closer than ever before (with one or two exceptions) to the pantheon of lovers.

I am saving every bit of the *Met Bulletin*. Thank you again, love. It too is ours — as all great beauty is.

Charles

Beautiful Tommy, a dancer with the Joffrey Ballet, was now seriously in your life. I had met him in New York at your place. He was gorgeous, child-like, sweet, and had one of those mind-boggling bodies the dancers build — rock hard bum, and solid beautifully-proportioned torso. You told me that he wanted to go to bed with both of us. A threesome!! Whoa, that was not something I was ready for then — I was still in the honeymoon stage with you and passionately in love. I am sure that you had the event with Tommy and someone else, I would think that it was Robert, who would have jumped at the chance. Must admit that I was shaken a bit by Tommy's beauty and sweetness, but thought of him, as I did the Pepsi kid, as just a playmate to keep you happy between bouts of passion with me. I had been pissed at the Pepsi kid because he was in New York when I was there, and you pushed him at me a bit. He was pretty but silly and sexless to me. Tommy made me a bit jealous, but then I remembered what we had shared that far, and felt on firm ground with our love.

And, to my relief in fact, Tommy was moved back to the chorus in your life after an incident involving a can of mace that you had given him for protection.

The "enormous head" was a papier-mâché head that got stuck in the door of the 104 Bus as its owner tried to drag it off with him. It must have been used in a parade or show somewhere. We stood at 86th Street and Broadway and belly-laughed at the visual absurdity before us.

February 5, 1973 (Zanesville)

Love,

I'm still here — the flu flattened me for 5 days (out of school for three) but has moved on. Jesus, was I sick — one of those crazy times when death seems at the doorstep. Luckily, I had penicillin pills to beat the infection. When I felt myself getting sick, I drove to Pgh. and stayed at my Mother's.

In spite of the difficulty I had getting there, it was a wise thing to do. As it turned out I was too sick to even do the simplest of things.

Your second letter was waiting for me when I returned. I like the sketch; framed it and it now hangs in my room on a wall with all our other things — including a leaf, Antinous and Beppe, the things on that wall help me sleep at night and cheer me in the bleak mornings.

You said so well in your letter what I often tried to put into words. Perhaps it was that very quality — our god-like love — that lifted our bodies that glorious night and sent us toward the sun. We had preludes to that night — signs and moments of our unique love — we have both felt the vibes — but the release came in a gushing torrent of ecstasy. Truly we were gods that night. You literally were transformed into a god and as you held me — each time you pressed against me — we shed another layer of mortality — until for that ultimate eternal moment we, as gods, soared like speeding stars playing in our heaven playground — naked children of our father sun devouring the pleasure in each other's body and rollicking in the joy of our love.

Oh, what I would give for you to be here with me now — to sweep down and say, "Come, love, the sun is waiting for us."

It is already February — the sixth month I've been in Zanesville. Even now I can detect the longing for spring in the kids' eyes. They are starting to anticipate the summer and freedom. If they only knew what a comrade they have at the front of the room. Summer and freedom! How good that sounds in February. Summer and Andrea. Let's plan to go somewhere — the two of us — for a week or two. Maybe we could jump in the car and go to Nova Scotia — or to Tamworth if the house is finished, or anywhere — just so we can be together — to walk, laugh, love, talk, sleep and hold tight to each other. Fauns may be pleasant distractions but where is the joy.

I miss you so, my love,
Charles

February 10, 1973 (Zanesville)

Love,

We talked tonight but I thought I'd still write you a brief letter — my Valentine's Day greeting!

Now I shall look forward to March and our weekend. It is very indefinite at this point, but we'll see. My first trip to you in New York was in March.

When we talk I feel so close to you and what's happening in New York. It's as if I'm visiting Zanesville but my home is New York. The answer, of course, is that my home is where you are. It is you that makes me complete. When I think of living closer to you — which is often — I try to imagine the adjustment that I will have to make and the change it will bring to our relationship. In the isolation of Zanesville — or even in Oakmont — I have been able to picture just the two of us. In the quiet of my apartment, I can structure my world around "Andrea and Charles." New York, however, will not allow that for either of us. Oliver, Pat, Robert and a myriad of others will never know that we are lovers who have tasted fruit of the gods — that we have sanctified ground from Maine to Ohio. Constantly, we will have to pretend that friendship — or at the most, to the keen-eyed, that a once passionate affair still binds us. Only we shall know the truth. Perhaps, rather than being detrimental, such a situation will keep the edge of love glistening — for we will still plot for our time— still hunger for solitude — still anticipate our flights to the stars.

A recent review of *Last Tango in Paris* claims that Bertolucci is exploring the idea that the possibility of a "great love relationship" between two people is no longer possible. That the individual is doomed to isolation, and relates only briefly, sexually. How empty life would be if that were true.

Fortunately, it isn't. Bertolucci, like so many others, misunderstands the existential precept which first documented man's isolation. Sure, we are alone — family, church, tribe, the old verities have been torn apart by the 20th Century. But they have freed us to love, not stopped us from loving.

Unfortunately, that message was misread by the masses when they swallowed up the flower children into the plastic world. They thought the message was free love; so they made Gucci copies of the culture's clothes, and set up switch clubs in the suburbs. The message was freedom to love — there's quite a difference. The poet e.e. cummings knew exactly what the flower children meant when he said, "to be free man must realize that he is more important than any institution which he belongs to…"

Nothing sacred was lost when all those institutions crumbled. We were set free to love — free to realize that we are more important than all institutions combined.

But the isolation scared everyone — so the kids flipped for Jesus and tried to recreate the institution that squelched love and freedom for 2000 years — they once again made themselves less important to an institution and felt secure in something "bigger and better than themselves." And the others, like Bertolucci, made statements in art about the void we created. What a joke. But it really doesn't matter because such a beautiful revolution was doomed anyway. Such freedom was never meant for everyone perhaps. Poets understand it, some other artists — that a few gadgets, a Freud, or a Sartre cannot destroy the potential in man for love that only the Greeks seemed to really understand. No one explained it better than Socrates who talked of the level of love which culminated with the highest form of love — that between two men who are free and neither one usurps the other. Needless to say, I think Bertolucci is wrong.

You are probably right about it being a mistake to have the Hartford guy here for a night. He probably thinks I was being coy to mention the sex bit over the phone — maybe I was merely protecting myself. There are days when I would go to bed with practically anyone to get out of here, but I'm sure now that you are right. That, in the first place, it is not worth it for merely the possibility of a teaching job, and, in the second, that it would be a horrible mistake to get into an employee-employer relationship with him. Shades of Drew! I'll drag out the cot and play it by ear.

Your Yale weekend sounds great — even if you do have to sit through the Mass again.

It's 1:30 now — I'll be incoherent if I write more — besides oversleeping come 7:00 AM — so goodnight my wonderful love — in my dreams you are mine alone — I share you only with the sun.

Charles

The Hartford guy came — he was not happy. He still offered me the job, but I turned it down. He went home to his wife and kids, a bit frustrated I think.

Bernstein had invited you up to Yale to spend a week as he put together his Mass premiere. You remember you did not like it but did like his assistant, John M. When I visited you in March John was staying in your apartment for a few weeks, again while he was working with Bernstein. Another Faun, perhaps. I liked him a lot also, but that was all.

March 1, 1973 (Zanesville)

My love,
Your last letter came and brought not only love, but seems it threw

in spring for good measure. Lord, how I needed both. The job has been rough; I'm adding all kinds of electives to the senior high school English program — Modern Poetry, Modern Novel, Science Fiction, Mystery, etc. —

Anyway, in order to start the job-hunting process I had to request a reference letter be sent to Univ. of Pgh. for my credentials file — so rumors and pressures start about whether I am leaving or not — whether I'll be here to see that "my" programs come off. My practical side won't let me tell them that I'm leaving until I have another job, so I'm just ignoring rumors and denying queries. Oh, for the foolhardy courage to say, "Yes, Goddammit. I'm leaving and I hope to erase from memory this whole nightmare." Enough of this — But on that day, I needed exactly what came — a letter from you telling me to remember where I belong — where I have always belonged. I am determined this time to step into my own reality completely — not to merely guard it — long for its fulfillment — or enjoy it 4 or 5 times a year — but to say, "Charles has emerged totally into the now of his life — no more waiting for tomorrow or bemoaning yesterday." I must break into it now — if nothing more my exile has allowed me this time to search into myself again and find the essence of the boy got who covered by layers of social causes. Oh, I shall still be Daddy to Lisa — son to my mother — but the emergence will only increase my understanding of even those roles. Our love was the beginning of my voyage back to find — what in some miraculous way I somehow believe that you saw. It has taken me a long time — several unscheduled "trips" — to even break through to what you instinctively or even unconsciously touched in me. I have had no Don Juan to lead me — but your eyes were my guide; in them, I saw my better self. I have been afraid, cried, walked and talked for hours (as you know) and, here, I have been like a man in prison, but always those eyes have whispered, "Love, come, be warm." And it is not merely a romantic dream — it is a new reality.

The reality business is creeping into the letter because I just read the article on Casteneda in *Time*, but it is true. I absolutely believe that because we both were capable of expressing a love beyond normal reality, we were swept into it and nurtured it into existence. As you said before, we cannot even talk about it in terms of "love" because the very words are mockeries of our love. It is not even the poetry of Crane or Cavafy — it is in their minds only. Hadrian knew it and experienced it, and never recovered from its loss.

Soon, love, you and I will bring it to Zanesville — may Alexander, et al., forgive us. Perhaps they will laugh with us later.

I will take off Monday 19th — but will probably not be able to manage it the next week. I've written to Teaneck and *Current Bio.*

Bring the grass — I'm not sure that it's worth the risk at the airports — but I guess they wouldn't search that thoroughly — you decide. Just come!

If it finally comes out in the *Times* that Hoving made our vase in a ceramics class at the West Side YMHA, I give up on art. It is still one of our treasures — It's not just a clay pot nicely painted or worth one million to us, but a statement about Greek civilization: love and life concept.

Goodnight love,

Charles

Oh, I hate to bug you with this, but is there a chance that you could get Tebaldi's autograph for Dr. Huzzard — you remember my old teacher.

Apparently he cannot get it through regular ways. Anyway, he is a special person to me and I thought I'd ask you. His

dream is to have an original photo from her to John Huzzard.
I'm sure that all you need now is to be asked to run around
after Tebaldi to get a picture — but forget it if it is a chore.

March 2, 1973 (New York)

This would have been a week to test our love — wow — if we were
living together — you probably by now would be on your way back
to Zanesville. I've worked 10 to 6 every day and had a show one
evening. I've been so tired and irritable that everything has bugged
me. Above all that fucking cabin. We wasted so much time because
I'm busy and Pat won't lift a fucking finger — yesterday — being
a great day — he was in the park on the bicycle (Shit) all day. I've
tried to impress upon him that it all must be done now but no good
— so I think the bottom of this horror is that we probably won't
have a cabin. I'm determined not to do it all myself, as usual — I've
not been able to work on my Haydn opera at all — Miss Taylor has
been pressing (she is about to be told to go fuck herself.) Tommy has
gone off to live with one of his leading ladies (poor child) and I must
sing a dress rehearsal of *Carmen* this morning with a perfectly ghastly
conductor (who must be borne because he is married to Horne) —
and then rehearse *Rosenkavalier* until 6.

If you get the impression that I'm irritated (you are right). If you
were here we would probably be fighting by now — do you think
we could fight? Could you say anything to hurt me? Could I hurt
you? I would rather die! That's my problem with Pat and everybody
— afraid to hurt them so I tie myself down — pull myself down —
keep myself down — instead of passing by — "fuck you" and going
on — free — going on — on holding on to you — free and going
on — into our realm. Only you could console me now. I could lie

on your chest and have you read to me — your voice coming to my ear through the rumble of your chest — This should be my consolation — This now is the only thing which could soothe and calm me. To sleep there — this is the only true rest for me — to lie curled in your arms — deep in your soul. To hear you say, " rest, let me read to you, and rest." That is my drug —

Andrea

March 5, 1973 (Zanesville)

If only I could be there now to show you that we would not fight — that I would comfort you — love you into sleep — that I would be your rock when you need strength and your pillow when you need sleep. Would we fight? Well, we will never live together but let's suppose — I would hope that we would not fight — but that is naïve — the pressures of daily contact would occasionally produce a battle because we are strong individuals. But is that bad? I would hope that we both could reserve the right to say, "Fuck you!" and slam a door. Whether it ever happened wouldn't be important — that we both felt secure enough to blast off would be. Only those who live in glass houses are afraid to slam doors (to paraphrase a bit.) I would hope that we both would be laughing about the whole fight as we burned a candle to Antinous that night. Although, I cannot even imagine yelling at you, let alone ever doing anything to hurt you. I realize that living together would bring new tensions to our relationship. Again though, I think a person must feel secure enough in love or whatever to know that he can let loose. There is much more than a semantic difference between saying, "Fuck you!' in an angry moment and being "fucked." The fly-by-night (no pun intended, well — kinda) lovers who have one "great love affair" after another, don't know the difference. They destroy each other piece by piece and then wake-up in bed with someone else bemoaning their lost love. But we are not of that order. Back to the point. You cannot hurt people. Those who know and love you realize that, so don't hesitate to let loose — even with Miss Taylor — although, "Fuck you, Miss Taylor" might be a shade too harsh, something like "screw off, Miss Taylor" may do the trick. Seriously, love, don't let people rob you of release; it's not good for your mental state.

Aren't you entitled to let go; you can't do it at the Met. Should you be muzzled at home? I would puncture Pat's tires — to stop him for a minute and say, "Look, if you want this fucking cabin you better plan it now or I'll simply use my half of the property for a wild game reserve and stay at the Holiday Inn when I go to Vermont."

Everything I start turns light. I love you — I loved your wild, Fuck this, Fuck that letter. I know you were raving mad when you wrote it, but it came to me gushing with warm, vital blood. You were screaming out in the letter — taking your stand — I love it. In the process of writing you reached for the very freedom you were craving. It said to me that in the midst of chaos your mind turns to me as mine does to you. There are times when I am overwhelmed by my love for you. It used to frighten me — now I welcome it and wrap my soul in its warmth.

The fauns may play in our garden and run off with leading ladies, but I shall die with your name on my lips — sounds like an aria's about to start — but I can only regret that the words are flat from ill use. I know that your name shall be there; I have been to paradise with your heart touching mine and then touched eternity with love — I shall love only Andrea and hold him in my heart of hearts.

Soon you shall sweep away my loneliness with one touch of your hand to my hair.

I wish they had left the vase alone; now, it's the "vase that was stolen" or the "*New York Times* Vase investigation" instead of "that magnificent Greek vase at the Met." Maybe in a couple months people will get back to the vase. I hope the *Times* doesn't decide to investigate our Unicorn tapestries and plaster them all over its pages with affidavits from a wrinkled little Lebanese lady who claims she did them on her Singer and smuggled then to New York disguised as place mats, where they were miraculously put together by a seamstress in Brooklyn.

Strange reply from *Current Biography* — still don't know the verdict on assignments. I'll enclose the letter — easier than explaining.

Do you believe this! Friday I was called to a meeting at the Superintendent's office very hush hush — intimidation time — castrate the English teachers. It seems "people are upset about my hair" — it is causing undue talk — blah, blah, blah — "vicious rumors" etc. He rambled on — hinting once about only "queers" have long hair and live alone — etc. — small town gossips — so forth. I let loose, in my best Irish tradition about Zanesville — in fact, I said Goddamn Zanesville — and his "hint" of homosexuality demanded that I not continue the discussion without a lawyer present. After he regained his color, he backed off two miles. Again, I felt like telling him to stick the job, but I'll wait. I know I am leaving — that is enough.

I hope these last two weeks let up for you. I shall listen to you Sat. I will try to be with you mentally.

Goodnight love,
Charles

Obviously, my days in Zanesville were numbered, as you recall. I did not cut my hair.

March 6, 1973 (New York)

I can't tell you how your letter which came yesterday was welcome. I'm sure you were thoroughly depressed by my last one, but I really felt that way — I can be so set upon. However, that's all over now — *Carmen* (ugh) don't miss this week's broadcast — *Carmen* is out of the way and will be unveiled to a complete black audience tonight. Now only *Rosenkavalier* remains, and by the time you see me on the 18th it too will be gone. I am trying to have the 20th off also. If I can, then you can take me to Columbus when you go to "check" your schools in the early afternoon. Or put me on a bus as you did that poor unfortunate creature up north. In any case I must be home to cover that evening — I quite frankly can't wait. The Memphis trip will be so bad because I really won't want to be there. I'll leave there Sunday at 12:30 PM, and be in Columbus at 3:45. It's the only even semi-direct flight — with a 30-minute stop in Cincinnati. If I leave earlier I go to Indianapolis and wait two hours — besides the Ball is a late affair and I don't think I can leave much earlier. I'm surprised that I found any connection at all. Now I must find a direct Columbus-New York for the 20th. Then sit here three days until you get here. It's either feast or famine. Anyway, I will be at the hotel with you as often as I can, and I don't care what Carolyn thinks. Is there some way we can put her out of the way for the weekend? I'm getting a new Cavafy translation this weekend; I understand it's much better than the old.

Our "house" is still crawling along. Newest problem — price hike as of Feb 1. Now the fucking thing cost $1,500 more — can you believe that? I wonder sometimes if I am doing the right thing — but then it's always worth something, and can be sold for a profit I hope — much love — must run to *Rosenkavalier*.

Andrea

175

Carolyn had asked me to join her choir one last time for the spring trip to New York. We stayed at the Taft as usual, and you managed to come down several times. And, then, you went to Memphis for a concert appearance; afterwards you flew up to Zanesville for two days before returning to New York.

March 24, 1973 (New York)

What can I say about my visit? Perfection — no — there can be no more perfection between us than just being together. Zanesville, who saw it? Was it there? I think not — for those two days — Zanesville was transformed into a bower of art and love — we brought Cavafy there and worshiped him. It's true then — when you are with someone you love, nowhere is ugly or lonely. For those two days Zanesville was a paradise. My paradise is in you — in lying in your arms, in looking into your eyes, in listening to your voice. And always when I am feeling lost, comfortable and content with you, I must leave. I never will get used to you. We never will have enough time to explore each other and the things we love. Not even in our entire lifetime. That's why our love is so eternal — we have always been torn away from each other, and even eons are not enough for us to fathom this immortal love we have for each other. Shall we try this time around? For I despair at the thought of waiting in dark limbo for you to come and wake me again. Will the gods ever say to us, "there you two, take each other and go off forever, become one forever for you were one at the beginning. There is no Faber, no Andrea, no Antinous, no Hadrian, no Hephaestion — No, you are all one, you are all Love."

My soul, what a pain to be without you — how hard everything becomes. How unnecessary. In this horrid week coming, you should be here beside me — this is yours as well as mine. The pain, the joy — whatever — is yours.

I need you to sustain me — to love me — to comfort me. I know that can't be — I shall keep close to my soul the memory of our love — it will warm and comfort me.

Faber loves me.

The Cavafy experience, where we seemed to enter into the soul of the poetry, was so powerful that it scared me. We seemed to take our bodies on psychic sexual journeys. You — perhaps tapping into your Greek genes — welcomed this ecstatic passion without question, only celebration.

April 1, 1973 (Zanesville)

Love,

And now the pen again, or the phone, takes me momentarily out of this place and near you. How second-best it is after our total sharing of souls.

I felt strange the day after our "Cavafy experience" — childish that I seem to let it get the best of me instead of taking it with much more élan. That is the main reason I wanted you to leave some. So I tried it. Nothing — oh, the medium-high, nice light feeling I used to get when I first tried it years ago. But nothing compared to the world I go into at our times, when I absolutely cannot contain my mind. Perhaps, one explanation is that I <u>believe</u> in all the things I say to you — all the poetry, the whole thing is real to me, as real as the unquenchable (is that right?) Satyr that Cavafy released in me, as real as the pain that smothered me and the loneliness of lost love that poured from Larry's painting that night. I become a sieve for these emotions because inside I actually believe it is all possible, how naïve perhaps; how unsophisticated perhaps. But I prefer it to chains holding me to strange walls and rooms that contain no faces. I would not trade one night with you — past, present, or future — for all the orgies the Continental Baths has hosted. I don't know what is in your head all the time — although I sometimes see it in your eyes. But I know what is in mine, and I know that with you our love begins through my body and goes into my soul. Although I have no scars from shackles, I've been around a bit (god, what a dreadfully unoriginal way of putting it), and I know that no one, no time — from the first nervous touch on Tony's thigh to a couple threesomes with tricks in Pgh. — no one, ever came near my soul — transcended beyond the moment into all- time where I feel part of the world where I have always lived — the world where Antinous lived — the world where Cavafy idealized his boys. He knew it was there; he wrote about it, so did Crane. Michelangelo put it in stone. We have lived it for four years.

We have had our Fauns, as you like to call them. There was Marco for me and I am glad that I finally admitted to you how much he and I had between us — glad you asked at last. There has been Tommy for you, and Oliver for me. Must admit that my relationship with Oliver, unlike with Marco, has love as a component. He has a small percentage of the love I have to give, the little that is left after I happily give to you all that you will embrace. Am I cheating Oliver then?

I think not because he and I come together at a level of love that suits our needs; we don't look to the gods to help us celebrate our love. It's only you who has reached in and tapped "the mother lode" (That smacks of a Freudian slip — just ignore it.) within my inner being.

If some day you tire of my love, the great crevice you opened and filled will close again and I will know only the love of Fauns.

It did bother me that you spoke so casually about "indestructible love" — I believe our love must be guarded as a precious jewel or other treasure. I know you do too.

Sorry if this letter is sort of down, love, but I was awfully depressed when you left — always down from losing you only to snatch a few more days in a month or so — thank you for calling me. I hope you know what happiness it brings to some pretty empty days.

Charles

April 4, 1973 (New York)

Indestructible? Indeed, yes it is!

That doesn't mean we shouldn't care for and protect it — but indestructible it is — not without built in faults and flaws which any man-made thing must have — but solid and indestructible as all things made by the gods are. We didn't make our love, it didn't grow. It was always there, it will always be there — even when we are not. It is not only indestructible but it's immutable.

I knew about Marco. I rather sensed it, and it didn't matter — such things don't to me — however, knowing Marco as I do, I would not say "Faun" but rather "Centaur." I was indiscreet to ask — perhaps it's my desire to share with you. I want to know of you — not out of jealousy, but out of desire to know all of you. I'm sorry that Oliver is denying me that part of you, which is his. Do you think he knows that I could not help but love him, if you do?

> But we who serve art,
> sometimes with the mind's intensity,
> can create pleasure that seems almost physical —

but of course only for a short time.
That's how in the bar yesterday —
mercifully helped by alcohol —
I had half an hour that was totally erotic.

(C.P. Cavafy, *Half an Hour*)

"Cavafy tells us in effect that the artist, by intensity of mind can know that which the lover will probably never know, however tangible and however realized his erotic commitment," says his translator Edmund Keeley. And Mr. David Stivender agrees. Does Cavafy really think that? I think not.

Cavafy's intensity of mind is of course his imagination — and the whole verse reeks of failure — do they mean he would rather have his imagined love, than the real thing? What if it were Cavafy himself who was the real lover — then it must follow that his real love is better than this imagined lover? What about "almost" tangible? Again failure. Cavafy never mentions the word "lover." He meant something totally personal which had very little to do with "lover." Those two (Keeley and Stivender) should learn to distinguish between "sex," "erotic" and love. What Cavafy felt was "erotic" and is a totally different thing. So few can distinguish the difference between sex and love — we do — I have sex with <u>you</u> because I <u>love</u> you, and not the other way around. I love without sex. I love eternally — with great depth — on many levels. I could never love anyone because they were great sex. Nor could I have sex with anyone simply because I love them. That's the perfection in our relationship — it is "totally erotic" — there is no way that I can get enough of you physically. I think Zanesville showed that, and it is totally love. We have as yet only scratched the surface of what we have for each other. There is a complete dimension there which we have not even explored. That will come, when we have set aside the hysteria of having only a few hours together. That will come — I know.

The Boulez thing is over — I had a success out of it — but I am glad it's over.

Now it's almost sure that Pat will go on the 12th — can you make it? —

My love
Andrea

This was a confusing letter. After all these years, some of the references escape me. I do know that you talked a lot with David Stivender (chorus master at the Met) about Cavafy's poetry. David was brilliant and you and I both respected and liked his insight into music, art, literature.

The line in the letter that resonates strongly with me is "we have as yet only scratched the surface of what we have for each other." That was indeed true; so much was to come.

April 10, 1973 (Zanesville)

My love,
Just finished a couple more applications. I hope all of this is not as futile as the running around that I did last year. It seemed that I was always going after something but wound up with only Zanesville. Nothing yet from *Current Biography* — strange business. I don't get it — why hedge around about the thing. If I don't get closer to you, I don't know how I'll survive the years ahead. All these precious days — time defeating us and here I rot

in Zanesville. Zippy must come through for us this time. He must bring us together.

Your letter about Cavafy took much of the gloom away. You are so right about the poem and about love — ours is truly a culmination of imagined and real ecstasy, and as you say, a mountain rather than a ship.

If spring would come back (I'm tempted to put my winter corn cobs on the door again.) then I would find it easier to face these seemingly endless days of loneliness. The smell of fresh life that oozed out of the ground a few weeks ago has been smothered again by harsh winds and snow. Eliot was right, "April is the cruelest month." It is a deceiver and a cheat — a tempest of despair while we wait for rebirth of our god and ourselves. Easy to believe that more people commit suicide in April than any other month.

But it shall not overwhelm me this time or ever again while I have your love. Each time I struggle with my despair, I seek your love and it rises up to me. When your letters come, or phone calls, or, after your visit, your cologne on my robe, and I am caught up again in our wealth of love and I believe that I will escape the nightmare of loneliness and be with you. For I have been lonely for years — it seems a thousand — and even now as I write this my heart beat increases at the very thought of our love voyage. Oh, my love, I hunger so for you — you are the great mystery — I will not miss you this time — with all the strength and courage I have I will struggle towards our destiny. I must be near you; I know that better than anything else right now. If it meant walking out of this apartment and away from everything — then it would be that way, and I would not look back — only forward towards your eyes and the mystery of quiet nights along the Rubicon and your touch against my smooth body as I cried in your arms —

Sorry, got carried away — it's late. Still not sure about this weekend. As it stands, Oliver plans to come here Sunday and we will drive to New York.

I'll talk to you.

Love,
Charles

April 28, 1973 (Boston)

My love — where are you now? I would like so much to be with you. We could be together on your trip to New York — I could make your trip so short (isn't all our time together short). Is it raining where you are? Here in New England the sun has come out — it's late morning. What is it like in PA where you are? I hope the horrid weather we have had in the past week s not affecting you. The TV just said that it's clearing in PA. I hope you have a comfortable trip. I also hope that it's fruitful for you. At least in the field I want you in. Don't compromise. You can have a brilliant future if you will just accept it — be selfish. It is in you to be what you want. Zanesville is over — it served its purpose and now it is gone — now an open clear future lies before you. The only consideration you have is Lisa. I say only because I can adjust to whatever your future may be. I will go along, for I love you, and will be with you. She is affected by anything that you do.

I am trying again for the house — damn it — I'm sure I can swing it. I have convinced Pat to go ahead — but of course I must go it alone. I wish <u>you</u> were here to help. I'm sure you would and could. Unfortunately, Pat's job in California fell through, so now he may be much with us, but we must make him understand. He must allow us to have our life together. I'm sure it can work out — it must. As he accepted Tommy, whom he dislikes, he must accept you whom he likes. I think Cleveland will help. I want this obstacle to our happiness to be removed — after all you're not a "Dancer."

I love you —

Andrea

You were on the Met Tour in Boston so our letters started to get jumbled in the time sequence of responses and so forth.

This is the first time that you suggested that Tommy — the Joffrey dancer — had been woven into your life to such a degree that Pat had to accept him even if he disliked him. I did not realize that Tommy had moved from chorus to soloist so early.

April 28, 1973 (New York)

Love,

Here I am in the Queens, alone, tired and a little flaky. Writing to you will bring you closer to me right now and I need to feel that you are with me now. Sorry this letter will not be waiting in Cleveland for you, but in a way I'm glad I waited for this moment to write. God, how I miss you my love — and New York without you? — a monotonous village. So tonight I shall gather you into my arms in my dreams.

The drive yesterday was a nightmare. Why do I have such horrible trips from Zanesville — when I easily managed scads of trips to NY from Pittsburgh. For 10 solid hours it rained and for much of the trip the road was covered with fog. Besides, I was upset because I called the guy at Macmillan and his secretary said he would be out of the office for 3 weeks so that must mean they decided on someone else for the job. Also, after spending $70 on the car it acted crazy — jerking and swerving and almost dying out. At one point I stopped to turn around and go back. I've been upset all week anyway. Not sleeping well — wanting so much to get out of Ohio and on with life. I literally thought yesterday was crack-up time.

I wanted to start crying and screaming and just stop holding together — bearing up — being strong and all that rot. But instead, I talked myself out of the breakdown and decided, "Damn it to hell, I'm not going to be stopped now, I'm going for the golden ring or I'll die trying; I love you and belong near you and I belong in New York." Anyway, I "talked" the car all the way and then there it was, soaring into furiously churning smoke, our jeweled bridge. It was fantastic. Powerful, elegant — defiant. And then you were with me. I held you — us — tightly in my mind — all our beauty together. Our love — the love I saw in your eyes when you came towards me at the doctor's office or when you were waiting on the corner to take me to lunch. You were tired, hassled, but you came downtown to spend an hour or two with me.

Oh, I should have wrapped my arms around you right on that corner and shouted out to all New York that here in your arms is my soul — here is my Andrea — my Sun. It's too bad that Hart Crane never saw our bridge on such a night. Perhaps he would have found the elusive "word" he sought.

Well, I arrived in the Queens at 1:30 AM. Oliver was here but he had to go to JFK at 6:00 AM for a flight to Germany. I was so exhausted I could not imagine being able to drive to New Jersey today for the teaching interview. But I had a very trippy dream. Almost an enactment of my anxiety. I was in Pittsburgh. I felt the total physical experience of the streets and places I know so well, but

I was being drowned by the city because, in my dream, I kept saying to myself that I had to wake up and come back to consciousness because time was running out. Well, I woke up in time to call New Jersey and tell them I was still coming for the interview. Miraculously, I felt that I had once again absorbed and worked through an anxiety attack.

Now, I had the problem of the car. It chugged and sputtered for 70 miles — wanting to quit but I insisted it get me there. It did.

The interview was all right. But it wasn't the important thing to me. What was important was that I went. That I pushed myself beyond the anxiety and even pushed the car — which, by the way, I had fixed in New Jersey. The principal took me to a garage. Nothing really wrong — "something" in the motor was loose and was bumping against some wires causing a short in the circuit — thus jerking, back firing, etc. It cost me $20 for him to tighten the thing. The mechanic couldn't figure out how I made it without the engine conking out. Logically, he said, it should have stalled when the circuit shorted. "Fritz" is the mechanical version of Hilla. So, I felt relieved and calmer as Fritz and I buzzed back across the Jersey Turnpike. Then, and I'm not making this up, or exaggerating, as I drove along the Hudson toward our bridge, with Manhattan's skyline cut out across the river, a glorious, stupendous rainbow appeared out of the drizzle and grayness and spanned Manhattan from the Cloisters to somewhere Downtown. It was incredible — a dream — something out of a Disney movie. I couldn't keep my eyes off it — a rainbow over Manhattan — a crazy symbol for a hopeless romantic — I actually started freaking on it. I had to pull off to the side and put my emergency flasher on. It only lasted 5 or 10 minutes but it was spectacularly appropriate. I had to write you tonight about it and about the whole day.

It is ironic that tomorrow you will be in Ohio while I'm here. Usually there are more than enough people in this apt., but this weekend I'm the solo tenant. I have an interview — teaching job — on Long Island on Monday, then I will head to Ohio. Oliver returns on Tuesday.

Speaking of Oliver, I hope my relationship with him isn't as confusing as my inarticulate explanation of it last week. How ironic that I assumed long ago that your relationship with Pat was a fact that I would have to accept and adapt to — that it would always be "Andrea and Pat" for all practical purposes — and that I would never share that particular phase of your life. So, I figured that such a "for practical purposes" relationship was also better for me then doing a bar thing or something. So, Oliver and I became a "thing" — one held together by bracelets, jade rings, gold chains, the trappings of most ephemeral gay love affairs. I keep telling him how little we really can share — for innumerable reasons — and he keeps insisting he gets VD from serving coffee. Amusing, but typical I think.

You said that you were surprised that I talked to Oliver the way I did during an argument last week. I was not cruel — only honest. I have always been honest with him. Obviously, he finds it hard to be honest with me. But what about you and me? No, I have not been honest with him about us — and have lied to him in connection with us — but only as far as our relationship goes. He knows we have a special friendship, but it would be ridiculous to try and explain more than that now or perhaps ever. Can you imagine yourself explaining us to Pat? And he is far more able to understand — or maybe not — than Oliver. Well, I still don't know if it makes sense. I'm just trying to brush away the slight questioning I saw in your eyes a couple times. Know, my love, that you are the essence of all the love of which I am capable. My soul has been a storehouse waiting to pour forth into your eyes. When I see you, touch you, share you, there is no Pat, no Oliver, no world but ours.

Goodnight, love, until Cleveland,

Charles

You recall that Pan Am reconsidered and gave Oliver a job as a steward based in New York, as he wanted. His apartment (shared with other Pam Am employees) was in Queens (have to laugh that, not being a New Yorker yet, I wrote "the Queens" which must have caused a chuckle for you).

I was definite now about moving to New York, and, as I told you, I would probably get an apartment with Oliver.

May 13, 1973 (Atlanta)

I'm sure you have wondered why I haven't written. I'm sure you think it's the excesses of life in the South. No, I've had a lot of time alone. I've needed more. After each of these famished bouts of ours, I've need a lot of time to recover. I have to re-live or re-love (thank you Dylan) each moment — to try and understand. You probably think of me as a jaded person, indeed I have done much in my life, but each time we bout it takes me about a week to recover. I simply can't understand. What is it that happens to us? I understand perfectly where we are mentally, but I can't figure out this physical thing which has grown into us, and keeps growing. I'm afraid of it — for fear we might lose it; I'm afraid to expect it for fear it won't come. What will it do to us should it not? I like to understand everything that is happening to me, but this I can't. I have never felt this before. It's as though each session we have is like a trip — all consuming

— exhausting — my head reeling. It takes me days to recover; it's almost like withdrawal. Will it last (my god don't let it ever stop)? When we are together will it change? It's almost like a combat to see which shall please the other most. I have become completely disinterested in other sex. I have been surrounded by beauties all week — and I know it wouldn't work.

I want to feel your body pressing into mine. I want to encircle your thighs with my arms. I want more sleepless nights spent worrying your body. When did we become this way? Do you know? Which one of us changed? Was it the compassionate drug (thank you Constantine)? Please help me to understand this, for I have to admit — that it frightens me a bit. I fear for me — I fear of being hurt. I fear for our relationship, for such a change cannot fail but bring change somewhere else. My god how I wish you were here.

Andrea

You were referring to our time together in Cleveland; I think that you had a couple days free and so we stayed in the hotel room and had sex, delirious astonishing sex. I thought that you had put some strong drug in the wine or something, but you swore you had not, and that we had just smoked some grass, period. So, we were both puzzled. The Met tour was halfway over.

May 15, 1973 (Zanesville)

Love,
Your letter arrived today — a much-needed contact with you. Rejections on two teaching jobs because I don't have NY certification. My reaction is mixed — half relief and half fear of not

having an income in September. I need the confidence that you give me.

How totally open I am with you — no one has ever known me so completely. I would let no one else see the unedited rambling of my mind that these comments represent – they are at times so self-conscious and indulgent.

But it is all part of my complete, absolute trust in our relationship. I never dreamed that one day both my soul and body would open like great vaults to spill out into another's arms. You have had my soul for years — now you have my body. Don't you recall how I questioned you so much about whether our love-making was affecting you as it was me. I felt consumed in its flames. Oh, the trips — the first flight — were ecstasy beyond anything I ever imagined. When you rode with me into the sun I was sure I would never come back. But beyond those times, something else happened which continues to expand. I can't explain it — it's weird maybe. I sort of trip on you — when we are in bed I feel strong — possessive of you — and all my love for you pushes towards desire for your body to go — fly — make it as only we can. It's a culmination of all that has gone before.

It scares me to read that you fear for our relationship because of the "change." Nothing has changed, love. What I gave you in my dreams before, I am now able to give in reality. I was afraid to ever release such passion — to ever need a touch of a particular person so completely. But I brought it out — or you did — or we did — or Cavafy did — or whatever. It represents only the other dimension of our love. Hurt you, hurt us? One thing I do know and that is that I will never hurt you — never could — "I too am Andrea." I cannot imagine a change, love, because I waited a life time for our love, and, though time destroys all else, I shall never let time, nor circumstances, nor others diminish its passion.

I believe our love was written in the stars by poets — dreamed by Emperors, and feigned by second-rate affairs. That even we, both "somewhat jaded" by what passes for love, are amazed by it. But I refuse to contain it — to be cautious about it. I will only nourish it — celebrate its splendor. If our "bouts" do not come in time — then I shall ravish you in my dreams again — but whatever comes will not hinder my love — that you possess totally as long as I have it to give.

Charles

[Enclosed note with the letter:]

As always, your voice was like a warm touch of my other reality — the true and cherished one. I was upset about the "hair" business; I realize I over-reacted — probably confirmed their thoughts — but my god, must I sit calmly through my own dissection in this town. It has only bought so much of me and I will give them no more. And, yet, I am scared. I worry about getting a job — surviving again. Last year's famine has left scars. I guess they're always piling up on us, but those are still pink and raw. It was a bad, humiliating time. I suppose it would help if *Current Bio* came through on a regular basis — it would be a touch stone at least. I hope we will talk some of these things through; although, I promise I will not burden you with more decisions — more complications. I guess I can only talk to myself for so long — eventually it's more an echo than a conversation.

It won't be long now before you are here — next to me in this bed. I've waited so long — through the darkest days of winter — for those hours with you. Good luck in Memphis. I'll call tomorrow about your return ticket.

My "Witch" told me that I would be happy in '73 — so I must count on the occult. I've tried everything else. That happiness must include you — so she must mean that we will be together more by the end of the year. I hope Zippy is paying close attention and doing his share.

What can you bring me? Bring me the Greek islands swimming in the blue of your eyes — bring me the poetry in your voice — bring me the earth and its passion in your body — and the sun in your soul — as you always do — then I shall rise up out of this desert — bring me your love and let us fly with it —

Goodnight love,
Charles.

Oh, I decided to pass on Carolyn Bruno's offer on a trip with the students again in late May. I would have to pay my own plane fare from Columbus and I don't think it is worth it to have to run around NY with the kids to see a few shows and probably only spend a little time with you.

The "Witch," of course you recall, was the Reverend Mary, a gifted psychic, amazing and never wrong.

May 27, 1973 (Minneapolis)

My love,

Your letter came the morning after you talked to me. It was so wonderful to read. So comforting. I suppose what it all boils down to is my ignorance of the extent of the passion in you. Was it always there? Our first sexual encounters were almost innocent, compared to the madness we now feel. You seem so calm, that I'm reassured. My fear was not of the passion, for that I can accept from you in limitless quantities and return in kind — so great is my love and need for you, but I was confused by this violent change in you — is there anything else down deep inside you there to surprise me? If there is, I pray that it be as magnificent, as all consuming as welcome as this. Our love now leaves me exhausted — satisfied and trembling against your body. Nothing gives me as great pleasure; even now as I think about Cleveland my body warms with excitement — and I long for your hands — your hands to calm me again. When we met, I felt boundless joy, that I had found you again. I was immensely happy and content with our love. The gods had favored us above everyone — they had given us each other — little did I dream of the extent of the entire gift — as I sit here perched on the 12th floor looking out over these flat limitless lands, I realize there is no extent to their gift — like our universe it has no limit — one cannot see the edge of our love. I reach into the heart of our love, grasp the frightening core of immortal fire that lies there, and thrust it burning and searing into my loins. I accept their gift without question — I lift you glowing, to my forehead, and together we streak across the heaven — for all to see. The fire of our love bathes my body with cleansing purity. I open my arms to it, I embrace it, I am content. I cannot tell you I love you. We are one, and we never need speak again.

Wasn't that one huge masturbation? I won't reread it, so please excuse the mistakes. I love your daily writings. I'm particularly fond of the one on love, and the one that ends, "I wonder where they are, Greece or Italy." Truly beautiful.

Along with your letter came a phone call from our builder — bad news — the banks in New Hampshire find themselves short of money, because of the dollar crisis. So, they will no longer make construction loans. Are you ready — our loan was all cleared, and now this. We called at least six other banks — the same. Does this smell of depression or not? They will ruin the economy of the area if all these people are thrown out of work. We have decided to finance the building ourselves. Our money in the bank earns 5 ½% and the dollar drops 8 ½% — so there is no reason to save. We will at least have a value in the land and building. What a time this is to build in, but the excavation will start on Tuesday — now we are committed to continue. Do you get the feeling that fate is trying to stop this construction? I have thought of this — perhaps we should not build. Still, if one were to stop every time a few problems arise, what would ever get done? No, perhaps all these problems, all this effort is to make me realize the value — the Baraka — for Tamworth. I believe in it; I love it. I want it with you — to focus our love there.

Hope you will come to Philadelphia.

Andrea

May 30, 1973 (Zanesville)

Love,

That was some letter! It prompted the sexiest, wildest dream I've ever had. If possible, it increased my longing to be with you. If only I could get my spirits up — the loneliness after Cleveland has been oppressive and pulls me down to despair. All the questions which faced me last year at this time are here again, still to be answered. What to do? Where? How? But I will be all right, love, once I am settled again. Surely, after enduring this much I can manage several more weeks or even a couple months of confusion. I am just nervous and anxious about the next few months. I'm not sure that I could take much more loneliness like this. In the middle of chaos, like the eye of a hurricane, is the certainty of our love. It alone sustains me and makes the present endurable.

Each time I read your letter my head spins in the world, our world, that you captured. The only surprise I have left is the depth of my love — you have shared its scope with me when it gushed into our arms and we raped Cavafy of his dreams — soared over Crane's bridge — and turned Shakespeare's sonnets to children's rhymes.

Oh, love, I need you so — I am so incomplete without you here I will write again soon.

Charles

June 2, 1973 (New York)

Would you believe that early this morning I was in City Hall Park reading your letter — what a marvelous consolation it was and is for me. Promptly at eleven I delivered the money to the lawyer (I suppose we must know people like that.) I went home and at 1:30 he called. All the charges except the possession of stolen vehicle were dropped. He was paroled to be tried on July 31 — no bail. I then spoke to Tom who was incoherent. I told him to come directly here — after all the fuss with the parole officer — he arrived — looking dead. He had not eaten in two days or slept. He had been kept with fifteen men in a cage 5' by 8' — they were junkies and all sorts of scum. He was beaten twice — once when he wouldn't give up his watch and again when he wouldn't dance for a big black. They took him out after his second beating and put him with the prostitutes — then the scene as they tried to seduce him, calling him queer, became pure Fellini. He is in such condition as I have never seen anyone — he has cried on and off all evening — talking about the way the police treated people like animals — beating an alcoholic with handcuffs, etc., etc. I can't imagine this won't have some permanent scar on him. He is so unstable as it is. The intoxicant charge was the mace which you sent me. I had given him one when he went to live in the village.

So, it is all over. I must get my money and forget the whole thing.

I really don't like the idea of you living out there with Oliver — all right — as a way out for a while to share with him. But to live there — no. Be near me — I think if you are going to lean on anyone here it should be me. Come where you can be near me — where we can in a few steps be with each other — not painfully close. You don't need to have an apartment when you arrive — you can stay with Oliver, stay with me, stay in a small hotel, 'til we find just the right place for you — we'll look together. You must be comfortable there. And it must be near me — unless, of course, it's in some other city because of work there.

Have no fear, New York is made for you — you will be so perfect here — you have passed through the dark night — now cross your rainbow into my arms.

Thank you for being with me this morning.

Andrea

You had called and told me that Tommy had been arrested. I don't recall all the charges, but he was with that strange woman that he hung with who probably stole a car or something. Tommy was charged with carrying mace, which was illegal in New York then. Anyway, I do remember that you took one thousand dollars in cash down to have for the lawyer, or for bail to do whatever you could to get Tommy released. I don't think I ever saw Tommy again, after the episode. He left the city to go to his parents; took a leave from the Joffrey and then later on joined the company again when they moved to Chicago.

Don't remember if you ever got your money back.

June 8, 1973 (Zanesville)

My love,

What a horrible nightmare. Tommy will, as you said, carry its effect for some time....mostly fear I would think. Such an experience is like dropping down to hell and seeing what humanity can be reduced to.

You are so goddamned beautiful. You go through this mess and then write me to do more "leaning on you." Who does Andrea lean on? Do you realize that you can lean on me? That I see your needs so often when you're not even aware.

At 11:00 on Tuesday or was it Wednesday — this has been such a long week I forget — but I did think of you and Tommy. My vibes were good for him. I thought the lawyer was a rip-off but knew that the consequences of being wrong were too great — you wouldn't take a chance on his being kept in jail. You did the right thing — the only thing you could do because you are what you are and, as Frost said of his road "and that has made all the difference." Love, humanity, conscience has no price tag.

My timing is always off. I wrote to *Current Biography* last week and yesterday received a copy of the June magazine with my article in it. No letter yet, though. It is a relief to know that they did publish it finally. I think it was held because of additional info. being added from an article that came out in January about Pavarotti.

Tonight my mother and Lisa are coming for the weekend. My mother has been anxious to see where I've been living that has made me so miserable, although I hardly expect her to understand the reasons.

I'm sending this check because I must start paying you back the loan — and my bills are getting down enough now that I can. It's nothing, but it represents more than the $25.00. And it has nothing to do with your financial bind right now. You are always doing things for me — sharing part of the things you have worked hard to enjoy. I enjoy them — treasure them because they are from you — and know it makes you happy to share. However, when I asked for the loan it was exactly that — a loan. I know the money is not that important to you and it by itself is not of consequence, but I must pay it back as I can because it will help me to maintain the equality that is an important part of our relationship. This may sound crazy and if I had tried to explain it in Cleveland you would have still insisted I keep the money. One of the strengths of our relationship — among many — is that we can be one without absorbing each other. There is an exquisite balance. The other way is the easy way — to simply say "it doesn't matter to Andrea."

But that is deceptive. Of course, it doesn't matter to you. But it does matter to the relationship. I am not an opera star, nor any other kind, so I cannot balance the relationship through stature — it must be done by maintaining a kind of integrity regarding you. Oh, it's too vague in my own mind for me to explain it. But I do understand the need, so don't return the check.

Most relationships — men or women — lose the very thing I'm talking about. One party takes the easy way merely because it's easy and not realizing that the price is the loss of balance and the eventual destruction of the relationship because this change in the relationship sends the stronger party out seeking the balance he originally had. In other words, I'm sending you this check to keep you out of the baths (or something like that.) I give up.

Now, I must put in some time here. I have to get the apartment ready for my visitors. I love you.

Charles

June 10, 1973 (New York)

My love,

I long so much to look into your eyes this morning. I have finished my lecture (success) and my first Benoit anywhere (*Bohème* — success) and now, I must start thinking of *Maritza*. I'm very tired, and long to rest in your eyes. I need the calm of your arms — I need to be quiet and listen to the music of your voice. I feel very deprived. I have worked very hard, suffered a bit with the Tommy thing, and can't have the oasis of the one person I need and love. I don't ask much, just your arms when I need them.

Star has returned, so Tommy now seems to be settled; he found a new girlfriend two days before she returned, and seems to have a good job at Wolf Trap doing *Most Happy Fellow* which he seems to be anxious to do; it will be only for a few weeks but lots of money, and a fun place. We went to the monument several days ago, to watch the sunset and be cool. I finally got through to him — that he could only dance and should only dance. He was thinking of not dancing anymore — after the Joffrey experience. So he's very happy again. He has accepted the fact that he must still treat his illness, and that he must above all dance. Thank god.

Enough of him. I hate to waste our time together talking of him but I'm sure you realize how much of my life has been filled with this the past weeks. Had a letter from Robert; he seems to like Hawaii and says he will stay there until he tires of "Paradise." I think he will be back in the fall. Caleb went through without stopping, called from Maine. Visited Tamworth — the floors are covered over, so the wall will go up next — then roof, and we have a place to stay. He saw your article on Pavarotti — he had Midler in the same issue. My god, will the next few weeks never pass — 'til we can be together. Pat will go to Spokane on June 26th. So if you can, or will, perhaps you will come to me — can you, will you.

Andrea

You were very kind to Tommy; looked after his spirit and mental health, and did not simply use him as a sexual object, which if I remember correctly you told me that a lot of guys did. I don't recall the trouble that he had with the Joffrey, and I thought I remembered that he did finally go to Chicago with them. All so long ago, I am not sure of what became of him.

Robert had gone to Hawaii after an operation in hopes of recovering fully in the sun. And apparently it worked because when he returned to New York, all traces of his cancer were gone. We rejoiced.

June 20. 1973 (Zanesville)

My love,
I'm glad that we talked today. Though I can do little to change things for the better, I now know what has been troubling you, and at the least can offer you encouragement. If I have learned one thing well in life it is vigilance with which I have struggled, and continue to do so, to discover and preserve my individuality — my unique being which is my only true distinction. I struggled against destruction from an alcoholic father who brought such pleasantries into my life as lost weekends, lost love, and death in a city jail, after having been arrested for drunken disorder.

But, also, there was beauty — I clutched it, determined to rise to it and shout my triumph. I never do. Don't fear, I'm not going into a chorus of "Nobody knows de trouble..." We all have known pain — a few it makes beautiful — some it curses or cripples. Why the difference? I don't know. In some strange way, I believe that my determination — even as a child — has maintained me through this struggle. I remember fighting with the therapist — even under hypnosis (he told me) that I would <u>not</u> sacrifice my identity for a marriage or any ideal established by society as a norm.

In *The Stranger* when Camus's main character, Meursault, is waiting for his execution he suddenly realizes, as he looks out his cell window at the sky, that the only significance to life, the raison d'être, is his uniqueness, his separate identity, apart from the sky. We look to the sky for confirmation of our significance by relating to it, by finding our place in it. Rather, he says, we should glory in our separation. Of course, I accept that that philosophy requires great courage because it places the burden of responsibility squarely on the individual. One cannot cop out on life and "excuse it away." When my therapist told me that one cannot exist fully on the periphery of acceptable social adjustment, I quoted this from e.e. cummings: "But man, to be free, must realize that he himself is more important and more real than any ideal that limits or classifies him."

And so the struggle continues — but I am resolutely determined that I will live only this way. The homosexual, particularly, must hold on to the integrity of his existence; otherwise, he becomes a rather pathetic creature with sad eyes and empty arms — frantically looking for something he knows he lost years ago but can't remember what or where.

Sorry to get carried off so, but you know how strongly I feel about this. Never would I want to hurt Pat or suggest that you do. But I believe that no one can "punish" another person into relinquishing his identity — his right to life. It is asking that one negate his very existence. Love cannot require the destruction of the beloved. When we speak of the glory in our love — the exchange of our souls — it is a celebration of our unique identities — a marriage of two not into one — but into two. That is the glory — the miracle — to join yet remain distinct. Any common love — a marriage of two to one as they say — is merely a usurping of one personality by another — a spiritual cannibalism which passes for bliss under the protection of stupidity. I glory in your unique strength, and it is that combination which shall take us to Valhalla time after time. You are right, my love: you are strong — overpowering (sometime I will tell you how strong you seemed during our first flight — incredible.) You could have a Tommy for breakfast, lunch, and dinner and it would bore you in a week. But you know that, and realize your own zest for life, for youth. If only Pat could. I would never expect him to understand us, just as very few could without trying to reduce us to something we're not. My strength is far less apparent, but is always here for you. I love you, Andrea — Pat shall not trouble me in the apartment again. I hope you can find a way to talk to him — you must insist.

I miss you,

Charles

At last, June came and by the fifteenth I was done with Zanesville. You got a flight to Columbus and came to help me close my apartment so that we could drive back to New York together. I felt that you were a sort of "deus ex machina" coming to lift me out of the dreadful tornado-riddled plains of Ohio and into a new life of love, beauty, and passion. We went to Manhattan for a few days. Then headed towards New Hampshire and the little cottage being constructed in the foothills of the White Mountains in the village of Chocorua, town of Tamworth.

III.
NEW YORK, TAMWORTH AND BEYOND

June, 1973 (Tamworth)

Yesterday should have been ours — what I had wanted for our first Tamworth visit was that the two of us should have walked up the road together, and finally came to our Tamworth — all that confusion — Caleb mugging, that was not the way I wanted Tamworth to be for us — I wanted rest, peace, and love. I'm sure you saw it all there, all the beauty I saw and loved there. I'm sure you saw what Tamworth means to me. You couldn't help but see. I'm sure that had we had a second alone you would have told me. I wanted that great solitude for us — I wanted it alone for us — now this summer we shall not have it. I still have that vision for us — now more real since we have seen Tamworth, only us, alone on our hilltop — alone through those woods — shutting the world of our personal problems out. No checks for you to wait for — no job to get — no Pat — no Hilla, no operas to learn — only Faber and Andrea who have finally found their Tamworth. Unlike Mr. Cavafy — the voyage will not have been all the arrival is about, for Tamworth is a goal for us, a real one — it represents — your liberation from Zanesville — it represents our final physical union, and the peace and success we will have in our life together.

Our flight through time — searching for one another has had a marvelous flowering in Tamworth — there in our woods, they all stand, Antinous and Hadrian, Alexander and Hephaestion, all our gods rejoice and say — "Our children have found each other — there under the pines, as in Hellas, they shall love in Peace."

Andrea

Yes, those checks that you referred to were from my contract in Zanesville.

I received a check once a month through the summer. August would be the last check. However, because we were together all summer, I had saved some money to keep me afloat until late in the fall.

We left Tamworth in late August. You had to return for rehearsals and get ready for the coming season. You and I discussed our plans and you asked me to stay in New York with you, in your apartment temporarily, and perhaps that would give us time to decide what to do. I agreed to stay with you and Pat; however, I wanted the situation to be up-front: we would sleep together in your bedroom and you would talk to Pat about our love for one another. A big ask, I knew. You agreed to that.

September, 1973 (New York)

In one of your letters you said, "I will never let Pat bother me in the apartment again." I'm sure you didn't realize at that time how difficult that would be. Surely he knows we love each other, surely he wants me to be happy, surely when he knows my only happiness is with you, he will help us. He seems to be our only problem, and that seems to be only one of his pride. Surely, we can find a way to save his pride — if not, then we will simply go away. For I will not surrender this happiness. I have waited too many ages for you. I have sat through many dark years waiting for your bright light to rise in my eyes, for your warmth to wake my body — nothing — and no one can stand between us. It is only a question of finding the way of less pain. I'm not sure it isn't direct and honest. Please don't be depressed or discouraged. Hold on to me. I will try to be strong, and with your added strength and love — this final, small barrier will be crossed. Then I will say to you — there is our sun — fly into its golden warmth with me — fly again.

Fear of being lonely? How can you ever be lonely again. After so long a time how can you be lonely now? We have come to the end of a very long period of waiting and loneliness for us both — now we have each other. Yes, we really do, we shall never be alone again — I promise you that. Now with your help, with you to lean on, I can free myself from the entanglements of my past life — it will be long, it will be difficult, but I count on you to be strong with me, as I tear away years of unhappiness and mistakes. Our goal is right there now in sight — we already have each other — now we must be patient as I try to free myself from the clay around my feet — then we can fly, free and alone. You must know by now that that is the only thing I want and need — to take you in my arms and fly to our waiting gods. Surely after all you have suffered — this little more can not be too much — now you are not alone — I will not let you be alone — it is Faber and Andrea — and will always be, as it has always been.

Andrea

October, 1973 (New York)

Last night for the first time I heard threats to our relationship, "If it doesn't work out..." — is there even a remote possibility that between us — Faber and Andrea — something won't work out? That thought never entered my mind — can it be that the unhappiness you have had with the "situation" has made you doubt? Have you seen something in me which has clouded the vision of our destiny? If you have please be honest with me, I beg that of you, tell me what it is, and I will rip it out. For our gods still blind my eyes, and I see nothing but our love and our future. Oh, I'm aware of your unhappiness. I try to shield you from it; it hurts me. But don't let Pat with his small annoyances (heat, music) hurt us. I will not — keep our vision in your eyes, until I can remove you from him — you are not part of our life, Pat's and mine, he cannot touch you — he must not. Laugh at him as you did last night, and you will see how stupid and petty his habits are to us. Be strong for a little longer for us and for me — I am not so strong as you think. I need your help, I cannot make this change without your help. You must remain the individual you are — you must find a job to be free. With that off your mind and with us in our own apartment, what can there be, to make our relationship "not work out?" Can it not work out? Am I Oliver, are you Tommy — are we also like the millions of others who lie to each other for a few months of imagined happiness — you must assure me that that isn't true, for I am placing my life in your hands, and such ultimatums as "I may go to Florida for a few months" really devastate me. I dreamed last night we were in my mother's home together, where I was born. I was crying like a baby, and instead of comforting me, you were angry. At the moment I too am very con-fused — plus your situation and Pat I must handle my work, which is very emotional — help me, I have no one else

— help me — let me lean on you — be strong for me for a little longer — help me to find the way out of this labyrinth for us — only for us.

Andrea

Two months sharing your apartment with you and Pat was pushing me to a point of despair. He got nastier every day;

the archness, which he wore like a great crown, crossed into the realm of vicious sniping and so forth.

I struggled to stay calm. Your notes saved me and reassured me that we would eventually free ourselves from your past and the complications that ensnared us temporarily.

November, 1973 (New York)

Strange that you should have the idea that when I constantly have you with me I will <u>need</u> outside stimulus like Tommy. I wonder why you think that? My past record, indeed! But that was B.F. — the past years since I met you — well what could I do — I have a very strong need for sex — and seeing you twice a year was not enough — but what will I want with a Tommy if I have you near me. Our life together is perfection — sexually and otherwise — I <u>need</u> no one and nothing else but my Faber — that is my completion — as long as I can get my hands on your body — the body of the only person I want — why would I put up with some pale imitation? Youth? Forget it my love — there is no youth, no age, only Andrea and Faber standing ageless in eternity. I'm glad you don't feel "threatened" — but that fact will never alter the complete lack of need I feel for anyone else — only my Faber — my homo Faber.

Andrea

We got a laugh out of that tag: Faber "the maker."

And, then, it did finally happen. We started to look for an apartment as a couple. In order to salvage Pat's pride and appease your guilt somewhat you decided to give-up the wonderful rent-controlled apartment, including your piano, and many prized possessions — not your gilt bed, however, that and the Antinous lamp came with us to our new apartment in December, 1973, also on W 89th Street. My "Witch" proved right, just under the wire.

I started a new teaching job — needed a decent salary and New Jersey offered it — in Ringwood. My MA and tenured experience paid off. Bit of a tough commute — did not fit our Manhattan life style and your schedule at all.

February, 1974 (New York)

What can I give my love after I have given him all — there is nothing I withhold from him — to give. So I will give him something which is not mine but which I love — a poem on giving. Francis Quarles, canticles 2.16.6-7:

He is my altar, I his holy place
I am his guest and he my living food.
I'm his by penitence, he mine by grace
I'm his by purchase, he is mine by Blood.
He's my supporting elm and I his Vine
Thus I my best beloved's Am — Thus he is mine.
He gives me wealth — I give him All my vows:
I give him songs He gives me length of days –
With wreaths of grace he crowns My longing brows —
And I his Temples with a crown of praise –
Which he accepts: an everlasting Sign —
That I my best beloved's am That he is mine —

For your birthday my love 1974
Andrea

March, 1974 (New York)

We must guard our love, we must use it like a purple laser beam to cut through Ringwood 5:30 AM, Watergate and no gas. We must nurture it, hold it close in our hands, pass it only from one to the other — nothing must be allowed to touch it from outside — not money, nor other people. It will be buffeted — I know how envious others can be — but nothing can harm us — for ironically, now that the world around us has turned into turmoil — where before was calm — inside, we have found peace, and love in each other — cupped in our closed hands we stare at its flaming core and are fueled by its warmth. What is immortal cannot be changed.

> You would come home after midnight from the Met most nights; I would be fast asleep with the alarm set at 5:30, and you would write me a note and leave it on the kitchen counter. On top of that, my love, you would crawl out of your gilded nest and make tea and a bit of breakfast for me. When I left you went back to bed for several hours. You were so loving. We both knew that I would have to find something in the city; "Ringworm" would have to go.

April 24, 1974 (Boston)

You seem troubled by my talk of fidelity — you need not be — it's not that I'm trying to force you into anything — nor am I trying to make it too important. It's only that this feeling is so new to me — this feeling of contentment — I have lost all desire for the way I lived up to now — and I love the feeling — I revel in this exclusivity — I'm so very happy with this new way I feel — I treat everyone differently — I see these tour cities differently — it's like a rebirth to me — and I love it — that's why I mention it so much to you — not that I expect fidelity from you, but because I want you to share this new joy with me — naturally I would be hurt if you had sex with anyone else, but it wouldn't destroy us — but of this you can be sure, if I go to bed with anyone else, it would hurt me much more than it would you — for I am now so happy that I would be crushed if I ever felt that I needed anyone else.

I am so happy with our life that I want no other — for the first time I am a complete person — let's celebrate our completeness and not worry about anything being too important — everything is too important to me if it concerns you — my Faber — my love — goodnight.

Andrea

April 27, 1974 (Tamworth)

My love, here we are at Tamworth and I'm alone in our bed — our sheets which we left so long ago — our pine boughs still lie on the red tables — how strange to see so many things which we left so long ago — after our so idyllic weekends — we have lighted a fire — we have cooked dinner — all is well, all works — we have drunk wine — but still this house of love cries out — where is Faber — our gods in outrage cry out — why did you come without him? My only answer is "I have come to tend you — I have come to care for our house of love — don't be angry — I love him more than when we last worshipped here — we have not forsaken you — even though I am alone he is here with me — he is always with me — and I with him, and together we are always here with you. We love you still."

My joy is how much Robert loves the house — he was really surprised at what we have done. All is exactly as we left it — not one sigh has intruded upon the love we left here. I open my arms to you — I clasp you to my heart — heal it for me — for it burns for lack of you — you my love — my god.

This morning at 5:00 I rose up at sunrise to watch the day break at Tamworth — I opened my window and leaned out to look to my right — all the birds were up and one whose voice I will never forget, greeted me with such a sweet song — it was three notes of great difference in pitch — then followed by what can only be described as the tinkling of crystal chandeliers — it was unearthly beauty — he sang to me for a while, and then left me to the canaries. What a greeting. What a marvelous portent for the summer, for us, for Tamworth.

I wish I could have seen him. I'm sure he was not beautiful, but, my god, what beauty he brought to me. Now — all the tree trunks facing the sun have a golden streak on them. Day has come — outside my window the lantern which we drove into the snow stands high and dry. The feeders must be filled so my sweet singer will return. My love, see all this through my eyes — share this as you have all else. Stand with me, and let the golden sun consecrate our love. Let him always find my arm around your shoulder —

I called today — I found I could — but you didn't answer — what a shame to not speak to you from here.

Andrea

That was the first time that you heard the Wood Thrush, and your description was so perfect. We listened to that song morning and evening from then on, in absolute wonder at its beauty.

May 2,1974 (Detroit)

My love — I wish I had beautiful things to write of — like my letter from Tamworth — but here — no bird sings, and the sun just seems to be there. This morning I was awake at 5:30. I think your vibes are reaching me — and even here so far away I wake up with you — as much as I hate this place, I'm surrounded by your love. It warms and comforts me — there is no Detroit — only Faber and Andrea — there is no Ringwood — only Faber and Andrea — your raison d'être is not me there with you, but my love for you which is always there — wherever you are — we are never alone — we have our great universal love — we who have conquered the ages, cannot be defeated by Ringwood and Detroit.

I know as you do, that I have your love — I am also sure that I do not have your body — I so long for that — my body pains for the closeness of yours. I long for your physical love — and the weekend in Atlanta seems so far away — I am so starved for your love — notice I said your love. Even now — bored, lonely, and so wanting love — I want only you — only you — come to me — take me to that land where our love dwells. Take me in your arms, and let us evoke our gods — and sacrifice to them with our bodies — not five weeks — but eternity.

Andrea

May 3, 1974 (Detroit)

Have I told you how grateful I am for your love? How marvelous it is to love you? The way I thrill when I look at you — how I am constantly stunned by your beauty — I find myself staring at you, enthralled by you — grateful for you. Do you know what your body looks like to me — what joy it gives me to see you naked — to see you so beautiful before me — a work of the gods, and you are mine. Do you know what your nakedness feels like to me — the shock every time I touch you — the joy and completeness of feeling you press against me — the absolute insane madness I feel in our love-making.

The calm quiet oneness we have afterwards — when I take your deflated passion in my mouth, and feel you leap and I smell the love still fresh on your body.

The penetrating heat I feel when you are inside me — there where you belong — so close — closer than any human has ever been — since we last loved — there in Alexandria — there in Athens — there in Rome. Now let us take our love to Atlanta — there our gods await us — they prepare our altar — they light our sacrifice.

Andrea

May 5, 1974 (Detroit)

Now my week of cloister is over — this long day is drawing to a close, and soon we will try and perform *Hoffmann*. I have packed so that I can sleep as soon as I get h– o–m–e — back to the hotel — imagine calling this horrid hole "home?" Today being Saturday, I couldn't even get tea — coffee — or food.

Tomorrow at 8:30 AM we will all board our huge plane and fly off to Atlanta to begin my vigil — counting the days until Friday — at least there is sunshine and beauty — and, after my wait, love —

It's hard to imagine only two weeks have passed — it seems like years — my god — so long — was I really at Tamworth — it all seems like a dream now -where is reality? I seem to be suspended, hung here away from you — waiting for reality to return. Haven't we waited long enough? All these ages — and now to have to wait so long again.

Still with you working as you do — I wouldn't be much with you — but I could be there to comfort you at night and in the morning. I miss that — and I hope you don't feel abandoned — it is hard on you — I know that — I love you all the more for doing it — I know you are doing it for our dream -I love you so much — and I always shall no matter what happens — rest in my love — let it comfort you.

Andrea

May 5, 1974 (Atlanta)

What can there be for us but success? Where can we go but up — I feel so very positive about our future — wish you too could feel this — this wonderful up I feel every time I think about us. You must know that your success is right there waiting, you have only to reach out and grasp it — don't hesitate, don't doubt. Your future is not Zanesville, not Ringwood — can you for a moment doubt our future? Yours is there, grasp it and pull it to you — you have more talent, more ability than most people walking the earth — and you know that. Don't be satisfied with what comes easiest — or first. You have an incredible instinct for what is right for you, you have me to stand behind you — you have everything — you have found immortal love — now grasp the rest — you deserve it — it's yours — there is nothing in our future but positive action and up, up, up to the stars — which are our destiny.

Andrea

May 7, 1974 (New York)

How strange it seems for me to be in New York writing to you. For so many years spring meant your tour, but also our stolen moments in Cleveland. Last year we said farewell to Cleveland. But who would have predicted this dream we are sharing. Even now I wake up sometimes, startled by a sound or the sense of being alone, and can't believe that I am in our apartment — our apartment — incredible! I searched for you through all my years of loneliness — perhaps beyond even my consciousness — and now those dreams are ours to share as we share everything.

The phone rang tonight. Again, I was sleeping and only vaguely heard it. I hope you don't worry if you do call and I don't answer. I'll be all right.

This one I didn't tear-up. I'll just continue. I'm sorry I was so low when you called, but your voice did help. Also, I took your advice and kept awake until 9:00.

How wonderful it is when you tell me you love me. And your letter from Tamworth was so vivid, it carried a bit of that paradise with it to 89th St.

I want so much to be there with you, to spend entire days doing nothing but talking, walking, and loving.

Spring is wonderful here, too, and the cherry blossoms we looked at before you left have ravished the hillside far up the river. I see them as Mike and I drive down the West Side Highway. How I long so to turn and see you there sharing them with me. But, instead, only Mike is there babbling about his latest hysteria.

You are the only one I can share my beautiful experiences with, whether it be blossoms, tapestries, vases, or sex. With others the attempt at sharing is a loss, one of perhaps privacy or intimacy, or emptiness. But with you, my love, I do not lose, but I gain. I unite with my beginning again. In you I am one with my entire soul. All poets have sung about love like ours, the union of the souls, but few ever knew its glory. For some reason, and I do know it when I swim in your ocean eyes, the rare love came to us. It haunted us — spirits from Attica and Rome — while we sensed the difference. Then, when it came I knew, we both knew — something inside us was feeling complete for the first time.

Oh, how much I love you — and somehow we sought the strength to seek our love. Miles apart, and lost on different paths, we began our quest and, then, one day in December — the month that breaches gods and brings the sun back — we caught that dream. My head has been reeling since. If only you could know — know totally the completeness of my love — you would never again for the rest of your life feel a need for another. We are the loves of a poet's dream. We are the stuff of dreams, my love. How sad for me not to spend with you each day, each second, of this parade of death.

I miss you — my soul waits — my love,

Charles

May 9, 1974 (Atlanta)

I am here in my room — drunk from two things — alcohol and your letter, which the kind gods brought to me this morning. We have done *Hoffmann* (great success) and I am home [sic] — I have had some Bourbon and re-read your letter — my god I am so unworthy of such love — I have never regretted that you didn't write me on tour because I know how tired you are — I have so much time to kill — but my god, such a letter — it is worthy of us and our love — it is a classic. I will never give it up — I will hold it up to the world and say, "so am I loved — my life is worthy — for this man has loved me" — whenever you doubt your ability I will give you that letter — if I should ever doubt or be lonely I will read that letter. Oh, blessed paper to receive such love.

I am more demonstrative than you are — then I'm more theatrical — but you my love are more profound — and I will spend my life trying to be worthy of your love. I apologize for any moment of doubt or lack of trust — I place my life naked and vulnerable in your open hand. I give you my strength and take yours in equal exchange. We are one and it will always be so — as it always was.

And now I wait — how can three weeks be so long — you are in school now — I wonder what you are feeling? I am more fortunate than you, I will be busy with my luncheon this morning and my opera tonight. I wonder what it will be like, that first moment when I hold you in my arms? I will probably be reduced to speechlessness like an idiot.

I think our gods will be very happy that we bring them to Atlanta — it's a city for gods — warm, lush, poetic, and full of love — they will probably say "Now this is more like it, what is this Cleveland and Zanesville?" But still they beautified our lives there — now we shall bring them with our love to new beauty — here amidst the magnolia and peach trees we shall offer up our love to them again — and take them on our trip of ecstasy.

Now rest my love — there's a water heater in the bathroom and tea — milk in the tub — Tab also — relax and wait — I am holding my breath nearby, and will rush to you as soon as I am free —

Andrea

P.S.

There is an ice machine down the hall to the right. If you are hungry call room service and sign my name and room number. I LOVE YOU.

I flew to Atlanta as we planned; it was midway through the six weeks of tour. I arrived at the motel while you were at the theater.

May 13, 1974 (Memphis)

My Love, here I sit in another strange room — I'm all surrounded by windows looking over the Mississippi and Memphis — I have a nice little terrace on the river with white lawn furniture on it — across the room on a table my magnolia looks at me — mocking me — saying, "remember it was only this afternoon that he made love to you and we watched, now we are both alone in this strange land." I hope it opens tomorrow for I'm leaving on Tuesday at 4. I don't think it will last that long. Marshall Parker was waiting for me at the plane. Jeremy had told him when I was coming in. He was very sweet — he and his lover Tom took me to dinner. Now I am back here — lonely — sad.

I remember every moment of this weekend — every caress, every kiss, every touch — all our love making of this Atlanta visit seems like some ritual sacrifice to our gods, to give them life again — to bring them to us, alive again through our love. This is the eternal nature of our love. It had a beginning, lost in time — then it lived so often through the ages — and now it lives again through us. The care of the precious gift has been given to us — we hold the love of all the ages in our hands and our gods watch, waiting to see us worthy of this gift — they cannot help but be pleased.

May 15, 1974 (Memphis)

My Love — the sun has risen on my last day in Memphis — which is also my second. Out my window I can look down this vast brown river — with its clean white tugs pushing up and down — so gay with their banners flying — they seem to salute the lush green cliffs as they struggle by pushing their incredibly long lines of barges.

There is a strange sort of beauty here — I've never heard any Memphians speak of it — but I think If I had been born here on these muddy banks — I would feel a great love and nostalgia. I think Twain felt it — it certainly is one of the most evocative parts of our country. What a shame we have a country that cares so little for its past — even here where the past was probably cruel — there is great beauty.

My magnolia has opened fully — it's filling my room with perfume of Atlanta — in its lemony beauty I can feel you so close to me again. I can relive those warm damp nights. I must leave it here. No matter, at the end of next week, I will no longer need to be reminded of anything. I'm going to write our names on its petals — so wherever they go, they will carry the sign of our love. They made our weekend so beautiful — they deserve to bear some symbol of our love. They will carry our message on their perfume to our gods: Andrea et Faber omnia amavit.

Soon my love — soon — again

Andrea

May 18, 1974 (Dallas)

And now Dallas —
I arrived Tuesday at 5 PM with Sutherland, Bonynge, Chester and Tourangeau. Ted and Bill picked us up and then had us all over for dinner — we swam until midnight. This morning Ricky, Chester, Bill and I went antiquing. Then Bill and Ted took me along to a dinner with some friends — really those two are so Texas — they ordered new white Cadillacs for our arrival. Ted's arrived — but Bill's isn't here yet, and the company arrives tomorrow and he will

have to meet the plane with last year's car. I managed to get them two tickets to opening night tomorrow. They're very pleased. I hope to get to Neiman's tomorrow, then Friday more antiquing.

Saturday a Flea Market — and Sunday at 6 we leave for Minneapolis to begin our last week — then I will start my daily countdown of days — then hours then minutes until Sunday morning — what time will it be — perhaps 3 AM — perhaps later — but I will be home — finally back into our home, into your arms. What a rest that will be — to be in your arms, to close my eyes at last to rest in your arms where I belong, where I long to be. I have sung my way through these many miles of Hades — I have played my lyre always searching for you — crying for you — and now once again I see the light ahead — I know that you wait there in our cool glade — before our green wall — to welcome me, and our summer back again. We will raise our sun high in the sky again for our gods to see — summer has returned. Faber holds Andrea in his arms again — the world has recovered from the turmoil of winter again and now the fields will laugh — and flowers will bloom, all because Faber holds Andrea in his arms again. The world rests, grateful for their love.

Andrea

May 20, 1974 (Dallas)

I'm truly very weary — I'm packing my bag for the fifth time — to go off to my fifth city — I have only three more shows — one lunch lecture, and three parties to go, and I will be home — and I am weary. What I wouldn't give for one peaceful day there alone with you Ted and Bill have been very kind this year, but very trying — Ted has had his face lifted (at 41) and talks of nothing else — Bill talks of nothing but the fact that Ted has had three convictions for drunk driving — and may lose his license. They both talk of nothing but their new cars. I'm weary.

I saw Jane briefly, backstage. Then I called her hotel and she had checked out. I did want to see her for lunch at least!!

There is one plus in being here — every gardenia in town is in bloom — every hedge — every pool — every yard. The whole countryside is a perfume of gardenias. I have brought arms-full into my room — and all night long their fragrance wafts over my bed and comforts me. It says "be patient." I am, I have been — but I don't know what shape I would have been in had you not come to Atlanta — probably I would have had to fly home by now.

Miss you so very much, my heart breaks when I think about you — or fantasize our love — such perfection — such satisfaction — I ask nothing more of you but that you love me the way you now do, for as long as we have this time. When I fall exhausted from your arms, there is not one desire left in me — only one whole being — perfect in you — you are my life — you are my breath. I live not for you, but because of you —

Andrea

May 21, 1974 (Minneapolis)

This past week I was subjected to a barrage of boasting from my friends.

Perdue had "the most beautiful boys," "with the biggest cocks." Best "had something last night you wouldn't believe." All this brings back memories of past tours to see all the new members running around with each other to bars and baths. I was never quite as rapacious as all that, but I must admit that I wasn't immune to a pretty face or a well turned muscle. I don't affect a sanctimonious air with them, they think they are happy — and in some lost hopeless way they are — but I feel a great sense of relief — of contentment — a release from fear — both physical — and of disappointment — a relief from having to compete. I no longer need all that. I sit very quietly and think of our love, our gods — I read your letter — I send waves of love to you — waves of gratitude. Do you think it possible that this frantic search which we all do, is really looking for what we found. Could I have been looking for you in all those pretty faces and well turned muscles? Could Perdue and Best actually recognize a Faber or an Andrea if they found them? I don't think so. Some spinning arrow somewhere, stopped and pointed to that stage in Ken High — in that instant the whole universe changed. Things that had not been said or thought for years, were. Our lives — Phoenix-like — rose up, as we joined in our flight to our sun — to our eternity.

Andrea

May 22, 1974 (New York)

My love,
I hope you get this before you leave. I don't know if I had the right address.

When I got back from Pgh. and your letters were waiting, they soothed the difficulty of coming back to an empty apartment. They helped me to face this final week of waiting. How funny it is that we even talked of "being faithful" and I have thought of no one or nothing but you for five weeks.

I will admit to being jealous of the young numbers — the Corys that you know in the tour cities. But it's only because I think of the future. There will always be young numbers out there and, eventually, I will worry about my loss of "youthful" appeal. If I could give you — or us — one gift I would give us the eternity of our present youth. I would love to remain as I am now for you. Perhaps, though, you realize as do

I that the eternal joy in our love is beyond the physical — it's in our souls. There, we unite as Faber and Andrea and we can always reach for that joy. Our love grows from beyond our own knowledge, beyond the mere shells of our bodies. In that realm we are youth — in all its supple pleasure and desire — we are eternal lovers and, remembering that, we can defeat all foes, even time. I waited all my life for this — maybe a few other life times — I shall love you into the next.

I am young in your arms as you are in mine.

I'm waiting, my love.

Charles

May 22, 1974 (Minneapolis)

My love,

This will be my last letter from this tour — it's Wednesday and I doubt if you'll get this by Saturday — but I'll miss writing to you — It has been my escape from frustration and my way of staying close to you. This morning I have my last lecture — tonight *Rosenkavalier*, Saturday *Turandot* — Oh, I'm so tired, and it's not over — Monday *Hoffmann* — Tuesday *Turandot*. How's that for a home coming? But nothing matters except that I'll be with you — I only regret Monday night with you but we must make Sunday and Monday memorable — I can't wait to walk through our door into our apartment to see our furniture — our plants — our bed again. Then to take you in my arms, and soothe away the weeks.

I have reached the end of my long trip — I have been in the dark, except for our days of sunshine in Atlanta, and now just ahead of me I can see the light at the end of the tunnel. I can feel a cool breeze from Elysium; it brings your perfume to me, and I know that you wait there — arms open — I have found you again. My music has protected me through my trip and has brought me to you — my goal — my destiny — my life — my love.

Andrea

We had an idyllic summer at Tamworth; Lisa came up for a long stay, Hilla came by as part of her musical adventure in New England, and so on.

Our letters stopped, except for the tours. However, you did leave notes for me every so often.

I decided — with a bit of pressure from you — to resign from Ringwood and to do some part time work for Pinnacle and for Alex Jackinson, a literary agent. Not much money, but we didn't have to get up at 5:30 anymore.

November 26, 1974 (Pittsburgh)

My Love,

Do you think I have forgotten how to write to you? Forgotten so much of what poured out of me in those seemingly endless letters: all of those lonely nights when I would bring you by sheer will power into my bedroom, with only my pounding heart accompanying your entrance. Perhaps, sometimes I do lose sight of my own poetry, of my own dreams, but if only I could know that I am not a fool to be swallowed up by my dreams. You have been so patient with me about so much — even now you continue to comfort my ego about writing, when I so abruptly want to stick my head in the hole of rejection. You must sometimes think that I am weak or silly — what would I do if I really had to face rejection. But my love, I am building what was taken from me — my Equus. You somehow know that and don't push. For that, I am and will always be grateful.

One thing you must know, and I hope always will, that I love you from the depths of an endless world — it has not died — it lies in me and I stupidly cannot release it at will.

Therapy — or whatever — pushes it back to my subconscious. But the ecstasy of that love is there now as it was the first time we sailed the heavens together. Let us find it forever. I am not afraid now of being lost forever to it. You are here for me to return to and I shall love you as Alexander loved Hephaestion, Achilles Patroclus, and Hadrian Antinous. I shall love you as only poet's dream. Whether myth, pot, or dreams are required to take me back and unleash my soul doesn't matter. You must believe, as I do, that beyond that line of daily reality lies our eternity, where we meet our destiny in each other's arms.

Permit me voyage, Love,

Charles

March, 1975 (New York)

I wish I could sort out the images that flash through my mind and body when you make love to me — the flashes of blinding light — not pure light, but brassy light reflected off armor struck in the heat of battle. Then the incredible strength — like towering columns holding monolithic cornices which press them into the earth with their weight. Your body becomes hard and solid as though eons of memories were pressing into it, it reaches out to me and screams into my body, remember — remember.

Then the memory returns — the clashing armor, the titanic columns all fall together into a compressed atom which explodes in my body — and we fall, joined together into those dusty corners and green blue glades where we have waited for so many eternities —

Andrea

April 30, 1975 (Detroit)

Today I sat on the steps of the Detroit Art Institute — I had just seen an incredible exhibit of Revolutionary art — David, Ingres, etc. — such beauty and my heart was sad that you had not had that beauty — the sun was warm and hundreds of beautiful young students were coming and going — and I suddenly realized what I had been doing to you the last few days. I was keeping you from having beauty — I realized I should not — could not do that If I loved you — it was my resolve right then and there, that those dark days were over — you must have the freedom to accept whatever beauty comes into your life. I cannot in the name of love protect you from the very thing I wish to bring to you. So, this is my declaration of independence for you. Keep it, and if in the future I should slip back — show it to me.

Detroit, Michigan

Andrea Velis

Amendment!

The reason I think that I was trying to withhold beauty from you — was indeed jealousy — I was jealous that you might find beauty in or from someone else. So you see it was not so much sex itself I feared, but that you might find beauty in another person — as I said in the declaration — I have no right to deny you any beauty, wherever you may find it. Indeed, it should be one of my functions to bring it to you — I am not suspicious of you — for you have the right as an individual to find and enjoy beauty when you can. Nothing could be further from my feeling for you — than a desire to isolate you from any joy you may find in your life. I hope this resolve will blow a fresh breeze through our relationship.

Andrea

We were relaxing into our lives, feeling confident after living together that we were on solid ground, that ours was a solid foundation, not a dream built on romantic myths. You were worried that I was a bit frustrated, especially during the spring tours. Six weeks is a long time indeed.

May 3, 1975 (Tamworth)

Now he has made it to the top — Fritz has nudged his nose into the snow banks which still wall the house and breathed a sigh — it was last November that we had to leave him lonely at the bottom of the drive. But now, victorious he shot to the top and sailed triumphantly into his usual spot. Now he basks in the 70 degrees sunlight, while his rubber feet shiver in the snow. He probably says "Vaataa kindt of vorld is dis — in May schnoow? In Germany it vas never like dis." And he is right. Here we are into May and snow is still lying all around. But if you know where to look and push the pine needles aside, there are tender, new green things coming to life. High over our porch, in an evergreen two blue jays are putting together a nest. The chipmunks are scurrying around happy in the warmth of the sun. But if you stand silently in our forest, and look up against the sun, you see a shimmering and sense a trembling as though the whole woods were ready to explode.

The sun has stirred a memory — a memory of soft warm breezes — and languorous nights — of afternoons in a hammock, of Lisa's laughter as she searched the ground for mushrooms or stones. This memory will soon quietly unfold in billions of soft, furry waiting buds. The long white wait will have ended and summer will have arrived at the top of our hill — along with Fritz Triumphant.

Andrea

"Fritz" was a name that Lisa had given to our Volkswagen 411. We had a chance to drive up to check on the cottage right before the Spring tour.

Also in 1975, the Met had been invited to tour Japan for the first time; the company left for Tokyo from Minneapolis, the last stop on their Spring schedule, on May 25 and returned to New York on June 16. Of course, you remember the incident prior to the Japan tour, while you were in Boston I think, and I was in Pittsburgh visiting Lisa. The Maestro was not travelling with the company; he was in Pittsburgh for a guest appearance with the Symphony. Apparently, he went cruising in Mellon Square Park, which was across from his hotel, and he was arrested for soliciting sex from a minor. You called me from Boston and told me that word of his arrest had reached the company the next morning and everyone was gossiping like crazy about it. He spent the night in jail I guess, and got bailed out the next morning. I read about it in a morning paper, but the story got pulled by afternoon and off he went.

Another narrow escape for the Maestro.

You wanted me to go along on the trip to Japan; I balked at going as your "lover" as you may remember; however, we did manage between us to get me the job of writing the story of the Japan Tour for *Opera News*. My work as a critic for six years helped to convince Robert Jacobson the editor of *Opera News*, to give me the assignment.

January 20, 1976 (Note — Tamworth)

Walt Whitman, Walt Whitman, you flew the sinewy Missouri but never pointed your finger at Chocorua and our lake. You never shoed our drifts or heard the owl moving in our pines.

You loved, with your arm around the beloved's waist but never saw our team stuck to the wall. You never saw the moon pour love through our woods, and strike us with intoxication. Walt Whitman we blow through your leaves — we know you — shake your great black head and join us — for we are that love you feared to name, and we come to celebrate you.

Andrea

Tamworth Cottage

April, 1976 (Cleveland)

Here it was again, the face of the beloved. What had brought me here after so many years to find him among these treasures. There he was — not the heavy lidded sensual face I had loved, no, changed now, as they had thought him sensual those Byzantines — open, vacant eyes, arched brow — much to their style — still they had had seen his beauty and wanted to make him their own as many had

231

done over the ages. Still it was he looking out of the case — there among the gold. Twice now he has come to me this past month as if to remind me "now that you have found your love again in this visible life — do not lose sight of us — live again in our memory — do not let our love be forgotten."

We vowed, you and I, that we should live our love so that the ages would know again the wonder of their love — we must not lose sight of our vow. We must not let our daily life distract us for a moment from our goal. The stars must wonder at our love — the ages marvel and emulate, for we are the loves of poet's dreams, and our sacrifice moves the universe —

Andrea

April 30, 1976 (Cleveland)

It's three AM and I have just returned from the Ireland party — we ate Moussaka — which I described as Moussakaka. I think it was made with hamburger helper and canned mushroom soup. That was really as short as I could make it. On the way home — we were flashed by two cars going over 100 mph. Then, a few miles on, we saw the entire street blocked. They had wrecked into each other and were smoking ruins with bodies strewn all over — one of the giddy dames said we should stop, but I said no — imagine a grey limousine with chauffeur and everyone in evening clothes stopping on the streets of Cleveland at 3 AM? We found a police car further on and sent them back. Not my night — on the way out I was sent in Mrs. Ireland's car. She's 79 and once she left the theater, she never stopped for anything — not lights or passing cars or anything. I really feel grateful to be alive — it was horrible. Thank god I'm back.

I so loved talking to you tonight and telling you about the

Manship — I do hope you love it. Here's a small poem I found, I think it's Verlaine:

Voici des fruits, des fleurs, des feuilles et des branches
Et puis voici mon cœur qui ne bat que pour vous.

Isn't that so simple and sweet? I know a musical setting for it; it's titled *Offrande*.

I so resent this waste of our time — I've not sung since I last saw you — yet we've been kept apart. I alone in my hotel — you alone there — why? I'll tell you why — for money. I hope that someday you will be so successful I can tell them to shove their tour. I didn't come this far to be separated from my love. It's like holding your breath for two weeks. I miss you so.

Andrea

All I can say, Love, is that it was 3 AM and you were drunk and missing me. You loved every minute of your career at the Met. That was a blip of nonsense.

May 22, 1976 (Minneapolis)

Was it only a week ago we woke up Sunday morning to our destroyed Dallas apartment? It seems more like a year. Gone is that hot Southern sun that we had to close the drapes against. Here, it is grey and cold and Northern. Gone is our celebrants — our Manship, my love. I look out on all these silos and wheat fields, and dream of our grape-heavy vines in the south, of our pine woods in the Eastern mountains — and there far off the east our temples standing in the heat, smelling of thyme and hibiscus — waiting all these centuries to feel our tread again. There our moon casts the shadows of giant columns across sacred groves — waiting — there our stars wink above roofless altars — waiting — there the cool night air saves from the relentless sun, and its breezes blow flower petals against the dusty stone walls —where once we loved. They wait our return — all Hellas will thunder our arrival — look up, oh gods, look up at our silver chariot as it carries us streaking through the sky. Dionysus has sung our return; he has told them of our coming. He dances before us — and his flute warns the hills of Attica — Love has returned — great Bacchus lives – Friday minus 6!

Andrea

Andrea and Faber, 1976

May 24, 1976 (New York)

My Love,

How strange it seems for me to be sitting here writing to you. I've grown so used to simply turning to you across our bed, or simply picking up the telephone to hear your warming voice. I can't help but think of those years when paper such as this was our main means of reaching each other. So many nights I poured out my sadness or my joy to you, so much more of the former I'm sorry to say. And within days the balm would come into my hands as I yanked your letter from that beat-up mailbox at 610 Allegh. River Blvd. "My Charles" or "Love" you would begin, and at once the calm began to run through me, the reassurance that our love continued within those lines and waited, desperately most of the time, for its celebration.

Perhaps this letter can carry my love to you in that way, can sing to you through these lines of the celebration in my heart at your return. How frightened I am sometimes at the awesome spectacle of our love. I question it, never doubt it, but stumble over its monumental nature. I read the tragedy of other songs and other loves, of aging, of impotence, of simply wearing out the curiosity, and I shiver and say, "Can we be that different?" And yet I know we are. I know that each moment has been set by our lost comrades who dreamed our nights of revelry. It was our gods and their priests who sent the Bacchante, who said, "Lift your holy cup to toast the children of the God of life. Drink to their passion." It was they who took us to the woods. Who cried out to us in that summer madness, and demanded that we reach for the vine. Seared as we were, we clung to them, and they have blessed us.

If there is disillusion there, my Love, then I willingly choose its

madness over the world's sanity. I don't want anyone to write anything about "Wahoo" on my tombstone, rather let them read about
our love, let them learn of us and "Come, dance in the wine."

I wait for you, my Love, we all wait, for the celebration of our
souls and bodies as they reach towards each other's deepest passions,
while the heavens echo from the thud of the hoof upon the root.

Saturday, Love,

Charles

MY NOTES FROM OUR
TRIP TO EUROPE IN 1976

July 17, 1976 (Tamworth)

Before we left for Athens we had an experience that seemed to be a prelude to the spiritual aspect of our journey. The grass must have been very strong because I tripped out on it. I had a flight of imagination that filled my head with visions of Apollo and Dionysus and the reality that seems to exist beyond our known reality, very Timothy Leary, Aschenbach stuff. It was frightening to me, but you helped me to stay calm and let it play out, which it did in about an hour.

July 19, 1976 (Athens)

After 9-hour flight from JFK we arrived at 2:00 PM Athens time. Lambros Eutaxias met us and escorted us immediately through customs. He had his driver and car waiting to take us to our hotel. As we drove past the modern, baked cement buildings I was struck by the arid look of the land and the disheveled, shabbiness of the approach to the city. It gives the impression of all being built in the past 20 years, and very quickly with no concern for anything other than keeping the sun from broiling one.

Finally, Andrea told me to look to the left of the front of the car. There it was, perched as it had been for thousands of years, the Acropolis. The Parthenon, splendidly dominating the right side of the cropped mountain seemed like the only building on the top.

We went to our hotel, Attica Palace. Lambros would return for us at 7:00 to take us to see Patroclus Poppamichel at his Pleasure Interludes Travel Agency.

We checked into Room 406. Large, modern, no view — terrace opens onto back of an adjoining office building. Air Conditioning not working. Andrea and I tried to get us moved to another room. No luck. They promised to fix AC tomorrow. Very pretty boy came to assuage us. The Greeks have been at this too long not to use the right moves at the right time.

Promptly at 7:00 Lambros arrived and took us to Pleasure Interludes. Pat later explained the name is a product of New York PR agency. What else!

Nice man — bit pompous. We arranged for (3 nights, 4 days) tour of Classical Greece. We leave Thursday, July 22. Also arranged for 7 day cruise of Greek Islands and Istanbul, Turkey, which we will take upon returning to Athens from Italy.

Before meeting Lambros, we walked from our hotel to the Acropolis. As we approached the winding path we could see the ancient supporting walls layer upon layer of stone with columns or other forms encased in the walls.

The pinkish granite, rough and slippery started appearing right at the main entrance. We bought tickets (5 Drachmas each) and walked through the stone entrance and up the sacred steps into the main area.

I was struck by two overpowering impressions. First, the strewn rubble of ancient, sacred stones which were scattered around us as a result of years of savage abuse of the Temple and entire area. Huge squares of granite, fragments of columns, and fragments of pediments lay around the entire plaza. Second, tourists were swarming around the buildings, climbing, shouting, and snapping photos.

What had I expected? Hadn't I seen pictures of the damaged buildings, the strewn rocks and the tourists? Of course, I had. Perhaps, I was simply exhausted from the flight and the hectic arrival in Athens with its armed soldiers carrying machine guns. Whatever the reason, and as always my mind leans towards another reason still: the romantic one of loss and destruction of the sacred grounds. I sat next to Andrea on an overturned, numbered slab of marble, backed by a still larger piece which formed a crude bench, and I stared at the Parthenon. Slowly the pain rose in gulps until it pushed out of my eyes and then my throat in sobs. The abominable destruction of the temples tore at every part of me. I hated the sacrilege around me and the callous behavior of the guides as well as the tourists.

Ah, I was too tired for this. Andrea understood and helped to calm me down and we walked around the remains briefly, but I wanted to leave and return another day. Instead, he suggested that we go to the museum on the Acropolis. Again, I was constantly reminded of all the beauty destroyed. But the excitement of the museum's collection, particularly some of the fine sculptures, appeased my senses. We saw a beautiful marble head of Alexander at the museum. We both waited until the guard was distracted, then we touched Alexander's lips with our rings (the rings that Mark West had made for us with the raised initials of our man-god heroes, A&H, H&A, along with ours, A&F).

By touching our rings to Alexander's lips we wanted to sanctify our journey, to make it a pilgrimage of love between men, not a conquest; we declared it the First Blessing of our trip.

July 20, 1976 (Athens)

Slept late. Lunch with Lambros at his town house, which adjoins the original residence of Otto I, the first modern king of Greece. Lambros owns both houses and is presently restoring the king's residence as a museum. He took us for a tour after lunch. In addition to Andrea and me, Lambros included Pat (the travel agent), a Parisian antique dealer, and a young Greek-American who lives in New York. Lunch was good, Greek of course, served by two servants and overall pleasant. Afterwards, Lambros took us by car to his country home at Eleusis. He referred to it as his paradise and it is easily that. When we left the car at the entrance beyond a railroad crossing (Lambros's family fortune came from railroads) we passed through a gate into a forest of color. On both sides of the path were hundreds of flowering plants, roses of all colors, geraniums, bougainvillea, and sage. They were backed by trimmed hedges of green which sparkled under the intense sun. The rest was filled with climbing vines and evergreens. This cascade of color started at the gate and it became eventually clear as we neared the terrace of the house at the edge of the cliff, that the oasis spilled all the way down in lovely terraces to the green-blue water of the Bay of Salamis.

This creation is maintained by trucking in water about 13 times a day. There are four or five gardeners. The head gardener lives at the house along with his wife and two sons. He is still a beautiful man, and has a subtle smile when he speaks with Lambros, perhaps a hint of secret moments shared between them. (You told me later that they had been lovers for years before the gardener got married.)

We toured the house. I remember particularly the room dedicated to Byron with various Byron memorabilia spread about the room in cases. And there was a terrace off the room offering a spectacular view of the Bay of Salamis. And, at the bottom of the hillside, below the cascade of terraces, there was a small courtyard with a beautiful bronze Kouros, this was Lambros's great treasure to share with us. After lunch, we went back to Athens, and we asked the chauffeur to leave us at the National Museum, where we spent the rest of the afternoon.

Andrea and Faber, Eleusis, Greece

July 21, 1976 (Athens)

Early to Acropolis. I was more at peace today. Still disturbed, however, as we walked the sacred way into the sanctuary and were confronted by scrambling tourists even so early in the day. Finally, I sat alongside the Erectheum and concentrated on this, the most sacred of the high city's temples. The Caryatids were partially covered by scaffolding for restoration and only the back of the building, Poseidon's porch, was accessible, the rest was closed.

When finally a quiet moment came, I knew that we must pray at this spot. At the National Museum the previous day I had copied a prayer which was attributed to Socrates:

242

Socrates: Oh, beloved Pan and all ye other gods of
this place, grant to me that I be made beautiful in
my soul within, and that all external possessions be
in harmony with my inner man.

May I consider the wise man rich; and may I have
such wealth as only the self-restrained man can bear
or endure. Do we need anything more Phaedros?
For me that prayer is enough.

Phaedros: Let me also share in this prayer; for
friends have all things in common.

Socrates: Let us go.

I read this prayer with its most devout supplication to the gods of
the Acropolis. Andrea answered as Phaedros. Now, I was able to leave
Athens intact in spirit. We had respected the sacred soul of the sanctuary.

July 22, 1976 (Epidaurus)

Left 9:00 AM by bus from Athens for four day Classical Tour.

Highlight of first day was Epidaurus, the great ancient healing
and medical center, and home to the best preserved theater from the
ancient world.

We spent the first night at Nafplio on the Peloponnese coast. The
hotel was built on ruins of a Venetian fortress which guarded the
port. Our room faced the sea of Corinth.

July 23, 1976 (Olympia)

Stopped first for a swim then drove along the spectacular coast towards Olympia.

The monolithic pillars from the temple of Zeus are strewn like great slices of stone piled and then knocked down like chips from a stack before a gaming board. An earthquake toppled the columns in the sixth century. They remained in place though covered by tons of earth, until excavated in the 19th Century. The sanctuary of Hercules is in exceptionally good condition. The athletes prayed to Hercules before dedicating themselves before Zeus.

We gathered laurel leaves as we walked through the ancient grounds and planned to make our own offerings of the precious laurel to the gods throughout our trip.

At Olympia under a statue of Hermes with Dionysus was where we placed the first laurel leaf.

July 24, 1976 (Delphi)

Finally, we stood before the remains of Apollo's temple — the temple which was the most sacred sanctuary of his worship. The spot where the Omphalos stood over the navel is visible and the remains of the main altar stand just outside the front of the temple. Only a few columns are even suggested, with only one complete to its Doric cap.

The temple commands the entire valley which sweeps below it in a huge wave of silvered-green olive trees, which once provided financial independence for the sanctuary.

This sacred area cast its power on me even as we walked over little more than the rubble of its centuries of use. This had, in fact, been what the trip was about. I felt the presence of myself and the presence of the past which had made me seek this spot, regardless of how foolhardily. Andrea and I talked very little but we both sensed the importance of our reactions — each of us perhaps began to talk to Apollo as we stood within his seat of worship and tried to understand our identification with a past so long abused.

The Delphi Museum. My god, the charioteer thrust itself upon me before I realized exactly what it was. At first the drapery of his dress looks awkwardly placed and rigid, but study reveals the calm and exquisite strength of the work. The extended arm has reassuring strength in its easy hold on the bronze straps, and the pleated elegance of the sleeves preview the dazzling refinements of the head and neck. The eyes are as fixed and steadfast in beauty as they were when they looked down on the temple over 2000 years ago. The slightly parted lips still show traces of red paint and gilt still clings to the headband, mixing with the deep greens from oxidation.

The Antinous of Delphi stood in a small room by itself. Though damaged, the torso and head are in perfect condition. We could not get close enough to secrete a laurel leaf on the base of the statue until the crowd left and even then it was difficult because of the guard. Antinous got his tribute, however, and knows of our gesture. I don't know exactly what prompted us to start placing laurel leaves in or on the statues of special significance to our lives. We have always done similar tributes to places or objects that hold personal weight within our feelings; however, this trip took on an increasing sense of reverence, akin to a pilgrimage, and it reached a high point at Delphi.

I saved some of the wine from our dinner that night and the next morning we went back to the sanctuary. When we reached the altar in front of Apollo's temple and were alone, I climbed on the altar, placed our gold rings together on two laurel leaves and poured the wine over them as I prayed:

Oh, Dionysus — celebrator of the highest joy — though your springs are silent — the mountains still stand watch over your sacred temple — join with the wisdom of Apollo your passion to these tokens of love and bless them by making eternal their circle.

As you have for Alexander and Hephaestion, for Hadrian and Antinous, so do for Andrea and Faber.

You still reign over the hearts of joyous lovers and may this offering of laurel and wine celebrate your eternity.

As if Selznick were producing it, the wind rose up the valley and swept across us at the altar. We sensed the presence of soothing forces — our own or the gods' — we didn't know, at least at that moment.

Temple of Apollo, Delphi, 1976

As we walked down the road to start back to town we saw an eagle — alone and masterful — spiraling over the valley. He gyred upwards — as if Yeats were describing his movement. He disappeared into the overcast sky. Like some majestic messenger he seemed to be indicating an acceptance of our offering.

One other sign had filled the day at Delphi. We awoke to find a huge rainbow arcing the valley. Rain-less Greece, as at Olympia, had blessed our visit with the most precious gift of the sky to this thirsty land. Light rain fell even as we walked down to the sanctuary.

After leaving the temple we walked through the lower section — Athena Pronea's temple and surrounding buildings. Before leaving the sanctuary hillside, we went over to the nearby woods and cleansed our hands and rings in the Castalian stream, still rushing with iced mountain water from Parnassus. This was the end of the second blessing; we both knew it as the bus squeaked through the village street, preparing to skirt the mountain and head towards Athens.

July 26, 1976 (Piraeus — *Neptunia* to Brindisi)

By bus to Piraeus for 5:00 PM departure aboard *Neptunia* for Brindisi, Italy.

At about 7:00 PM we started through the Corinthian canal, leaving the Saronikos Gulf for the Gulf of Corinth and the Ionian Sea. Midway through the Corinthian Gulf — at a point approaching Delphi off to our right — the sun started an incredible, fiery descent to the sea. We were both stunned, but I could see that Andrea, who stood just a few steps in front of me with his arms spread holding the ship's railing on one side and a metal guard rail on the other, was captured by the sun.

You wrote about your experience on the ship, Love:

July 26 aboard the *Neptunia:*

I was transfixed — the sun seemed beaten brass — covered with gold — it seemed to hang forever, low in the sky. And I could look right at it — I was buffeted by the wind which seemed to me more as light than wind — I held tight to the ship to keep from being forced back by the light — yet, I looked straight at that golden glow — unafraid — I knew it would not hurt me — It seemed forever — I knew no sense of time — had I been there for a thousand years it would have seemed the same — the sun seemed to melt into the sea — much as [Michael] Ayrton depicted it — cascades of molten light seemed to boil out in waves and join the reflection in the sea. I felt such an incredible oneness with all that — I was that boiling light — I was mammoth as the sun — I was small as that gilded ripple of reflections — I was there, suspended forever — yet, I felt no fear, no pain at the possibility of it ending — only an incredible sense of familiarity — this I knew — this was no surprise. It's as if I had returned somewhere I always knew I would, and will go again. I knew the words I heard. They did not come in a clap or a god-like voice — I knew them — just as I knew that incredible golden, unbearable scene would turn blue and green and I would say "look there" and the dolphins would come.

I wrote this about that moment:

(Andrea) said Apollo had spoken to him in old Greek saying that he was the wearer of the Gold, and that we should rebuild his temple. What temple, where, and how was left to us to answer. This then was another, and most amazing, blessing which touched us as we left Greece behind and made for the open sea and Italy the next morning. After 10 days in Italy, we returned to Greece to tour the islands and Asia Minor.

August 11, 1976 (Rhodes — Lindos)

Once passed the medieval fortifications and enclosed passage way we stepped out to a sweeping view of the ancient steps leading to the temple of Athena. We walked to the top and had a spectacular view of the sea below. The acropolis was built high on the rock promontory, placing it ideally between the contrasting blues of the sky and the water.

Few columns were standing in the general vicinity. The main temple has been partially restored with four columns in the front and the side walls of the cella restored. There was a small theater on the side of the acropolis and hundreds of bases for statues. Andrea and I sat inside the temple, managing to be alone between tour groups. The emotional response was here for me to a large degree, not as pulsating as Delphi, but I did feel a sanctity about the temple where we sat and let our minds absorb the beauty of the place. It had originally been a cult of the earth goddess and was transformed into a sanctuary for the sky Gods. Apollo had a temple here also, but nothing but the base remains.

The view from the acropolis remains in my mind as the vivid impression of Lindos which I took away as we walked down the path, past the old women and children, past the mosaics, and back to the bus.

That night aboard ship we talked about the acropolis and the museum. Both of us had a strong emotional response to the Lindos acropolis.

I was starting to understand more fully the pilgrimage nature of our trip to Greece, and able to make sense in discussing it. Hadn't we, in fact, from the beginning started on a journey of self-knowledge? We had set out years ago to find our natures in the natures of other lovers. The links were constantly before us, beginning with Hadrian and Antinous, Alexander and Hephaestion, and Achilles and Patroclus. In our love we celebrated their eternal love. And in Greece we were seeing the force which prompted such celebration in two men uniting for the sake of each other's harmony.

I mentioned to Andrea my feelings about using my correct first name — Faber. The name he loved and always encouraged me to use. Now, in the spirit of this trip we have shared, I knew it was necessary to use my name as a sign to myself that I had definitely found the identity he saw in me so many years before and which he nurtured into the light of the sun.

9:00 PM we sailed for Kusadasi to tour Ephesus.

Tonight the sky's rhythms were breathing into me. Was it the spell of this sacred route in the southern Mediterranean, or the spell of my mind in the cosmic dance? Whatever — they were rising in soaring leaps: the waves, the stars, and the moonbeams.

We couldn't stand against the rail and celebrate the rising of the moon as we have done at Tamworth, like gods at play in the woods. We couldn't howl at the splendor of the universe and the splendor in our love. We had to restrain our celebration, a touch, soft whispers, and our imaginations were what we had here, but we knew that Tamworth waited in the pines of New Hampshire for our dance.

August 14, 1976 (Istanbul)

The Archeological Museum sits back from the street and has several acres of wooded area around it.

Of all the marvels in the museum — and we gasped with joy from one room to another — the one that won the laurel leaf was the Pergamon bust of Alexander. Its eyes are seering, deep visionary in their intensity. His lips are parted as if he is about to speak. His brow shows deep lines of a young man who lived intensely. His hair swept back freely, parting casually from the center and falling in waves to ear-length on the side and slightly below that in the back. His head is turned slightly, giving the bust a sense of movement, quickness in marble. The turn reminds me of the head of Apollo at Rhodes. Certainly Alexander's bust is as godly in aspect. It is Alexander. That he looked this way I have no doubt, and I prayed to him. When I touched the head I again understood further our trip. Who knew life or love better than Alexander? Who lived his myth on a larger scale? No man. We honored this bust as if it had been the reason for our journey.

We had sought only echoes of Greece — echoes which all romantics hope for, and, perhaps, receive — but our echoes were not the cries from a glorious but dead civilization. On the contrary, beginning on the Acropolis we became pilgrims — believers in what we saw. Shocked by its desecration, but blessed by its lingering sanctity. Alexander had greeted us at the museum on the Acropolis, and our pilgrimage included this walk to him in Istanbul.

We had stood in the presence of the god at Delphi — we stood in the presence of another aspect of Apollo at this bust in Istanbul. Apollo, Dionysus, Alexander, Hephaestion, Hadrian and Antinous

251

— all of them had shared this pilgrimage with us. Another blessing of the rings when we touched them to Alexander's lips. We returned to the *Solaris*.

August 15, 1976 (Delos)

Delos was the sacred birthplace of Apollo, for that reason the island became a center of commerce as a result of a large influx of pilgrims.

Three temples to Apollo were built at various times on the island.

The bases can still be seen. Because of Apollo's purification rites and hatred of death and blood, no one was allowed to die on the island. In fact no one could be born there either. Even today only care-takers live on the island.

We had come to this sacred spot as a final homage to the god, who is the Spirit of the Sun in man. The pilgrimage ended with Apollo's last blessing on Delos.

Reluctantly we returned to the ship at midday for the short trip to Mykonos, the last stop before returning to Athens and the journey home.

September 1, 1976 (Tamworth)

We celebrated to our gods as we had planned.

Andrea had made a Thyrsus from the pines of Tamworth, topped by a cone from Delphi.

With only our robes — the ones made for us at Delphi — we walked down the steps to the moonlight. I held the Thyrsus and we danced in each other's arms. We had brought our gods home from Parnassus. They joined us again at Tamworth. While the moonlight lit everything around us, we held tight to each other. I moved the Thyrsus behind Andrea's back and began rhythmically dancing and moving the Thyrsus around. We blessed the very ground that we danced on and <u>Each Became Both</u>.

Faber

Antinous at Tamworth

September 24, 1976 (New York)

You should be arriving about now. I think I resent your trips to Lisa because they exclude me. Not intentionally of course but because of my work. I could go with you — make the trip easier but I can't — so I'm left out of that trip you hate. We are so one — how can we not share that ? Here I sit with my crowned Antinous and my ready Thyrsus — alone.

It is 7:00 AM Sunday morning. Some child, bless him, has been in the courtyard screaming "NO" for an hour, so I'm awake after a not so restful night. Stayed up late with all those shows — then slept badly because my love is away.

This is the first time I've been without you since July — since Delphi — since Olympia — Rome —Venice — Delos — since our sunset on the gulf of Corinth — our eagle and rainbow — since our Thyrsus led us to the moon that magic night at Tamworth.

My mind has been very fat — laid out wide so that I can't think of what I wanted to think about. I have sought distractions but they don't help. I just sit here and don't think. I lay back and let waves of happiness wash over me like some huge tide of contentment. I am truly happy. You are working, and very well. You seem satisfied. I can see that what you are producing is great. As I see you do it, it's like planting a small pine tree right where you know it will grow. Now you sit back and nourish it, and watch it mature. Have patience my love — now the road is there — there is no other to confuse you. I stand beside you and light your way with love. Let us grasp our pine and follow its rattle to that searing land, let us plunge and frolic in our father's cleansing purity — he blesses our life as surely as he has sent us his eagle — his rainbow — his Dolphins — his words.

We are not mad — which I translate as — do not doubt — come my love, let us ride the fiery chariot.

This morning at 2:30 AM the Thyrsus woke me jumping and banging in the wind. I had to get up and close the windows — where are you now? What a horrid day I had — I shan't tell you about it, you wouldn't believe it. I will be with you every second of your drive today — come back to me my love — across the long state and bring the sun back to me. I will be waiting here — tired as you are.

October 20, 1976 (New York)

I think I'm far enough from my two-day depression to see a little clearer what happened. Two weeks before we left Tamworth this summer you started on a negative trip which has still not stopped. Tamworth represents escape from reality to us — no problems — you don't have to work — nor do I.

All the problems that beset us each day disappear. I don't know if Tamworth should be that — we should rest there, but our responsibilities are always with us.

Did those things really happen in Greece? Can you really write? Do we really love each other or are we fooling ourselves? You're getting old. I'm getting old. You even doubt my future because my love for you is ruining my career. I've had to prop up your talent, your ego — our love — our gods — add to that Miss Taylor's legs — her rent — Hilla's party and possible cancer — Pat's father and you can see I'm about to run out of props. Who props up Andrea?

The thing I have had to give me strength up to now is our love — no matter what has happened I could always lean on that — find comfort in that and joy — that I could live for. That one gleaming goal we have before us to lead us to give us joy — how could you ever for one second doubt that?

It is our most holy of holies — it must be protected, nourished, adored above all else— yes, even above Lisa for on it lies her happiness — her future. We must carry it close to our bodies and not let anyone desecrate it with their doubts. It brought us happiness — it brought our gods to us in Greece and Tamworth, it and it alone assures our future in this life and beyond. When you doubt, stop and think — what would we be without it? What would you be — and I be and Lisa be? Do you really want to go back to Zanesville — into

that lonely bedroom? The road we have chosen is the right road
— cast aside all those stupid thoughts — and fasten your eyes on
our goal — help me to reach it. I can only push you so far — they
are waiting there —our gods — waiting in their cool glens. We
saw them — how can you doubt? Can your manhood be threatened, when we have set ourselves a goal few other men in history
have attained? Can getting a job and earning money be more of
an attainment than acquiring a godhead — Alexander could have
stayed in Macedonia and been a good and perhaps famous king
— or conquered Greece — that would have been easy — but he
had our goal and attained the godhead. We have that godhead in us
— we have seen it. If we are "fooling ourselves" so was he, and all
our heroes — that road leads back backwards and to the weight on
your heart again — look up — see that light which has brought us
so far. Don't get tangled up in stupid daily mundane thoughts and
problems — don't compromise — we have this last final step to
take. Be positive and I can help you. Know that in you resides that
unquenchable godhead which drove Alexander and his love across
the world. Nothing and no one can stop us — the only danger is
from ourselves and that cannot <u>be</u>.

> And so, my love, you were worried about me because of all
> the things that were happening around us. Hilla survived
> her bout with cancer, Pat's father died and when he went
> out to Spokane he had a serious accident with his bike
> which caused not only physical injuries but serious brain
> trauma as well. When he came back to New York I stepped
> in to be a sort of caretaker for several months. I took him
> to all his medical appointments, including psychiatric ses-
> sions, and saw that he took his medications and so forth.

You know, love, it wasn't all altruistic on my part; I wanted him to get well and be able to go back to the Met and resume his life, for our sake as well as his.

You were happy that I was writing; and I was enmeshed in writing things that were way above my "pay grade" as Lisa might say. I was working on integrating ideas that had emerged from our trip to Greece. Particularly ideas about the dualism of our basic human natures, the male and the female, and how our culture forced us to repress one or the other, depending on our physical sex. *Initiation* was the title: "The result, in part, is that one's goal is thwarted. Instead of becoming an adult who is directed towards perfecting the harmony of an inner nature, one becomes directed towards maintaining surveillance over a repressed nature."

"Wherever there is repression (meaning that people have lost the intimate knowledge of a part of their nature) mistaken ideas — even delusions may exist in conscious minds." According to Danish psychiatrist Thorkil Vang-gaard in *Phallos* (p. 193).

The problem between us, love, was that I was upset not to be making any money. The writing I was doing could have taken over my life, the work I was doing with Alex Jackinson and his literary agency paid very little, and I was surrounded with your career, your A-list life, and it was eating at me to a point of deep depression. That was not what I had signed on for. I was not jealous; simply not able to accept the role that I was being handed, Greece or no Greece, Alexander or no Alexander. We had some rough terrain to travel for over a year and a half — troubled nights mostly in our apartment on 89th St. I don't think the grass helped me — it sent my mind into flights of doubt and suspicion.

November (?), 1977 (New York)

Dear Andrea,

What do I say after last night? Forgive me? Will that eliminate the pain and disappointment I brought you; no, I'm sure. And can I promise not to let such feelings sweep over me like a hurricane destroying everything in its path? How can I when I don't understand what in the hell happens. Oh, I know it is a complex thing, physical and mental, but it is bringing havoc to both our lives. There is something in me that lashes out at...? What?

Am I as Roz thinks fighting my homosexuality? Hardly appears that way when I take my love "home" for Thanksgiving, and totally expose my daughter to the relationship, and live unashamedly as his love-mate in a relationship that is often ego-impairing to me. My love is weakening because I am weakening, as surely you must be, after such evenings. I can't point to anything that happened and say, "that is the culprit." Something simply triggers this "thing" in me that makes me feel that you are "absorbing" me, that my life, even my thoughts, are not being shared with you but absorbed by you. Last night, I felt that way about our spirituality. I felt that you grabbed at that with both hands, wanting it all, and that you missed the actual meaning of the whole thing. I felt that even that monumental discovery of mine was indeed an illusion that you simply fed. You see, in order to navigate through this maze of thoughts which have come from our spiritual experiences, I must know and feel secure in that you are holding the ball of string.

I sometimes believe that you unintentionally use our spiritual experiences as sexual stimulus only. If last night was sincere — only you know that — then I apologize for those thoughts and congratulate you because you must have experienced a new sense of your self.

At least we are not yelling at each other. We are not running away from this difficulty. I love you! Yes, I do, and I am here because I choose to be here. Forgive me for not praying with you last night. I needed to do that alone.

We have come a long way this year, my love, and perhaps we have a long way to go. I will make no promises that I cannot keep. If I feel that my identity cannot survive the relationship, I will not continue the relationship.

I do believe that we have enough love to both survive and grow, but your ego (that mountain with a beacon to the world) and mine (a lighthouse off the coast of Egypt) must learn to stroke each other.

> I believe this and maybe have all my life:
> Oh, beloved Pan and all ye other Gods
> Of this place — grant that I be made
> Beautiful in my soul within.
> And that all external possessions
> Be in harmony with my inner man.

> May I consider the wise man rich;
> And may I have such wealth as only
> The self-restrained man can bear or endure.

> Do we need anything more Phaedros?
> For me that prayer is enough.   (Socrates)

With my love,
Faber

Sadly, Love, my doubt was a problem that only grew worse over the next several months. You were about to leave for the Spring tour. We had a really scary clash the night before you left.

May 12, 1977 (New York)

Love,

Yes, I can still use the word and mean it — in spite of the pain we are giving each other right now. I'm sorry that I was not a big enough person to write this last night because now there is not much time. Talking last night — as it has been for a while — would probably have not worked. It is thinking — reflection, that will see us through this. I hope we have not slipped beyond some crucial point. I don't feel that I have. I love you. I have faith in your strength, and I have faith in my own. You were protected and blessed at Tamworth, and, through me perhaps, given the wisdom to see through this maze. I await you, not the monster in the center, but the love — reality that you dreamed and spoke of. You cannot destroy me for that love; nor can I or will I destroy you for it. Oscar Wilde was wrong — we do not have to destroy the thing we love. We can find the keys to love and through the keys — our gods — nurture and embellish that which we love. My pain has passed, Andrea, I hope. Please do not stay back in that maze. Escape the insecurities which I know so well and have fought through with your help. I will not accept that I was wrong in loving you — that you will shy back in fear of me as a man, and regardless of what you said so often really loved the boy alone. Feel your own strength — your inner core of strength that I too have helped you discover while you were not even aware of it. If I have so hurt you — made you so insecure that you fled last night not to think but to hide, then you have abandoned me, love, for I have not now nor ever have given in to the maze.

I will call after I get my haircut. I would like to take you to the airport — but only if you think it best.

Please sign the other card for Lisa — the first one seems too adult, and she would enjoy the other one more I think.

Faber

May 18, 1977 (Minneapolis)

I've been wearing our amulet since you put it around my neck at the airport so very long ago. I've only taken it off to shower. At night while I sleep, I hold it in my hand and it comforts me, makes me feel less lonely.

I hold its strap to my nose, and I smell nights of ecstasy. I see the moon at Tamworth — I see us ranging through our home in New York — waking those long nights of worship. I see it hanging on Antinous and among the flowers on the wall — it breathes — Love! Love! — it cries "look at the stars through the trees — see my body with firelight on it — feel the heat of that sacred fire."

Thank you my love for giving me that comfort — for helping me to see the way out of our maze. I now bring you their gift — may it comfort you — may it bring joy to our life. Know as I do that it is their gift — how else could it have come here? Trust as I now do — <u>I know that it is a sign of their joy at our love — like so many signs we have had.</u>

Another tornado warning tonight — from my window I can see huge black clouds rushing past and hear a roar in the distance — that's how it passed three nights ago. If you were here we could get stoned and watch our gods at play. Instead, I have opened a bottle wine, and will set myself in to watch and wait. I'll have room service later. There is to be a big party after the opera at 11:30 — but the warning goes past that, and I'm not likely to dress up at midnight and go into a Tornado. Besides you may call tonight.

There was a party last night also and I dressed up and waited up for Ruta — but he didn't come until 11:30 so I didn't go. I wanted to be here when you called — I think it's stupid to dress and go out so late. I'm so tired of this rush, rush of sexual conquest I see around me, this parading of new tricks for everyone to see. "Look at me, I must be brilliant and beautiful or this cute trick wouldn't be with me." Poor idiots. Who would look at B..., Bo..., or Hu..., if they weren't with the Met? Ruta said after seeing the *Bohème* here, that all his friends who saw the telecast (he didn't) decried the fact that Corena was singing and not I. It seems Corena falls on Marcello when Musetta screams. I assured him, it was not Fabrizio or me, but the efforts and talent that you put into the rehearsals — that's quite a compliment for you since these friends are all actors and theater folk. Leona sang Musetta and she also was unhappy that I wasn't singing — she loved me in the telecast. Jack Matz was here with her. Didn't see him though.

Now I'll settle back and enjoy the weather. I love you so, and miss you so very much.

Andrea

The reference is to the first live Telecast from the Met: *La Bohème*. And to your close friend, Ken Ruta, the actor, who was then at the Guthrie Theater. Fabrizio Melano was the stage director for *La Bohème*.

The gift that had come to you in Minneapolis was a beautiful life-size bust of Antinous in plaster based on the Antinous/Dionysus at the Vatican which we had seen on our trip to Italy. I think that you told me that you got it somehow from a University Art studio — of course, we wanted it for Tamworth.

We had good periods and then I would fall back into my depression and doubt our path together. Michael Hall, our friend who was a major sculpture dealer, particularly with bronzes, saw that I had "an eye" as he said for quality in the bronzes; he was moving his gallery and asked me to work for him through the moving period, which would take six months or so.

I loved being around the art on a daily basis; Michael's life-partner, Bill Mills, was a delight to be around, and I was learning so much every day.

Instead of a rather small salary from Michael, I asked to be paid in sculptures, and he agreed.

October, 1978 (Tamworth)

Tamworth was the only place where I could find some calm and there I was best alone. There, too though, there were days when I thought I had to fight my way through this maze again to maintain my sanity. How had I gotten so lost in the corridors of love — or had I — was it a Freudian case number?

So, alone at Tamworth in that back area over the septic tank, while raking rocks and fighting madness I prayed to Zeus Amon to guide me, prayed to Apollo, prayed to the gods that had sent the eagle at Delphi to help me now. I went about the raking. Later, on the south side of the house I stopped raking because I heard a loud screeching. I looked up and a huge dark brown-black bird — a Golden Eagle — screaming with a piercing, shrill sound had landed on a top main branch of a white pine near the front of the house. I froze. The bird closed its wings — lifted its head around and screamed for several minutes. I kept saying to myself that I didn't believe this could be happening. I was in shock.

In celebration of that event before I left Tamworth for New York I climbed up to the roof at night — and while the brilliant stars and full moon witnessed along with the New Hampshire sky — I spilled my seed upon the roof and raised the Thyrsus on high in celebration of my belief in gods of life — and the spirit of the sun in man.

Faber

November, 1978 (New York)

How many eagles must you see? Must they come every year for you to believe? Must it come down and pluck out your liver before you believe? Believe — Believe — Believe in something — trust something! When you cried out in pain — when you asked for a sign — one came — that's all forgotten now. The message was very clear — Trust!! I didn't make the eagle, I was hundreds of miles away — it was your eagle — yet you forgot — you forgot Delphi — you forgot everything — all your mind remembers is pain and hate. The good, the promise, the prayers, all gone. Why believe an eagle, a Greek ideal when Irish doubt is so close to your heart — destroy everything — smash not build. Yet, look closely — when you cried on the Acropolis — that was not Irish. That was recognition — also Delphi — also the dolphins, also the eagle. That spark of beauty inside you — that thing that drew me to you — that thing which reached out to me — which joined me in our search — that thing, looked up in Athens and cried. It was not hate — nor doubt — now I beg you, let that come again — pray while you are there on our sacred hill, to find it again — was it bad? Is not that hate and doubt worse?

You are doing so well, the bronze thing is about to blossom — just now about to, and the Irish thing — the dark thing wells up to destroy — destroy before something good happens. Well, I have no darkness in me. The sun which <u>you</u> helped me find shines in every part of me, and I will not allow your dark side to destroy what we have so long sought to find. I will not allow it.

I love Faber as much as I ever have. The love that we found in Delphi and brought to Tamworth is still strong enough in me to fight. If you leave it will be a completely one-sided, destructive act on your part, and will have no help from me. I will only labor for the good of our love and the ideals we learned — only. You will succeed, your dark side will be destroyed and it alone. I will pray to Apollo to flood your soul with his light and drive all darkness from you. You have come out of the labyrinth unharmed. I will not now allow you to fall over a cliff. I will speak up when I see a wrong and trust that you will know right when you hear it. I think the way you are going is wrong. Your sexual experimenting is not on the level to honor ideals. I visualize the things you did last week, and I feel sad. Surely, this is not what you talked about when you talked of love. Neither of us should do anything which lessens us as men — or lessens anyone else. The way T. happened, and that experience was beautiful — the rest is not. I don't want you to do these things again. I have no right to ask you not to, I can only do it and trust you will understand why — you must only know people who are worthy of you — of me, of any of the things we believe in. We have reached a level of experience that is given few people. Let's not degrade it by our behavior. We have been given, if you will, a sacred trust. It involves ideals and wisdom and morals — let's never lose sight of that. All our experiences should be on that level.

I will fight — I have found new strength by only asking for it. I know I can't ask you to fight with me, but please pray for strength and see if through your prayers you can find again — some trust. You may not see an eagle again — but please don't forget that he did come.

There is no evil in what we have experienced — only wisdom and love.

Faber Kalos

Andrea

Tough letter to read, even now, Love, but all true. I was still wallowing in an Irish bog while you were already aloft with the Eagle. He came to me in New Hampshire; however, you heard his screech all the way from Tamworth to West 89th Street and you embraced its significance long before I did.

I had asked for help from our heroes to open a path ahead for me. I knew the eagle was a blessing but did not know what that meant as far as the path I had hoped to find. All I did know was that the path was not in the woods of New Hampshire but in New York with you. With that idea in my mind I returned to New York.

My tenure with Michael Hall — which had been an amazing opportunity to learn from him on a daily basis — had run its course. He offered me a permanent position as an assistant, but in addition to what I learned about sculpture from being around Michael, I also learned what a volatile personality he was, and how mean he could be to those closest to him.

No thanks.

You encouraged me, as always, to trust my own talents

and follow my eye. Remember that in Dallas in '76 we came across the Clodion Bacchante, and you suggested that I call Michael for his opinion before buying it. I said that it was time for me to begin trusting my own ability to know what is good in bronze. You agreed and we bought her.

In New York I continued to do my rounds of the various auction houses; they were clustered on the Upper East Side, with a couple far flung to the twenties on the West Side and lower Third Avenue.

I started buying some bargains that came through the rooms — remember, the good fortune was that Michael was in Europe all summer and returned in late September when the New York season began. We were thrilled when I bought the extraordinary statuette of the seated female drying her foot — our little Venus (who now has a place of distinction at the National Gallery).

But the path that opened for me for our next fifteen years together — my eagle's brightest note, you as a tenor might say — truly began one afternoon in February of 1979 when I came across an overlooked bronze statuette at a lesser-known auction house on the Upper East Side. It was tagged as a particular pope, by an unknown sculptor, unknown provenance. Just an old, rather tired-looking man. It caught my eye though. Even you questioned why I bought it; I told you that I would let him tell me why I bought him, and so I began to look, and look, and smile as the statuette began to reveal its secrets.

Within a week, you invited Michael to dinner (we remained friends) and when I brought the pope into the living room and placed him on the large cabinet he came over slowly, said nothing for several minutes, then lost his studied dealer's cool pan look and said, you recall, that he thought that I had found a bronze by the young Lorenzo Bernini. The eagle had landed at last — we both beamed. I had already done research on the pope and knew that Bernini was indeed working in the Vatican during that pope's time.

Within a month, Michael had acted as my agent in the sale of the bronze for his usual twenty percent fee.

The first thing that I wanted to do with the money was to buy out Pat's half interest in Tamworth. You agreed and that was done — that was another blessing for our relationship. Alone in our retreat.

Meantime, I took advantage of the knowledge that Michael with his brilliant eye was away in Europe for the summer as usual. In his absence I bought enough museum-quality bronzes of the 19th Century to begin a respectable career as a private dealer in touch with many curators that I had met over the years.

And now finally, as we headed into the '80s, our lives had come into balance — a balance that would last for the remaining years of our time together. The path that I had prayed for had opened next to your path; mine now, like yours, was one of art, beauty, and talent.

Now, Andrea, the last letter that I want to include is the one that I wrote to you from Pittsburgh in May, 1980. I was there to celebrate Lisa's birthday and to see my mother, who was unwell.

Love,

Here I sit on my mother's porch surveying so much that has become as slight as an echo in my life. As I look at these neatly kept houses — struggling against the encroaching Garfield decay — I realize how much we are caretakers, gardeners in life. (That sounds like a metaphor from *Being There* — did you see it?)

My mother looks much better, rested but not quite herself. Good for 80 though. She is bored or tired or both.

Went to the Christie's exhibition today. Quite a magnificent setting for the art collection — a Tudor mansion, complete with turrets, gables, ancient oak beams, and wonderful things. If we only had a bundle — it is a good sale. I like the Zeus and will go on Monday to see what happens. The estimate is $1,000–2,000 — I will pay $500. It has a fine quality — sensitive work — life in the eyes — a Baraká perhaps. If we get it fine; if not, fine too.

Your letters touched me very deeply. They had a Cavafy tone, particularly the one about the Love-Core. I wish I could gush forth right now a love song — but it would be a forced lyric. Oh, I love you. I know the Core. There is no Andrea other than you — nor do I want one, but I am in a confused, frustrating state — not in a bad, crippling state — maybe it's "40."

My confusion surely bores you by now — especially coupled with the tediousness of the tour and all the boring people. What confuses me is how isolated I feel, even in NY. I have so little in my life other than you and Lisa and bronzes. That, of course, is more than most people. I ran into Phil Mathews several times on the street. He would say something about thinking of me just that morning or whatever, as if I'm something pitiable that sits waiting for a phone call. I have other examples but they are all of a similar nature — and the irony is that I don't give a shit! Fuck Phillip, Robert L., etc.etc. It insults me, but I know that they are only spiting my indifference to them, or that they — most probably — like you and not me. You play — you court — you tease. I sulk — think — ask, and try to relate at a level which they find boring. The result: loneliness, but of a type I can deal with. I wonder, though, if I would have at least some friends in New York if it weren't for us or me not having a regular job. I slip into depression sometimes, thinking that our love has been a transaction that strips me of much more than I can give and maintain my "Self." Then, I look at the lives around me, or I try to reach into the Love-Core and it assures me that I am intact.

More and more I feel that I am seeing the destructive impact of this culture on being a man who loves other men. I, myself, push myself towards the sexual hysteria which serves as others' Common Core. I get hungry for it, but then, cannot satisfy the hunger because that, too, involves a transaction, one which erodes more than it enriches. When love/sex is experienced as a negative — that is, something that takes away rather than adds — it is as destructive as smoking or anything else that is Self- damaging.

I can experience any kind of sex, which you know, but if I feel that it is a negative, I must avoid it — that is simply "Self-protective." It enables me to love. If I had ravaged my body and soul with all the free sex that offered its self — regardless of how my instincts directed me — I truly believe I would be totally bereft of love — my soul would be empty — no god would or could hear the faint breath.

Sometimes, I also think that I'm only rationalizing — that I simply don't accept my "gayness" and just do the scene, that I act like a coward sexually — which is what a lot of "married" men do. But then, I think that is all bullshit because there is little that I am afraid of — the main thing — all of my life — has been damage to my soul — my Self. It is a mystery that I don't understand, but I know that it is my moral guide in some bizarre way, but this guide has little to do with the reality of gay-life as I see it — which in fact should be called gay-death — for surely it is a death dance in which flesh is the comic clown who mocks all the other dancers — them with their silly clothes, prancing walks, chit-chat, and empty souls.

I will not dance to that tune — Oh, I will die — that is the dance of life — but I will not die in life. I will not be a hollow man. You are not now and cannot be either for you have loved and loved me — our souls have kissed life within each other and that precludes going back. It is a difficult battle to maintain one's soul — to push it towards wisdom — to hold on until your knuckles turn white. As long as you and I are alive — Apollo is alive, Dionysus is alive, Alexander is alive, Delphi is alive. That is a different dance from one that mocks age — mocks wisdom — mocks love — and bludgeons its soul.

In the play *Bent*, remember that one of the gay prisoners says to his lover: "We won — we made love — we behaved as human beings. They can't destroy us." Well, damn it, they are having a lot of success with a lot of people.

Look what I've done — gone on for pages as if we were stoned on the floor at Tamworth. Oh, that has kept me sane — Tamworth, which speaks of our souls. That is where we brought the seeds from Delphi — that is where we are at our best.

Now, though, I understand how we as individuals must work as artists. We must each grow — you must be better next year in everything you do — as if you had made your debut only months ago — I must grow as a dealer into more confidence and panache in dealing with those people. I must keep the outside negatives in a proper prospective and not be so damned confused — which is where I began this, and where I better end it now — I hesitate to read what has just poured forth.

Did I say, "I love you?" I do.

Faber

New York, 2021

Last night I walked at Tamworth.
The moon light was there; I could see
each leaf, each pine cone under my
feet. I felt a great comfort, a great
warmth. I knew that behind me lay
our home, even though I didn't see it.
I knew that near me you walked,
even though you didn't speak.
I heard no thyrsus — no cymbal —
yet, I knew we prayed — that prayer
brought me comfort when I woke.

 I hope that you will remember
what I'm now saying — for I have
always felt it was important to learn
from others who have experienced
what we have not. Even though we
are more intelligent than they are,
they have had the experience and we

are ignorant of that. As you advance in life you will find that moments when we are happy, moments when we have felt intense love or experienced a dislocating happyness. These moments become like the core of a reactor — the reactor of living if you like, and they fuel us. Our love has given me this core. It is my experiences with you, through you that now fuel my life. If I sound, that I feel there are no more experiences, then I have expressed myself badly. I still receive so much from you, constantly. Even when you think you are not giving love — I receive it. Even when you hurt me, you cannot hide the love. For I believe, like that core, once our

LETTER FROM ANDREA TO FABER — MET SPRING TOUR (MID-'70S)

Last night I walked at Tamworth. The moon light was there; I could see each leaf each pine cone under my feet. I felt a great comfort, a great warmth. I knew that behind me lay our home, even though I didn't see it. I knew that near me you walked, even though you didn't speak. I heard no thyrsus — no cymbals — yet, I knew we prayed — that prayer brought me comfort when I <u>woke</u>.

I hope that you will remember what I'm now saying — for I have always felt it was important to learn from others who have experienced what we have not. Even though we are more intelligent than they are, they have had the experience and we are ignorant of that. As you advance in life you will find moments when we are happy, moments when we have felt intense love or experienced a dislocating happiness. These moments become like the core of a reactor — the reactor of living if you like, and they fuel us. <u>Our love has given me this core. It is my experiences with you, through you, that now fuel my life</u>. If I sound that I feel there are no more experiences, then I have expressed myself badly. I still receive so much from you, constantly. Even when you think you are not giving love – I receive it. Even when you hurt me, you cannot hide the love.

For I believe, like that core, once our love was lighted the rods of privacy and unhappiness were withdrawn: a life was started which cannot be extinguished. Whatever life may bring us — even if we are not together — this core will flow. The forces which lighted it

— the forces which we called to witness its kindling — are eternal. They are the precepts which create all — which make matter think. I have done much in my life, known many people, gone many places. If you think out there somewhere is another Andrea and Faber — or Faber or Andrea, you are wrong.

They have not scratched the meaning of love or searched the heavens for wisdom or beauty — they have not poured wine on that blessed hill. If irritations arise between us, let us have the wisdom to look beyond that. Look beyond the age — the habits — the drugs — look to this entity which now writes to you, and which stood upon that wind torn altar and pledged to the mortal part of you.

Andrea and Faber, 1980

IV.
CODA

Andrea died at 10:55 p.m. on October 4, 1994 at Tamworth cottage. We had had twenty-five years as lovers, and twenty-one years living together in New York City. Until that moment, it had been a fantastic fall day, one of those crystal-light New England days, the ones that draw the post-card photographers out of the woods. We had seen their cars parked along Route 16, and them standing in a row across the way at Sutter's Gate. That was the shot everyone wanted of Mt. Chocorua and the lake. One time Andrea found a greeting card in New York that had a photograph with a plastic overleaf that read, "Happiness is..." The view was the one from Sutter's Gate. The card found a home on our fridge for many years. Like the locals, we felt good about living in a place people found idyllic. We felt lucky.

That day we went to the Fryeburg Country Fair in the afternoon. We usually went every fall, and always enjoyed it, especially if we had a friend up from New York who had never been to an agricultural fair, with its pigs, sheep, bulls, and competitions. It's mostly a local event. The summer people are gone, at least the ones with kids. Andrea and I had arranged our lives so that we could spend as much time as possible at the cottage. We had built it 20 years earlier, and over the years had nurtured it as a sanctuary. It in return, became for us a transformation site.

We were alone on that Tuesday. We were used to being alone. Much of our time there was spent working around the cottage, which was situated by itself on about ten acres of dense woods. I worked a lot in the woods. Just that fall, I cleared finally the area, mostly huge white pines, that blocked our view of Mt. Chocorua. For many years we talked about clearing the view, but never tackled it. Now I had to do it by myself because over the past several years, Andrea had developed a heart condition which caused him to have severe angina. He was 67. I was 54. His family had a history of heart problems.

A few years earlier he had lost a brother and a sister from sudden heart attacks. He didn't talk about it much, and still enjoyed some light work in the garden, his beloved garden. We labored hard for ten years to get the sandy New Hampshire soil finally to sustain a respectable display of lilies, columbines, and primrose, all under the tall white pines.

We arrived at the fair about an hour before the Horse Pulling started in the main arena. Perfect timing for us. We walked around a little, over to get some Italian sausages and cokes. Then we went through the hog barn — utter paradise — and, last, through the stable where the work horses are kept. Amazing creatures. They're huge, mythic looking, with a sculptural beauty. For the fair they have been brushed to a glow, and their tails and forelocks have been braided.

From the stables we went directly to the arena and climbed gingerly through the crowded bleachers to reach good seats with a 50-yard-line view. For the next hour and a half we watched as the teams were brought out by their owners. A wooden sled, loaded with cement blocks to a certain weight, was attached to each team's rigging. The driver had about ten minutes to get his team to pull the sled as far as it could before the next buzzer. The top teams usually go the full length of the arena and back.

What we enjoyed so much was seeing how the horses worked as

teams. They must be alert to signals from each other and the driver. The closer their harmony is the easier and effective is their pull. Some teams are so attuned that you can see one horse compensating direction or energy if the other one missteps or falters. And those horses, the ones that achieve the longest distance, respond to the slightest gesture, sometimes almost a whisper from their driver. The teams that spook or never synchronize their pull veer to the side of the stronger horse, get little distance, and frustrate their driver, who whips them while yelling himself into a fit.

There is a lot of sexual energy in the experience also. We both were reminded of Mary Renault's images from antiquity of the psyche as the driver of the team of the spiritual and sexual natures. Our objective, like the teams at Fryeburg, was to achieve harmony for the pull. How simple it sounds, but it is true that for twenty-five years we had built our team skills along those ancient lines. Among those skills was using visual sexual stimulus, intimate shared-fantasy, our furnace of sexual imagination.

We watched as one of those top teams did their pull. Each horse, ears alert, ignored everything except the command of the driver and common language of its harness partner. At the finish, after the applause let up, Andrea said to me, "We've been like that, you know, a good team." I smiled and said, "that's true," and then I turned away to look at the arena so that Andrea would not see that I was teary-eyed. I don't know why I got upset by his comment. It just brought a sadness to me that subsequently seemed like a premonition of what happened six hours later.

In vain now I try to remember every moment of our last hours together. But I can't. It was all so ordinary. We stopped for things at the Shop'N'Save on the way home. I put together a fire while Andrea heated some left over chili. We had a glass or two of wine, walked around the house to look at the garden and to enjoy our new view of the mountain. Later we watched some TV; Andrea casually looked through his latest batch of mail-order catalogs. You name it and he had a catalog for it. I am reminded of that every day with my mail.

We were waiting for the 11:00 p.m. news to start. The phone rang. It was my daughter, Lisa; more accurately, our daughter, Lisa. She met Andrea when she was five years old, and as an adult can't remember a time in her life when he was not there with a loving hug or a funny line to help smooth the bumps. Lisa and I had barely opened the conversation when I looked over to the sofa at Andrea. He rose or lifted towards me; his upper torso reached forward, his mouth fell open his right hand closed into a fist crumpling the center of the open catalog in his lap. His eyes, those beacons roofed by dense brush, looked astonished as if they had been undone by the rest of the body, abandoned. They reached for me.

It was all in a second. As suddenly as it had lifted itself, his body collapsed back in the sofa, with his head rolling back on a pillow.

I told Lisa something had happened to Andrea; threw the phone onto the other sofa, and rushed to try to get him to respond. The only thing that happened was release of air in a gurgle — like sound. I grabbed the phone; told Lisa that I got no response from Andrea and had to hang up and call the Rescue squad.

Strange what comes to mind now. I remember saying, "Something has happened to my friend," and being aware that I was editing. I had no word that worked, not in New Hampshire. Words don't matter at such a moment, I know, but I remember that they were a factor, and at that critical moment the language itself distanced me from him.

The Rescue Squad, composed of local volunteers, came and tried to revive Andrea. They did not use shock devices, and did not acknowledge that he was dead. They took him to the nearest hospital in North Conway. From what I learned from the Death Certificate, it appears that Andrea died from a heart-attack at the instant when he clutched the catalog. Later, the emergency room billed Medicare and me for a couple thousand dollars for their efforts to "save" Andrea.

As the men took Andrea out the front door, I called Lisa and told her that we were going to the emergency room in North Conway. One of the men came back in and asked me if I would be all right. I said, "if he is all right, I will be." He seemed surprised by that. Then he asked me where the trash can was because he wanted to throw away a wrapper from some "K-Y". The letters pinged into my head. I shook my reaction, and told him where to throw it. Next, I closed the house so that I could follow the ambulance in my car. As I drove I tried to talk to Andrea ahead of me. Tried to will him to live.

Right outside of Conway, the town before North Conway and the hospital, a woman pulled in front of me and then drove at a crawl. At the first chance I passed her. It was over a double line. She started to follow me, and when I got to the hospital she drove in behind me. After I got out of my car, she started screaming at me for passing illegally. I yelled on the run that it was an emergency, but she kept howling. Strange behavior for New Hampshire.

Inside there was a counter at the end of a sterile quiet room. A man and a woman stood at the counter. I told them that I was there for Mr. Velis. "Who are you?" "Well, I guess you would say, Significant Other." In a detached, cold voice, the man, the doctor, said that Andrea "didn't make it." The woman took me over to an area that had been curtained off. He was in there. He still had on his clothing: an old blue terrycloth bathrobe, worn smooth in areas like an old towel, a red and white striped hooded sweatshirt that he liked to sleep in, black sweat pants, and his ever-present black ankle socks. I cried, talked to him, tried to contain my desire to scream. I touched his hair, ran my hand across his forehead, over his eye-brows, down his cheek to his lips and chin. "No, my love. No. No." After several minutes, I slipped off his medic-alert medal for his penicillin allergy, with an Italian charm attached, and then removed the ring he wore that had belonged to his father. I kissed him, then backed towards the curtain. The woman had been waiting for me; she took me aside into a small waiting room. She asked me which undertaker I wanted to use. I picked the name of one that I knew a neighbor had used not too long before. Also, I told her that Andrea wanted to be cremated. She said that I should call the funeral home the next morning. Then she walked with me toward the parking lot. As we approached the glass door, she casually mentioned that if it had happened, Andrea's heart attack that is, in Los Angeles or New York, a big city, he might have survived because of the time factor. She was deliberately lying, and increasing my pain. I don't know why.

The drive was a series of howls, relieved only by gasps for breath. When I entered the driveway the pain increased, and I just started to scream "No!" and cry. The cottage itself seemed to stand in disbelief that I had returned alone. In every detail, every painting, every piece of furniture, I felt loss and pain. I called Lisa. She had a friend staying with her, and he held her through the shock. She said that she would fly up from New York the next day.

My howling continued through the night. I tried to reach our neighbor, a friend, but she didn't answer the phone all night. No sleep.

At dawn I went outside and walked around the cottage, still sobbing, still shouting "No!" into the wet morning air. I did not want the day to begin; did not want the sun to rise on the first day without my love, the first day in twenty-five years when he was not part of my life.

At seven AM I began the calls. First, I called Andrea's nephew so that he could go and tell Andrea's sister, his only surviving sibling, what had happened. Between calls I would break down, or sometimes on the phone.

It went on that way all morning.

Lisa came in the afternoon, and the crescendo of loss increased, but was soothed by her embrace and our efforts to console each other.

With Lisa's help, I dealt with the demands of a death, the arrangements as we call them. We went to the funeral home, literally a large white frame New England country home, over in Ossipee, and arranged for the cremation. It would be done at 11:00 AM on the 7th. Lisa and I planned at that time to do a simple ritual ceremony on Page Hill, which was one of Andrea's favorite places to hike, and from which one can see the whole valley and White Mountains.

Our first ritual, however, was the night Lisa arrived. At dusk, I went out and placed a large candle-torch, a piece of bamboo about four feet high with a wax coating with wick covering more than half of it, at the North side of the cottage facing Mt. Chocorua. Just as I was about to put the torch in the ground, I heard a loud cry three distinct times. It was a sound that I had never heard before. Lisa called to me from the window to ask if I had heard it. She heard it clearly in the house. We both thought it was an owl. That seemed confirmed the next night when we saw a white owl at the back of the cottage, a new experience for us both.

The torch burned through the evening. As the time of Andrea's death approached, Lisa and I both noticed that the torch was doing something unusual. We watched from the window as the wax dropped in flaming gobs onto some stones. It had already built up several inches of wax. Lisa said "I think the torch is going to go out at the exact time that Andrea died." She was right. There was still light, however, from below. Next to the spent torch, on the top of the stones, another candle had formed, made from the dripping wax. Remarkably, a piece of burning wick had fallen into the soft wax, and it kept the flame.

My mind did not rest; another night without sleep. More calls with their comfort and pain. Another incredible fall day. Andrea's spirit seemed to surround the outside of the house. The flowers, the birds, the trees, the walls, everything reflected him. As I walked around outside, waves of crippling sobs repeatedly interrupted the goldfinch's morning song.

At 11:00 AM on the 7th Lisa and I were on top of Page Hill. We took some incense, cymbals, a Thyrsus, and some food. We decided to create a simple ceremony at the moment of the cremation. We used the incense to represent the fire which would carry Andrea's physical nature through its transformation. The cymbals with their unending tone blessed the moment, and acknowledged the sacred spirit within his body. The Thyrsus, with its pine cone that Andrea and I had brought from Delphi, we raised to the sky in celebration of life, all life. In that spirit, so much in keeping with Andrea's beliefs, we ate the food and talked of his joyous nature.

Back at the cottage, the calls continued. The press department from the Met called about the obituary. Language again became an issue. The word "companion" means nothing to me. It sounds like a pet. Why was there no word that described us in a true, positive, accurate way? They said that the New York Times would not accept any other designation for a gay partner.

When the reporter from the Times called, I tried again for

Life-Partner or mate, but he said there was no other way. The next issue was more upsetting. He said that the paper would not list Lisa as a survivor because she is not a blood or legal relative. I protested that Andrea had helped to raise Lisa from the age of five and that she was very much his family and a survivor. No. They would not do it.

That night I did not sleep again. Foolishly, I continued to think that I could function normally without sleep. I would soon learn otherwise.

Lisa and I drove to Portland to change our surroundings for a day, and to get the *Times*. The obituary was disappointing, not just because it didn't mention Lisa, but because it didn't include a photograph of an artist who made his career with his face as much as his voice, and who had had a truly illustrious career for over thirty years at the Met. (I think that was an oversight by Charlie Rieker, one of the Met's artistic staff.) The *Times* refusing to list Lisa as a survivor was the really upsetting thing, and I did not forget it.

The trip to Portland was not good. Lack of sleep was now affecting my emotions, and I kept having crying bouts. Also, I was getting increasingly anxious. I was beginning to over-value things, like the obituary, and to feel threatened. Lisa saw this and started planning our return to New York.

A week after Andrea's death Lisa and I drove back home. Our departure was frantic, more like an escape. By then I was exhausted but still unable to sleep or calm down. We talked about Andrea for most of the six hours.

The drive, of course, was also a series of strong memories. Dumb little things came to mind, like his waving to the Polar Bear balloon in Worcester as we whizzed by on Rt. 87. By the time we got to New York, I was not making a lot of sense and was very confused. Finally, the loss, plus the exhaustion, overloaded my system. Lisa decided that

I needed immediate help, so she took me to the emergency room of a West Side hospital.

Somehow I had to get to sleep. The emergency room was a mess, and that whole scene really put me in a hyper state, very afraid and disoriented.

The first treatment was a much needed sedative. At last, I slept. The next morning I was formally admitted and taken to the secured floor to join the other patients who had bumped into reality sideways. Lisa came to visit me that morning, but I was into a marathon sleep. She talked to my doctor and learned that the lack of sleep had brought on some emotional trauma in addition to the loss, and now it would require medication, rest, and maybe some therapy to realign my psyche.

The ward I was on was small, relatively calm, and well run. Everyone got medication after dinner. Some patients got noticeably antsy from the stuff. I probably did too, but was not yet aware of what I was taking, how much, or what it did to me. I slept well. Most obvious to me was the effect the medication had on my emotions. Andrea's death was isolated by the chemicals to some distant part of my mind. I knew about it, but could not focus on his death. My grief was put on hold. Instead, I could concentrate only on my present surroundings. Each activity on the ward, especially all the social interactions, filled my days.

I had three roommates, all much younger. We didn't discuss our reasons for being there, but I learned that one guy, a student at Columbia had tried to kill himself. Because of that, and because he was the son of a diplomat, there was a guard at our door around the clock. He was built like a football player, had a slight Eastern European accent, dark eyes, and brains. I enjoyed it all; I was still alive, to my surprise, from the heart down.

After a week, the medication worked and I could sleep and function normally. However, there were side effects, like slower speech, and some awkwardness. Andrea's death remained in some holding zone of my mind. When I was ready to leave, my doctor suggested that I see a grief counselor, a psychologist friend of his, Michael Piccuci, who was also gay.

I called him for an appointment.

First, I had to deal with the apartment. I had only been there a couple hours when we returned the week before. The medication was strong but so were the memories in the apartment. The cottage at Tamworth was our spiritual center, associated strongly with personal myths, but the apartment was the place where we stood in the domestic trenches of the Upper West Side; it was home. And so I entered into its emotional mine field. Andrea was waiting. His humor, his career, his love, everything greeted me, except him. Despite the pills, the grief was back full force.

My work as a sculpture appraiser and small private dealer, was a one-man operation, so I was on my own all day, and didn't have the diversion of an outside workplace. Finances, probate, therapy dominated the next months.

First, however, was the memorial service for Andrea on October 27. It was small and informal, about 30 people. I decided to hold the service at the Aids Chapel at St. John the Divine. Andrea died of a heart attack, but we used to go up to the chapel to light candles for our friends who had died of that plague, particularly our beloved Robert Leonard, who had been Peter Shaffer's lover for many years. It was a simple ceremony that included some of our personal ritual and poems or quotes which expressed our love. A larger memorial was planned by the Met for December which involved his colleagues, other friends, and celebrated mostly his professional life.

On January 8, forty days after Andrea's death, a third service was held for only a few friends which followed the Greek Orthodox tradition. It is a beautiful, ancient ceremony that concludes with a ritual meal. Andrea described it to me once and said that he thought it was a beautiful part of his Greek heritage.

The critical ingredient for the next year turned out to be the grief therapy with Michael Piccuci. That served as my life-line as I groped my way from the center of the maze where death had struck towards a new reality. Each week Michael coached me through my despair and loneliness. He suggested that I join a group of gay men, called Center Bridge, which met at the center on West 13th Street. I joined the group and for ten weeks got a regular infusion of hugs, brotherly support, and healing counsel. In addition I made a couple new friends. It all started to work.

After several months, I began to discuss with Michael the ritual aspect of my relationship with Andrea. When I got divorced in the late 60s, and ventured into the gay demi-monde, I kept meeting guys who felt lousy about themselves. This surprised me. I was not looking for something worse in life. On the contrary, I wanted something better, something that I had not yet experienced, satisfying love. Really, I went after love. To me it seemed a natural right, like freedom, the right to love someone of my own choice. I refused to accept the party-line that, because I sought the love of my own sex, regardless of the cause, it followed that I was some kind of low life. It didn't make any logical sense that if, while I was married, I was a decent, honest, loving father, son, brother, and husband, and I was, that now I should lose my entire self-worth because of my efforts to go after my natural love, the one that fate had ordained for me. Therefore I rejected, as best I could, the negative misinformation that the culture tried to dump on me because of my sexual identity and I kept on the look-out for sympathetic souls.

Each week I discussed with Michael how Andrea and I worked from the beginning of our relationship on each of us trying to feel whole, intact. To achieve that, we knew that we had to narrow, and perhaps eliminate, the separation between our sexual actions, which the culture placed outside the natural order, and our spiritual beliefs, what we thought about ourselves. We had to define for ourselves, re-educate ourselves about love. What did it mean to our souls, our spirits, when we made love to each other. That was what became the central focus of our intimacy. Not that our love-making became a seminar — by no means — but it did include a strong spiritual element. Over the twenty-five years we slowly built a belief system that found its roots in earlier diverse cultures, that took its heroes from those cultures, that sought to include our love in the natural order.

It was at the cottage at Tamworth that our love-making took on its deepest and most satisfying dimensions. We created what we called celebrations which were very sexual and included spiritual ritual. I told Michael how we imbued objects that we created or valued, and let them represent our spiritual and sexual natures, and how we let some represent wisdom, energy, harmony, fantasy, and love. We placed the objects into a ritual space, just a defined area in the cottage, and started our love- making with a prayer, hymn, or statement that we would write ourselves and place in the space. We intermingled sex, as rough or raw as we wanted, with fantasy, goodness, pure love, and nature. Something positive happened.

And it got better as the years passed. We remained our individual selves, be we went deeply into each other's psyches. We tapped into great reservoirs of fantasy, sometimes encased in trauma, but since we protected our emotions through love- ritual, that fantasy, even trauma induced, became a further expression of our love because of the deep intimacy we shared. To our delight, we realized that each time we made love that way, we not only had great sex, we also healed ourselves towards wholeness.

Serendipity, that's what Michael tagged our meeting, when he told me one week that he was starting a group with people in the later stages of recovery which would include a workshop on healing what he called "the Sexual–Spiritual Split." Based on my experiences, he wanted me to help facilitate and join the group: also, and this was the surprise, he wanted me to explain the use of ritual in my relationship at one of the sessions. Although I was quite shy at the thought of sharing intimate details of my relationship with Andrea with relative strangers, it seemed to me that I should trust Michael's judgment that Andrea and I had explored something that was unusual, if not unique, and should be put out there to the community.

In March, 1995, I made the first presentation. The group was all male, primarily gay. For about two hours I did an adult version of "Show and Tell." I stood before the group and explained the simple healing rituals that had enriched our relationship for so many years. I made similar presentations to three more groups during 1995. The groups were diverse, and they were enthusiastic about the things that Andrea and I celebrated.

Time combined with the therapy was helping; however, there was still a problem. The cottage in New Hampshire had taken on a symbolic role in my recovery. Since Andrea's death I had been unable to stay at the cottage alone. Twice I had gone up with a friend to check on things, and I had great anxiety, even with the medication. I went up once on my own, in December of '94, but I was traumatized at being there alone; all the horror of being alone the night that Andrea died lingered in the rooms. After no sleep, I got up at dawn. I knew that I had to leave. I went around the outside tearing dead impatiens from boxes and pots, and dragging tools and outdoor furniture into the crawl space. The anxiety was so severe that I decided the only way I could continue to function was to control my breathing totally, using verbal commands and calming thoughts. It worked.

I got the house shut down for winter, and left immediately for New York. I did the breathing control for the entire trip to keep alert.

By spring of '95 it was obvious that I should sell the cottage for emotional and financial reasons. With its recently revealed view of the mountain it was only on the market a few weeks, when a local couple made an offer which I accepted.

I was faced with going up and confronting for the last time the pain that still echoed within the cottage. I told Michael that I was very troubled at the prospect of being at the house by myself, and also by the thought of actually selling the place that had played such a major role in my life with Andrea. For me the sale represented another loss, this time of my memories. Michael advised me to trust my own instincts, and let them guide me through a ritual separation of the cottage itself from the memories and beliefs experienced there. And to remember that they were not part of the transaction.

Michael's advice became my guide when I returned to the cottage in August of '95. I didn't sleep much the first night. Early the next morning, I walked around. I saw the empty bird feeders, the overturned flower pots, the empty wooden window boxes, and the gardens layered with the winter's cover of brown pine needles. The cottage never looked this bleak before in high summer. I sat down on a bench, and with no sound from me the tears just started rolling down my cheeks. Within a few minutes the tears stopped, and I looked around at the areas of green pushing through the needles in the garden. The lilies, though stunted from lack of water and care, were reaching for the sun. They had survived the cold despair of winter. And the goldfinches were back; even the hummingbirds. Everything, even Andrea's spirit around the house, was pushing me to accept the cycle.

Later, I drove over to Spider Web Nursery and bought some flowers for the cottage, enough for the pots, and boxes. I worked all day outside. The air was filled with the scent of damp pine as I raked the needles. Andrea always said the smell reminded him of his student days in Rome. It took a couple hours to plant the red impatiens and pink begonias around the cottage, and, finally, to fill the feeders with niger seeds, and mix the liquid for the hummingbirds to fight over. Throughout the day, as I used my hands to work the soil for the plants, or cleared brush, or raked, I felt something coming back to me. I felt the restoration of balance and acceptance that had been missing. I had come back and made peace with that October night. Each act that I did contributed to my feelings of completeness. I knew that I was doing the right thing.

For a week, before Lisa and a friend came, I had time to fill each day with healing, to say "Yes" and to banish the "No" of October. I went through a series of rituals which I believe allowed me to take with me the passion, memories, and sacredness of the cottage when I left on August 15. And on that great ancient female feast day, one that we had spent on Delos in the summer of 1976. I celebrated finally the joy of wholeness which we had learned from the woods, sky, and nights of Tamworth. Each day I realized that I was healing myself by each ritual; each moment of awareness of my authentic feelings about life and death, Andrea's as well as mine eventually, brought back in focus my present life.

That focus has remained. It keeps me aware of the responsibility that I have to my relationship with Andrea: to go on living, remaining part of the cycle. If I have learned anything from the journey that we had together, it is that our love has a unique part to play in the larger natural order of things, and that it too is crucial in defining human experience.

Written for Michael Piccuci Ph.D,
New York, 1996

V.

ANDREA VELIS MEMORIAL EULOGY

by Peter Shaffer
Metropolitan Opera | 7 December 1994

We all, I think, become haunted houses. If we are lucky, that is. I mean nothing fearsome by this. But if our lives have been rich at all in friendship, the chambers of our memory tend to fill up in age with good and ghostly tenants — obligingly repeating for us after death their best moments in <u>our</u> lives. Such moments are not usually those when they triumphed most distinctly — were applauded for their skills, occupied stages or walked up happily to receive awards: though in the case of Andrea Velis these scenes were also his — but more likely the <u>smallest moments,</u> almost insignificant to outside viewers, when they were <u>themselves.</u> When they betrayed the tiniest gestures of affection or inner strength, whose recall on the screen of the mind's eye can assure us, over and over, of the best part of existence.

I was thinking of Andrea a morning or so ago, sitting in the Argo Restaurant on West 89th Street where he and I often met to eat our plates of tuna fish in pita-bread, amidst the effluvium of disinfectant rising from the floor: an unluxurious lunch which both our heart-conditions prescribed — although truth be told, I tended to defy that prescription in favour of hamburger much more often than he did. As I sat I saw him quite clearly, wearing his flat cap, his contained and ordered shape bespeaking the order in his life: the order which enabled him to fulfill so exactly in this increasingly chaotic nursery we all inhabit, the ambitions of a mature gentleman.

That is indeed who Andrea was: a mature artist and a <u>gentle man</u>.

Gentleness seemed to me to be the element in which he lived: gentleness and culture. This last word often sounds inadequate to me — it emits an over refined, and rather precious signal, almost prissy. But there was nothing remotely precious about Andrea. First and foremost he was a <u>working man</u>: the best thing for anyone to be. A working man who served an art. He moved through life in a palpable cloak of urbanity: a mysterious garment which almost concealed the intensity of his dedication. Only when you spoke with him did they quietly emerge — the depth of his addiction to music: the certainties of his hard-won and long-loved knowledge: his sweetly inexorable standards of excellence. I respected him for these above all — because the love you feel for a man's dedication binds you to him in a very pure admiration which enlarges the admirer.

Andrea was given to me, as it were, almost like a present. He was perhaps the oldest and best friend of my own dearest companion, Robert Leonard.

Robert must surely have been known to some of you here as a vastly talented voice- teacher, life-enhancing and life-creating: qualities which would attract Andrea most strongly of all, as they attracted and fuelled me endlessly, over fourteen marvelous years with him. It was Robert who took me up to Caramoor to hear Andrea sing in *Curlew River*, that brilliant Church Parable of Benjamin Britten. I liked him immediately — not least because he sang so devoted the astonishing cadences of a composer I revere more than any other contemporary. As I came to know him better he revealed to me, almost shyly but with obvious pride, that Britten had corresponded with him, and sent him words of encouragement. I told him how I myself years before had lurked outside Britten's house on the shingle-strewn sea-front at Aldeburgh. Hoping for a glimpse of this genius as other youngsters my age might stand waiting to see a pop-singer pass or a film star. He understood immediately and only two summers ago in England I remembered all this when I watched Andrea sitting in the opera house at Glyndebourne becoming transported by the cold-washed interlude of dawn which begins *Peter Grimes*. In this sense — a constant experience of transport — music was the staple of his life: as his performances of it, always prepared and delivered with such high intelligence and self — submission, became a staple of life here in this house, which was his second home. He <u>knew</u> music. He breathed it. He reverenced it. And he made it.

I sat in that restaurant and thought how marvelous to be so defined. To have an avocation so connected with absolute glory — because music is surely the most absolute of the arts — and yet so demanding in its practicality. His public life was all practicality — people who had studied with him told me how practical he was; how clearly and simply he used his own vast experience to coach others — and his performances (like Justice is supposed to be, but seldom is) was always, in the great phrase, <u>seen to be done!</u> Theory and practice were one. Theory, practice, and service. And all of them, were informed with that unfailing shy kindness which I shall remember best of all.

I said that I felt I had received Andrea as a present. It seems to be the perfect word. After my dear Robert died, Andrea entered my life more and more — and old as I was, and strange to say, in some palpable way he assumed what was for me the infinitely gratifying role of a kind of Guardian to me. There was always a denied father, or uncle, or even mother in Andrea. At least once a week

I would find myself walking from the river side where I lived on 89th Street to spend the evening dining in the cabinet of wonders otherwise known as his apartment. Indeed on occasion he would show me his own "wunderkabinett" — an astonishing array of small antique objects. Treasures of all kinds collected through his working life, always displayed, it seems to me in memory, in a jewelled and amber light — he himself smiling like the Prospero of the cave, conjuring sights for my delectation. And the truth was that among all these prized things unwrapped from lacquered boxes and silk handkerchiefs, there was always one treasure on view much larger: he himself. He was, may I remind you, a Treasure himself. He was called this by no less an authoritative oracle than *New York Magazine* when it listed in an article the ten most cherishable treasures of our City. From that moment he was known to me, and I'm sure many others, as "Tresh". It delighted him — hard as he might try to look degagé, and off-hand. He wore the appellation like a chain of office — and kept it in the kabinett of his own heart.

What a heart it was! I shall always see him padding around the room — he was a padder, Andrea — almost slyly pouring too much white wine into your glass, or spooning too much exquisite risotto onto your plate, and then sitting at the head of his table in the hall that served as his endearing little dining room, watching his guests with secret pleasure.

One time he passed to me down the table a photograph of himself as The Duchess of Crackenthorp in the *Daughter of the Regiment*, and then with seeming irrelevance asked me what play I was working on now. I mentioned the idea of one I was thinking of writing. "And tell me," he said, in the clarion tones of the Dowager Duchess, "do you think there could be a part in it for an older woman?"

Someone said to me last week that the trouble with memorial

services is that the people who speak at them do so only about themselves. This of course is vainglorious, and trying. But in one serious sense it is inescapable — because those who speak tributes to the dead must seek to prove in some way that isn't egotistical that they are actually <u>worthy</u> not only to have been their friends in the past but now to be their representatives. The dead can only live through us: we have to be their conjurers. They can only speak through us: we have to be their voices. We have above all, to live <u>for</u> them now that they can no longer do so for themselves. And I would like just now to finish with one word to the most concerned person in this room — Andrea's dearest companion Faber Donoughe.

Faber, I know that now — at this moment — life must seem unreal, numbing and inexplicable, and painful beyond measure. But I can assure you of one thing — abstract as it will appear to you at this moment. You are very lucky. Even in your pain you are very lucky. "Blessed are the mourners" is not just a pious phrase: it is a good, real truth. Lucky are the mourners. Because the very misery you are feeling now is the exact measure of the tremendous fortune you have had. Think of all the arid lives around us — arid because of the lack of what you had in abundance and indeed <u>gave</u> in abundance. You made each other. Your life now must exult in that. Lucky Faber, to have had Andrea.

And lucky me, too, in a smaller way, to have known him too. A couple of years ago when I showed you both a little of the English countryside I enjoyed, I watched you standing together in a circle of prehistoric stones at Avebury, watching a white peacock spread its shivering tail and shake what seemed to be pearls into a beam of sunlight. That beam <u>embraced you both</u> — and it is as I see you — joined in your love of beauty, both of you, and of myth and legend,

and of whatever startles meaning out of the bushes of ordinary existence. In fact, in your love for each other, I might say, you now are
the custodian of that love. <u>His</u> guardian.

God bless you always, Andrea, for having been my friend. And the
friend of so many here.

Peter Shaffer and Andrea, New Hampshire, 1991

VI.
APPENDIX:

New York Times Obituary
Correspondence

Mr. Arthur Ochs Sulzberger, Jr. President
The New York Times
229 West 43rd Street
New York, NY 10036-3959

Dear Mr. Sulzberger:

Throughout the year, the Times has been celebrating its patriarch, Adolph
S. Ochs. I would like to suggest, in a serious manner, that you take the
opportunity of your centennial to honor, in a significant way to your
community family, the matriarch, and I quote from her obituary which appeared
February 27, 1990, who "nurtured and bridged the generations of the family
that has controlled the Times since 1896," Iphigene Ochs Sulzberger.

That Mrs. Sulzberger cared most about two things, her family and her paper,
was obvious from the Times article. She cared also about Barnard, and it
was while an undergraduate at the college that my daughter had the
opportunity to meet her, and to take delight in such an extraordinary woman,
a "life-force" my daughter said. My only comparison, I replied, was a
similar reaction to having met Mrs. Roosevelt in the early sixties. In addition
to Barnard, my daughter shared with Mrs. Sulzberger her status as an only
child, which, as you might expect, promotes a strong bonding with adults who
are close from early childhood. So you might imagine, then, how very painful
was the incident that follows, and, in my opinion, what a departure from the
guidance of a woman who strove, and I quote again from her obituary, "to
preserve family ties," and who was dedicated "to progressive values."

When my life-partner of twenty-five years, a man who had helped raise my
daughter in every way, died in 1994, your editorial policy did not allow for
her to be listed as a surviving family member. Granted, my inclusion itself,
though I find the designation, companion, unacceptable, is a major achieve-
ment. But, surely we can now move on to a more family-based policy, one
which serves to re-inforce many families as they are, rather than as we imagine
them, at the close of the century.

In the gay and lesbian community, we have had enough pain and exclusion from
the plague that has stripped us to the bone. What has arisen in comfort for our
losses has been, quite simply, love and family. We have seen caring heroes
emerge from shy, quiet shadows; we have seen fortified families form among
casual friends. Our artists have shown the world these transformations. And,
yet, the "paper of record" encases us on microfilm as if our deaths occur only
in isolated, unconnected lives, with "approved" survivors only listed, while
those who share our daily lives – our joys – our holidays – our deaths, are
excluded.

Please honor further the memory of Mrs. Sulzberger, and her maternal spirit
at the Times, by changing your policy to allow non-traditional families,
primarily gay and lesbian, to include their designated-family in obituaries.

Let us lose no more daughters. Iphigene, I think, would approve.

October 3, 1996

The New York Times
229 WEST 43 STREET
NEW YORK, N.Y. 10036

ARTHUR O. SULZBERGER, JR
Publisher

October 7, 1996

Dear Mr. Donoughe,

Thank you very much for your thoughtful letter.

The Times moves slowly, but it does move. It was but a few years ago that even "companion" would have been unthinkable. I believe, in time, we may move further.

Sincerely,

P.S. Your letter had only one substantive error. My grandmother, Iphigene, would be absolutely appalled.

October 10, 1996

Mr. Arthur Ochs Sulzberger, Jr. President
The New York Times
229 West 43rd Street
New York, NY 10036-3959

Dear Mr. Sulzberger:

    I do apologize for being mistaken about your grandmother.

                        Sincerely,

                        Faber Donoughe

P.S.   Apparently a lot of people were.

August 18, 2001

Mr. Arthur Ochs Sulzberger, Jr.
Publisher
The New York Times
229 West 43rd Street
New York, NY 10036-3959

Dear Mr. Sulzberger

Perhaps you may recall that I wrote to you in 1996 requesting that in your capacity as Publisher of *The New York Times* you could help people like me, a gay man whose family included his adult daughter and his lifepartner of twenty-five years, at the most painful and stressful times we encounter in life, when one of our family members dies. I sought a change in the paper's obituary policy of excluding from the survivor list those who are not related to the deceased through blood or law: a policy that I believe increases the pain of the loss to a non-traditional family. When my lifepartner died in 1994, the journalist from *The Times*, rejecting my pleas, insisted on excluding from the surviving family list my daughter, who for twenty-five years had been in essence a daughter with two fathers, my lifepartner and me. This exclusion, in addition to the obvious direct hurt, expands into larger pain because of the impact it can have on the mourning process: if one is not a "survivor" then one has had no loss, and one needs no comforting or consoling. That, in fact, was the experience that was troubling to my daughter.

You can imagine, then, with my past experience with this policy, my disbelief when I read the obituary of Mr. Robert S. Jones (*NYT August 14, 2001*) and came to the final paragraph:

Mr. Jones was also survived by his dog, Scout.

May we now assume, Mr. Sulzberger, that you indeed have changed the rigid policy of the paper regarding this issue of survivors and that the Lesbian and Gay Community and others can define their own families? Identify those they know as the survivors of the deceased? Surely, if there is room for Scout there is room for the rest of us.

Sincerely,

Faber Donoughe

WILLIAM BORDERS
News Editor

September 11, 2001

Dear Mr. Donoughe:

Arthur Sulzberger has asked me to reply to your letter about our offensive obituary reference to the man who was "survived by his dog. Scout." The general view around here is that including the dog in that obituary was a foolish feature-writing excess, and we wish we had not done it. It tended to demean real survivors in other obituaries.

But the larger point, of course, relates to the kind of situation you describe that occurred with the death of your companion in 1994. I apologize, all these years later, for the pain we caused then to you and your daughter.

Newspaper policies change along with the changes in the society they cover, and we have certainly changed in this one. I don't know if it is any consolation to you, but I am certain that if we were faced today with the situation we were faced with seven years ago when Mr. Velis died we would handle it differently, and I hope we would include your daughter in the obituary.

The New York Times stylebook, which we adopted in 1999, includes this directive, in its passage on how we should handle obituaries:

"The Times should not be the arbiter of what makes up a family: if the survivors regard a more distant relative or even a friend as a member of the subject's immediate household, mention the relationship."

If that had been our practice in 1994, I am sure we would have handled the question of Mr. Velis's survivors more sensitively than we did. I am also sure that the thoughtful arguments you made at the time and subsequently, helped us to change our policy in the right direction, and I thank you for that even though it did not help in your daughter's case.

I stress that none of this supports or defends our including Mr. Jones's dog, which we should not have done. And I thank you for helping us once again with your thoughtful and sensitive letter.

Best regards.

William Borders

ACKNOWLEDGEMENTS

My deep gratitude to those who helped, guided, and shared this journey: Jonah Rosenberg, Consulting Editor, and Craig Rutenberg, June Mikkelsen, Susan McIntosh, Rimli Sengupta, and, especially, Mathieu Guertin, who encouraged me throughout, and, as always, to my daughter, Lisa, for her love.

ABOUT THE AUTHOR

Faber Donoughe is a New Yorker. He has lived in Manhattan for nearly Fifty years. Prior to moving to New York, the Pittsburgh native began his career in education, teaching drama, speech and English for six years. Concurrently, he was a free-lance arts and entertainment critic for a daily paper. After obtaining an MA from the University of Pittsburgh, he joined the Drama Department at Carnegie Institute's Education Division, where he organized drama events and art exhibitions and taught classes. In addition, he wrote for "Carnegie Magazine." After moving to New York in the early '70s he continued with various free-lance writing in the arts, working for "Current Biography", "Opera News", and the Jackinson Literary Agency. In the late '70s he worked as an assistant for Michael Hall Fine Arts in Manhattan and that eventually led to an independent career as an art appraiser and dealer in sculpture.

He has one daughter from an early marriage, and shared twenty-five years with a Life-Partner who died in 1994.

Made in the USA
Middletown, DE
17 November 2021